WAVES OF HATE

By the same author

Field Gun Jack versus the Boers
(Leo Cooper, 1998)

Sea Killers in Disguise
(Leo Cooper, 1999)

WAVES OF HATE

Naval Atrocities of the Second World War

by

TONY BRIDGLAND

NAVAL INSTITUTE PRESS
ANNAPOLIS, MARYLAND

First published in Great Britain 2002
by LEO COOPER
an imprint of Pen & Sword Books,
47 Church Street,
Barnsley,
S. Yorkshire, S70 2AS

Published and distributed in the United States of
America and Canada by the Naval Institute Press,
291 Wood Road,
Annapolis, Maryland 21402-5034

Library of Congress Catalog Card No. 2001098492

ISBN 1-55750-439-3

Printed in England by CPI UK

CONTENTS

ACKNOWLEDGEMENTS

The writing of a book such as this can be both exhausting and exciting, even though some of the stories in it are far from pleasant. Exhausting because its preparation involves many days of often fruitless rummaging through archives and exciting because when that rummaging does prove fruitful it tells the prospective author that it is all going to be worthwhile – that is the carrot which spurs him on. But the real peaks of excitement come when one finds a person who was actually *there.*

I was fortunate enough to find and talk to several such people, and their contribution to this book has enriched it, I hope, in a way that no pearls in archival oysters ever could. It is a pleasure, therefore, to record my especial thanks to them. For several of them, an horrific wartime experience in the prime of their youth in mid-ocean has resulted in a lifetime of recurring nightmares, and the help they gave to me so readily cannot have been given without a considerable amount of mental discomfort.

Others have helped by making available to me their private papers. Without their help, too, the task would have been impossible and I am greatly indebted to each of them. There were many others who have assisted and guided me in a host of different ways, from the translating of German to the lending of a photograph or the imparting of some specialized knowledge in one field or another.

Together, they comprise a sizeable group, and it is not surprising that, owing to the nature of the book itself, they are scattered all round the globe. I hope they will forgive me for naming them all, *ad hoc,* in one list.

My sincere thanks to each of the following, in no particular order: Bess Cummings; Dennis Allen; Lady Margaret Stirling-Aird; James Wolfe Murray; Tom Barclay, South Ayrshire Community Librarian; Dr Iain Gow; Ashley Aslett; Michael Ward; Captain David Gibson; Alf Hunt; Jack Hughieson; David Wilson; Patricia Garvey; Harold

Payne; Jim Allaway, Editor of *Navy News*; Ian McGregor of the Meteorological Office; Yvette Pritchard of the *Shropshire Star*; Rob Ford of the *Sunderland Echo*; Violet Stoker; Billy Short; Yoshinori Miyuki and Akira Takizawa of Tokyo; George Clarke; David Hogg; Horst Bredow and Jack Showell of U-Boot Archiv, Cuxhaven; Gordon Dixon; Frank Hunter; Tom Fowle; Jean Rochester; Edith Henderson; Eric Halfhide; George McGinnis of Florida; Doug Spon-Smith; Allyn Nevitt of California; Ron Taylor; Simon Riley of Stornoway Coastguard; Helen Jones of the University of Massachusetts Library; Rodina Stephenson; Finlay Macaskill; Tamara (Toni) Horodysky of USMM Veterans Association, Berkeley California; Marsha Coke of the Medsearch Committee of American ex-Prisoners of War and Bob Baird.

As always, the staffs of the Public Record Office, Kew, the Imperial War Museum, London and the Public Libraries at Hastings, Rye, and Newport Gwent rendered invaluable and patient assistance. Tom Hartman provided his usual sterling service with the editing and Gina-Marie Bridgland applied her customary patience to the preparation of the index. My thanks, of course, to all of them.

I have made every effort to obtain the necessary permission from the copyright holders to reproduce the photographs which appear in the book. This has been granted whenever requested which is acknowledged with due gratitude. In the one or two instances where it was not possible to trace a copyright holder, I hope that inclusion of such photographs will not be met with any objections. If that should be the case, however, I shall be only too pleased to acknowledge the matter in future editions.

Tony Bridgland
Rye, East Sussex
April 2001

INTRODUCTION

The industrialized world never quite settled down to be at ease with itself in the aftermath of the Great War. The 1920s and 30s saw the rise of both Nazism in Hitler's Germany, arising from the bitter resentment caused in that country by the oppressive unfairness, in German eyes, of the 1919 Versailles Treaty, and Fascism in the poverty of Mussolini's Italy. In Soviet Russia, first Lenin and then Stalin mercilessly propagated their various brands of a new-found religion called Bolshevism, whilst in Japan an ambition to crush China and compete with the United States and her Allies created a surge of fanatical aggression which was eventually to give birth to the nightmarish Greater South-East Asia Co-Prosperity Sphere.

The First World War had given rise to scenarios of horror on a scale which had never before been witnessed by mankind. Passchendaele, the Somme, Gallipoli and Verdun are names which have become indelibly etched on the bloodstained scrolls of history. The war at sea, too, had created its own special brand of nightmare. True, major clashes between the mammoth Fleets of the belligerents were few – Jutland, the Falklands and Dogger Bank comprised, more or less, the sum total of them, and at these the carnage was truly horrific. Smaller scale skirmishes apart, and escapades such as the Zeebrugge Raid, it was the day-to-day grind of convoy work, often in terrible weather, accompanied by sights of burning, sinking ships, drowning men and half-dead survivors in lifeboats, on rafts, or simply clinging for their lives onto spars and bits of wave-tossed wreckage which painted the fuller picture. And often in the background lurked the dark, silent sinister form of their assailant, the new weapon of war called the submarine.

During the world's first Total War several events had taken place at sea which shocked whole nations. Such happenings as the sinking of the *Lusitania*, the *Baralong* affair, the murder of Captain Fryatt, the attack on the stranded submarine *E13*, and the sinking of several hospital ships including the *Llandovery Castle*, all gave rise to an escalation of hate on both sides. But the International Laws laid down at the Geneva and Hague Conventions had, in theory, made retribution possible. These Conventions had created a new concept – that of 'war crimes' and 'war criminals'. To the victors fell the power to seek such retribution when peace came at last. With a display of quaint decency, even naivety, that was already long outdated, the Allies agreed to a series of selected alleged 'war crimes' to be heard at Leipzig, with German judges. But many of the accused had long since absconded, never to be heard of again, and the handful of cases which actually saw a conviction were given sentences which were farcical in their levity.

In the face of so many dangers to world peace, the major powers did, with commendable foresight, display initiative by putting in place some measures intended to minimize the chances of another World War occurring and, failing that, to humanize as far as possible the conditions under which any future global conflict would be fought. But these could be no more than paper promises – mere Treaties. They could never enforce strictly the Rules of Etiquette and Chivalry in War that had existed from time immemorial, albeit having been steadily on the wane since 1914.

Indeed, by 1939 any real likelihood that these Rules would be adhered to, cricket-fashion, by any of the more ruthless characters on the world's stage existed only in the Elysian minds of the Peace Movement and the gentlemanly Neville Chamberlain school of thought, which, as was to become famously known to history, were so utterly and disastrously mistaken.

On 6 February 1922, at the end of a three-month Conference on the Limitation of Naval Armament in Washington called by President Harding, a Treaty was signed by the U.S.A., the British Empire, France, Italy and Japan, the signatories having expressed their desire "to contribute to the maintenance of the general peace." New capital ships were to be restricted to 35,000 tons standard (aircraft carriers 27,000 tons) displacement, with armament not to exceed 16-inch calibre. The U.S Navy and Royal Navy were to be permitted to build capital ships up to a total tonnage of 525,000 each, with the other nations allowed somewhat smaller limits.

Importantly for the objectives of this book, Article XIV stated that "no preparations shall be made in merchant ships in time of peace for the installation of warlike armaments for the purpose of converting such ships into vessels of war, other than the necessary stiffening of decks for the mounting of guns not exceeding 6-inch (152 millimetre) calibre."

A Convention, the purpose of which was to adapt the principles of the Geneva Convention to Maritime War, had been hammered out at the Second Peace Conference at The Hague back in 1907. Article 16 stated – "After every engagement, the two belligerents shall, so far as military interests permit, take steps to look for the wounded, sick and shipwrecked, and to protect them, as well as the dead, against pillage and unfair treatment. They shall see that the burial, whether on land or at sea, or cremation of the dead, shall be preceded by a careful examination of the corpse."

The London Submarine Agreement was made in London on 22 April 1930. It brought submarines within the scope of existing international law as it applied to surface warships. This Treaty dealt mainly with the question of arms limitation, but Part IV established further International Law with regard to the treatment of shipwrecked crews of belligerents. Effectively, it extended the rules already formulated at The Hague. The London Submarine Agreement was signed by Great Britain and the Dominions, USA, Italy, France and, notably, Japan. Equally notably, Germany was a conspicuous absentee, although it adopted the protocol of Part IV later when the remainder of the Treaty expired in 1936.

Article 22 [paragraph 2] said "In particular, except in the case of persistent refusal to stop on being duly summoned, or of active resistance to visit or search, a warship, whether surface vessel or submarine, may not sink or render incapable of navigation a merchant vessel without first having placed passengers, crew and ship's papers in a place of safety. *For this purpose the ship's boats are not regarded as a place of safety unless the safety of the passengers and crew is assured, in the existing sea and weather conditions, by the proximity of land or the presence of another vessel which is in a position to take them on board.*" (author's italics)

The 1932 Geneva Disarmament Conference was overshadowed by the fact that both Germany and Japan had already walked out of the League of Nations. The Conference broke down in 1934 and, ominously, Japan announced that it intended to withdraw from the 1922 and 1930 Naval Treaties when they were due for renewal in 1936.

In 1935 the Anglo-German Naval Agreement gave Hitler the right to build submarines to bring the *Kriegsmarine* onto parity with the

Royal Navy's submarine fleet, subject to notice being given.

With the expiry of the 1922 and 1930 Treaties at the end of 1936, the major powers all moved towards naval re-armament. *Including Germany, they agreed to prohibit unrestricted submarine warfare against un-named ships.* (author's italics)

Come 1939, in April Germany abrogated the 1935 Anglo-German Agreement. August saw the mobilization of the Royal Navy and German U-boats sailing to war stations in the Atlantic. And on 1 September German troops marched into Poland, whose safe independence had been guaranteed by both Great Britain and France.

The paper promises had all been made in vain. The drama known as the Second World War was about to be played on a stage far wider even than that of the First. And the cruel atrocities that were to be enacted thereon would be of proportionately heightened inhumanity.

VIKTOR OEHRN, THE *SHEAF MEAD*
AND THE *SEVERN LEIGH*

Kapitänleutnant Viktor Oehrn, the handsome blond captain of *U-37* and holder of the Iron Cross Second Class, peered through his binoculars. He could see a steamship in the far distance, steaming westward at about ten knots. It looked like she had come from Vigo or Coruña. She had the appearance of a Levantine freighter. Painted grey. About 5,000 tons. There was a blue square with a yellow cross painted on her side. Swedish? No, somehow he didn't think so. She was zig-zagging slightly, no more than about ten degrees. Only ten minutes before, *U-37*'s wireless had picked up a warning from *Befehlshaber der U-boote* of "enemy auxiliary cruisers operating between 41°–42°30' North and 10°30'–11° West".

B.d.U's message had said that there were some German merchantmen sailing out of Vigo, and these were having to run the gauntlet of these enemy auxiliary cruisers. Oehrn was confident that this ship was not one of the Germans. She had a rather suspicious box-like structure abaft her funnel. More than likely this housed a concealed gun, and she probably was, in fact, one of the British auxiliaries. He decided to make a closer inspection. Visibility was poor, with a choppy sea, and by keeping a discreet distance, her lookouts would not be able to spot the low-slung Type IXA submarine on the surface as it worked its way around to bring itself ahead of them. It was 1252 on 27 May 1940.

Thirty-two-year-old Oehrn had taken over *U-37* from Werner Hartenstein just three weeks before, and this was his first war-time patrol in command of a U-boat. He had commanded *U-14* back in 1936, taking her into Spanish waters during the Civil War, but since late 1937 he had had shore appointments, first at the *Marine-Akademie* and later as *Admiralstaboffizier* on the staff of Karl Dönitz at B.d.U.

By 1445 the U-boat was ahead of the unsuspecting steamer. Oehrn dived and settled down to wait at periscope depth. There was a considerable swell, which made observation a little difficult, but as yet there was nothing to see in the periscope and nothing to be heard by hydrophone. Eventually she came into view. She was about three miles away. The hydrophones ought to have picked her up before she got that close but they were not always very reliable. The steamer was steering a course of 280°. Strange. Was she German after all? Oehrn was convinced that she was not. And the Officer of the Watch, who was an expert on merchant ship identification, agreed. He also thought she looked like a Levantine.

Oehrn rang for Full Speed, to keep abreast of the steamer. The distance between them had closed rapidly. It was now down to no more than a quarter of a mile. The U-boat's crew were already at Action Stations. The German looked again through the periscope. She had a small gun mounted on her stern! Good. But he could see no name painted on her hull and she wore no colours. Fire! It was point-blank range. 320 metres. He could hardly miss. There was a crashing explosion as the torpedo tore into the port side after-part of its target. Perhaps this would bring a little confidence back to the crew. Lately they had been plagued by a run of faulty torpedoes, but this one had run true enough. Maybe the new captain had brought them better fortune. By the time *U-37* had regained the surface, the stern of the steamer was well down in the water, her bows were rising up and her crew were taking to their lifeboats. Oehrn opened the hatch and had a look around. It was five minutes to three. The sinking ship's bows had risen still higher and her stern was now well under. Her boats had all got away and were lying some way off.

Suddenly two men appeared from somewhere in the now towering forward part of the ship. They tore down the hill of her sloping deck and ran straight into the water at her stern. Then one of her boats capsized. She finally disappeared, accompanied by another rumbling crash as her boilers exploded. An archipelago of debris floated to the surface, among which sat the crew, some in their boats, others clinging to bits of wreckage. The U-boat's sailors fished out a buoy from among the wreckage. It had no name on it but had been freshly painted. Cautiously, Oehrn brought the *U-37* closer still to obtain identification from her crew. He called to a man on a raft. The man did not even look up. "Nix name," he muttered, tersely. There was a young seaman in the water, no more than a boy, calling for help. His shipmates were close at hand in their boats and on their rafts. They would help him. All the shipwrecked sailors looked calm enough, although wet and tired. There was no display of panic, but all bore on their faces expressions which Oehrn interpreted as 'cold hatred'. He turned the U-boat away and resumed his old course.

When the new paint was scrubbed from the buoy they had picked up there was revealed the name *Groatefield* – Glasgow. It meant nothing to Oehrn. Was she an ordinary freighter or was she a disguised warship? He was still unsure. After all, she was painted grey, she showed no name and she did sport a gun, mounted aft, although there was little unusual about that. Her crew had displayed a high degree of discipline when their ship was torpedoed. They could have been Royal Navy, although none of them wore any kind of uniform. And as for that unusual box abaft the funnel, had it concealed a 4-inch gun?

In fact she was the Sheaf Steamshipping Co's steamer *Sheaf Mead*, 5,008 tons, port of registry Glasgow, rated + 100 A1 at Lloyds and bound for Philadelphia from Swansea in ballast. She had sailed on Tuesday 21 May to join a convoy which was assembling at Milford Haven. For some reason she had been ordered to leave the convoy at 0445 hours on 27 May, the day of the sinking, and proceed independently without zig-zagging.

Out of her crew of thirty-six, thirty-one men were to lose their lives through the sinking, either by drowning or exposure. There had been no panic when the torpedo struck. In fact some of the Lascar firemen insisted on going forward to collect their prayer mats and belongings before being urged into the boats by the Fourth Engineer. But before the boats could be got properly clear they were dragged under with the ship, carrying many of the men with them. The only men not seen to have left the ship either by getting into one of the boats or jumping into the sea were the Master and the W/T Officer. Some of the men trapped under the boats managed to get clear when they re-surfaced, but others were never seen again. There had been ample life-jackets on board, but unfortunately two of the regulation emergency rafts were lashed down on a hatchway beneath the derricks and went down with the ship. The sea was wearing a lumpy swell and survivors trying to cling to rafts and bits of heaving wreckage were continually being washed away into the water. On one raft there were the Chief Engineer, Mr Wilkinson, together with the steward, the galley-boy and an injured seaman who was badly cut about the face. By concentrated paddling for half an hour, they managed to reach another raft on which were the First and Third Officers and make fast to it with Wilkinson's belt. Together they struggled towards one of the boats, which was waterlogged and had several men clinging to it. They tried to bale it out, but it kept capsizing each time the boatswain tried to get into it. All the time the sea was getting rougher and all the time the U-boat captain and his crew cruised around watching the men being battered by the waves as they battled for their lives.

Wilkinson had been in his cabin when the explosion took place. He rushed to the engine-room to find it almost full of water. He returned to his cabin for his life-jacket and got away in the starboard boat just in time, only to be dragged under with the ship. It seems that he must have passed right underneath her, because when he came to the surface he found himself on her port side, only about five yards from the U-boat. From there he managed to grab hold of a piece of hatch cover and then onto the raft with the others. He wrote later, "The submarine captain asked the steward the name of the ship, which he told him and the enemy picked up one of our lifebuoys, but this had the name *Gretaston* on it, because that was her name before it was changed to *Sheaf Mead* last January. The captain was a young fellow of about twenty-eight, height five feet ten, about thirteen stone and well-built. He had fair hair and was rather good-looking with sharp features and was clean shaven. He spoke very good English with a deep voice. He was the only man in uniform. I think he had two gold stripes, and he wore a cap with a gold badge but no braid. There were about ten men on the deck of the submarine, all of whom appeared to be freshly shaved; they were very young, only boys really, and they wore blue and brown dungarees, or a kind of smock like that worn by fishermen. No one was in khaki, nor wearing forage caps. I did not hear them speaking German among themselves, and there was no sound of any wireless. The submarine must have surfaced very quickly as it was in full view when I came up from my room. There was no warning noise of any kind before we were torpedoed and no one appears to have sighted her; the gunner who had been on the gun platform until 1230 had gone below for his lunch and was about to return to his station at

4

1250. He was never seen again. [Author's note: These are, of course, ship's times.] She was painted a greenish-grey colour with no markings of any description and she looked absolutely brand new. (In fact *U-37* had been laid down at AG Weser of Bremen in March 1937 and was first commissioned in August 1938.) She was rather long, about 150–200 feet, with one gun well forward from the bridge. This gun was covered and not manned. There were two rows of slots along the side; we could see a man walking round under the deck on a level with the upper row of slots. She had cut-away bows but I did not notice a net-cutter. Two men stood at the side with boat-hooks to keep us off. They cruised around for half an hour taking photographs of us in the water; otherwise they just watched us and said nothing. Then she submerged and went off, without offering us any assistance whatever."

Abandoned far out into the Atlantic, in inhospitable weather conditions, the plight of the survivors was precarious. Exhausted by the battering wind and sea, they continued nevertheless to hold the violently rocking rafts together and to try to bale out the boat. This went on for two hours after the departure of the submarine. Then, suddenly, it seemed that salvation was at hand. A ship had appeared. It stopped no more than half a mile away. The relieved balers gratefully ceased their toil. They were about to be rescued. Or so it seemed. But then, heartbreakingly, the stranger blew two blasts on her whistle, turned and steamed away to the south. And to make matters worse, in apparent anticipation of being rescued, somebody had cut the rafts and boat apart.

Gradually, all three drifted farther apart. Eventually they began to lose momentary sight of each other as they slid into the deep troughs. Darkness fell. During the night three men on Mr Wilkinson's raft died. The Chief Officer, the Third Officer and a seaman were hanging on to a piece of wreckage. Their shouts became weaker and weaker until they were heard no more. Neither the waterlogged boat, last seen with six men hanging on to its grablines, nor the raft on which were the wireless operator and an A/B were ever seen again. On the Fourth Engineer's boat, they had no flares to attract the attention of any would-be rescuers, not even a light. He had been spreadeagled on its upturned keel and dived under several times to try to retrieve her flares, but had no success. All he found underneath her were five dead bodies – the Second Engineer, the cook and three firemen. Sickened and exhausted, he carried on clutching the bottom of the lurching boat for the rest of the night.

As the sun slowly broke through the morning half-light the next day, 28 May, it brought into view two ships in the distance. The Fourth Engineer blinked. One was the mystery ship which had cheerfully blown her whistle as she steamed away from them the previous day and the other was a submarine. Both were hove-to and seemed to be communicating with each other. But they steamed away hurriedly when a large group of ships appeared on the horizon. It was obviously a convoy and it would be passing the stranded men only about a mile away. He tried vainly to attract their attention, but a small boat is only a tiny speck on a corrugated sea at the distance of a mile and they were not seen.

But five men did survive to tell the tale. The captain of the Greek steamer *Francoula B. Goulandris* had spotted some floating wreckage early that morning and was keeping a keen watch for survivors from a sinking. They had been in the water for twenty-five hours when he picked them up – Mr Wilkinson, the Fourth Engineer and three seamen. They were safely landed when the ship docked at Cobh, Ireland. The unfortunate *Francoula B. Goulandris*, bound for the Virgin Islands on her next trip, was herself torpedoed and sunk on 28 June. Her twenty survivors were landed at San Sebastian, Spain.

The *Sheaf Mead* Chief Engineer's report formed a major part of the Prosecution case against Admiral Dönitz at the Nuremberg war crimes trials, when it was alleged that Oehrn had acted in an exceptionally callous manner towards the men stranded in mid-ocean, clinging to their makeshift rafts and upturned boats. The Fourth Engineer, the only other officer to survive, swore that "the submarine cruised among the survivors pushing them away with boathooks, taking photographs while they did so and laughing and joking among themselves".

Oehrn's dubious career was far from complete when he left the five *Sheaf Mead*'s sailors to their fate. In fact, by the time he returned to Wilhelmshaven on 9 June he had sunk ten ships and damaged one more in the course of a three-week patrol. Three months later, now working out of Lorient on the French Atlantic coast, Oehrn was stalking the high-riding outbound convoy OA200 in mid-Atlantic on 23 August. He had already sunk the 1,718-ton Norwegian freighter *Keret* that day, but he waited until just after midnight to select his next target. She was the 5,242-ton *Severn Leigh*, owned by the Kelston Steamship Co. She too was in ballast, bound for St John, New Brunswick, to bring another cargo of desperately needed supplies home to a hard-pressed Britain. Without any warning the submarine buried a torpedo in the steamer's side, which killed eight of her crew of forty-two merchant seamen and a solitary Royal Navy gunner. She was never to see England again. The rest of the crew took to their boats, but the submarine came nearer and sprayed a stream of murderous machine-gun bullets into them, killing eighteen more. Oehrn said later that his men had thought that the merchantman's crew were going for their gun, which had been reported to him, and that was why he had ordered them to fire. Several others were to die later by drowning or exposure.

A day or so later, the crowing voice of Lord Haw Haw (the traitor William Joyce) announced over the airwaves from Germany, "We have sunk the *Severn Leigh* with all hands." Many hearts fell in Hull, the *Severn Leigh*'s home port. "Let's not believe it," some of the braver ones advised. " Anything Old Haw Haw says is usually a lie." And it was this time, too.

On 5 September 1940 eleven-year-old Finlay Macaskill was helping his father on the family croft 100 yards from the beach at the little community of Taobh Tuath (Northton) near Leverburgh on the Isle of Harris, Outer Hebrides, during the lunch-break from school when he first noticed the sail of the lone strange boat in the distance. It seemed to be heading, or rather drifting, slowly towards the shore, lazily borne along only by the tide and the odd puff of wind, without any purposeful hand on the tiller. He shouted to the neighbours, who all came out to look. It was indeed a rare occurrence for such a boat to arrive at the isolated little collection of houses from the open ocean. The crofters' curiosity was increased when she drew nearer. There did not appear to be anybody at all on board. It was late afternoon before she finally scraped her keel on the beach. Finlay and the others rushed down to inspect her. She bore the name *Severn Leigh* on her bows and her sides were riddled with bullet holes. Slumped inside her were ten gaunt men. Eight of them were Europeans and two seemed to be of Middle Eastern or Indian origin. They were all in a dreadful state. Bedraggled and bearded, with swollen, cracked lips and glazed, hopeless expressions on their delirious wind-blackened faces. Some of them even appeared to be dead. Two, with wild eyes and dribbling mouths, were tied to the thwarts. For thirteen days they had rowed, sailed and drifted all the way from 54°31'N–25°41'W, a journey of some 600 miles as the crow flies.

In their weakened condition, they were quite unable to stand, let alone climb out of the boat. The two men who were tied up to the thwarts had gone mad after drinking sea-water and had to be restrained for their own safety. One of them was the captain, Robert Hammett, who, only a few weeks before, had earned the OBE when the *Severn Leigh* was involved in a collision in the fog-bound Firth of Forth. Surely, he above all should have been aware of the danger of succumbing to the temptation of sea-water. But desperate men do desperate things. Gently, the crofters carried them all to their houses, where the Macaskills, the Martins and the Mackays looked after them through the night. In the morning they were put aboard the old bus which served as an ambulance and rattled off on the narrow winding road to Stornoway Hospital. Sadly, after reaching the safety of dry land, one of the Lascars died on the sixty-mile journey.

One of the survivors, nineteen-year-old deckhand Bill Garvey from Hull told later how they had survived by living on condensed milk and a few biscuits. As long as they had had the strength to do so, they had taken down the sail each night to catch a few drops of dew in its folds. And once, they had managed to catch a couple of fish and sucked them to extract some of the body moisture. The most awful part came when some of the men, dying with thirst, broke the cardinal rule and drank sea-water, only to become dangerously crazy. In order to preserve the lives of the others, the captain had been forced to shoot them, only to succumb to the same temptation himself later. Bill Garvey spent several weeks in Stornoway Hospital. As were all the others, he was in a bad way, with his feeble body covered in painful boils. Later, he was sent to Campbeltown to convalesce. It was there that he met his future wife and eventually returned to Hull to raise a family of six children. But he never completely recovered from his ordeal in the *Severn Leigh*'s lifeboat and suffered from depression for the rest of his life, which came to a sad end at the early age of fifty-nine.

An official Foreign Office report entitled "Enemy attacks on Merchant Shipping 1.9.40–28.2.41" offers a different version. It says "nineteen died as a result of exposure during a thirteen days' voyage in an open boat. Five others, including the ship's cook, were left on a raft with only one biscuit and a small bottle of water between them. They were several times washed off the raft by rough seas. Two of the five died and were thrown overboard. Two others died later. A fortnight after the sinking of the *Severn Leigh*, the raft was found with the two decomposed bodies and the cook still alive." The two versions are not necessarily mutually contradictory. The FO report does not mention any *survivors* in the lifeboat. It seems that there must have been some, otherwise who was there left to tell the tale? And if there were, these were probably the men who ran ashore at Taobh Tuath after thirteen days at sea, which coincides neatly with the thirteen days in the FO report – the cook could well have become separated from them and then found on the raft at sea. The one point of issue would then be that both stories claim to involve the *only* known survivors. Extensive research has failed to ascertain the identity of the ship which found the cook, or the man's name.

Oehrn, highly regarded by Dönitz, was promoted to *Korvetten-kapitän* and appointed to command the Mediterranean U-boats in November 1941. In the course of operations off the coast of North Africa in July 1942 he was seriously wounded, captured, and sent to the British 19th General Hospital at Alexandria and thence to Camp 306 near the Bitter Lakes on the Suez Canal. An exchange of prisoners took place in November 1943 and he was returned to Germany via Spain. He spent the rest of the war ashore in various staff positions.

As for *U-37*, she was to finish the war in a mixture of fame and ignominy. Her score of fifty-one merchant ships and one escort sloop, HMS *Penzance*, sunk, grossing 190,477 tons from eleven patrols, put her second only to *U-48*, the killer of the *City of Benares* in the Second World War U-boat records. Her fighting days came to an end when she was retired to become a training boat in May 1941, and she spent the rest of the war in that capacity and for experimental testing. But when May 1945 came, with Nazi Germany in a stranglehold, she went to her end, scuttled in Sønderborg Bay, Denmark.

The case of the *Sheaf Mead* does pose a number of riddles for the historical detective, as does that of the *Severn Leigh*, to a lesser extent. Was *Sheaf Mead* a Q-ship, a lethal decoy set to trap unwary German submariners? Oehrn himself seems to have been unsure about that. He noticed the Swedish flag painted on her sides, but there was a certain something about her that told him she was no

Swede. He had received a wireless warning from base that enemy 'auxiliary ships' were operating in the vicinity only two hours before. And there was that strange structure abaft her funnel. Oehrn described it in his log as "a bell-like erection of sail and wooden lathes". Could it have been a clumsy attempt to conceal a naval gun by means of a dummy deck-house? It sounds highly possible.

She bore no name and there is no mention of any flag. Indeed, "nix name" was the answer that Oehrn received when he enquired of her identity from a sailor on a raft. And there are several versions of her previous name, which, it seems had been changed a few months before. It was *Groatefield* according to Oehrn's report about the freshly painted buoy. It appears as *Gretaston* both at Lloyds and in the Public Record Office file containing Wilkinson's report, although it is *Groteston* according to an extract of that same report edited by Sir David Maxwell Fyfe, KC. Frequent changes of ship's names were common practice in the murky double-cross world of Q-ships. To confuse matters even further, there was a ship named *Gretafield*, but she was a 10,000-ton Newcastle tanker and had been sunk in February 1940 on the Archangel-Murmansk run. And Newcastle has been wrongly stated to have been the *Sheaf Mead*'s home port by some writers.

Oehrn noticed that she was steering a strange course, not on any of the well-trod shipping lanes. It seemed to him that she had come from northern Spain when in fact she had sailed in a convoy from Milford Haven. The truth was that she had been ordered to leave the convoy early that morning and proceed independently *without zig-zagging*. Why, if not to act as a lure to U-boats? And why, in such circumstances is the code letter/number of the convoy not given, nor the name of its Commodore, who would have been responsible for making the fateful order? The behaviour of the crew after the explosion was highly disciplined. There was no panic. It was almost as if they had been drilled for such a contingency. Were most of them, in fact, members of the Royal Navy? The Public Record Office file containing Wilkinson's report is sufficiently detailed as to state that he was interviewed by the Shipping Casualties Section in June 1941. Yet it gives very little information about the *Sheaf Mead* herself. One would normally expect to be told who the owners were at least, but there is nothing of the kind. And, finally, there is no mention of any crewman's name, not even that of her Master, other than that of Wilkinson himself. Would the Chief Engineer not have used some of the names of his shipmates, quite naturally, when telling such a dramatic story? Or was the report heavily censored? If so, why? This long list of questions might even lead us to wonder whether 'Wilkinson' was the man's real name. It is all very mysterious.

As regards the *Severn Leigh*, why does the FO report not mention the beaching of the boat on the Isle of Harris? Surely Whitehall would have known about it. Why reveal the ordeal of the cook, but conceal that of the others? And again, why no name? OA was the prefix given to those convoys of ships from the Tyne and other East Coast ports, which finally assembled near Southend before setting off down Channel. The *Severn Leigh* was said to have sailed in OA200. In the Public Record Office there is a bound folder, ADM199/58. It covers the history of the OA convoys. On the first page an index of contents appears, written in a neat fountain-pen-wielding hand. It goes OA198, OA199, ——, OA201. And there is no mention of the *Severn Leigh* or OA200 in the weekly Naval Intelligence Reports.

Perhaps we will never know the truth.

2

SCHIFF 21

Cleverly disguised decoy ships had been put to extensive use by both sides in the First World War, although each side had a different reason for using them. The British employed them as lures for the U-boats which were playing havoc with their merchant shipping tonnage, while the Germans adopted the subterfuge of disguising armed vessels as innocent neutral merchantmen as a means of slipping through the tight blockade which the Royal Navy had placed across all the available exits to the world's oceans. The practice was not continued to any great extent by the British in the Second World War, mainly because they had found that the escorted convoy system was, on balance, a far more efficient means of getting their ships home safely, albeit still with horrifying losses. However, in 1939 the Germans found themselves faced with that same irksome blockade which had frustrated them twenty-five years before. The *Admiralstab* requisitioned several freighters and passenger ships for conversion into disguised armed merchant raiders, *Hilfskreuzer*, to break out and roam the oceans in search of enemy cargo ships to send to the bottom.

One was the 7,851-ton HAPAG steamship *Neumark*. They gave her six six-inch guns, plus four 3.7 cm and two 2 cm, fitted her with two torpedo tubes and loaded sixty mines into her racks. It was as much armament as was carried by many enemy light cruisers, although she would have been outpaced and lacking in armour if it had come to a running fight with one of them. She became known to the dockyard as *Schiff 21* but her official *Kriegsmarine* name was *Widder* – the Ram.

Her haughty minor aristocrat of a captain had been a U-boat commander in the First World War. He was *Fregattenkapitän*

Hellmuth von Ruckteschell, the fifty-year-old son of a Hamburg parson and a Baroness. With the legend *Narvic – Sverige* on her bows and the Swedish flag brazenly painted on her sides, the *Widder* sailed from Germany on 5 May 1940 and slipped into the Atlantic. It was to be her only operational cruise and it was to last for less than six months, but it was to be packed with controversy.

After two months spent roaming the sea-lanes, all that Ruckteschell had to show by way of scalps were the British tanker, *mv British Petrol*, which he sank without warning on 14 June about 500 miles east of the Windward Islands, and the Norwegian *Krossfonn* which he captured and sent into a Nazi-occupied French port under a prize crew.

Then, a little further south, on 10 July the *Widder* ran across the British freighter *Davisian*. One of the cargo ship's defensive gunners was on the gun deck. He swung his binoculars towards the vessel, which was on a converging course. There was nothing about her to suggest to him that she was an enemy ship, she was so cleverly camouflaged, as he explained later. When she was about half a mile away, without the slightest warning, she started firing at the *Davisian*. One shell hit her in the bows, another wrecked her funnel, and one more hit the fo'c'sle, seriously wounding Chief Petty Officer Plimmer and two seamen. The firing ceased after about forty shells had hammered into the *Davisian*, which enabled the wounded men to be carried onto the after boat deck, ready for when the boats were to be launched. One or two of the seamen moved to go below to fetch their tobacco and things, but this brought another rain of pom-pom and machine-gun fire from the raider, who had clearly misunderstood their intentions. The merchantman's Second Mate, Mr Jolly, gave his account of the encounter and the eventual ordeal that faced him and his shipmates:

"We were bound from Cardiff to Barbados with a full general cargo and mail. We were armed with a four-inch Mk IX gun and we were fitted with wireless. We were not flying the ensign at the time of the attack. All confidential books were thrown over the side by the Master. The crew, including the Master, numbered fifty, ten of whom were wounded.

"We left Cardiff in convoy on 23 June. After four days the convoy dispersed and we proceeded independently for Barbados, steering S 44 W. We proceeded without incident until 1.45 pm on 10 July when NE of Barbados we sighted what appeared to be a Swedish vessel bearing about two points on the port bow. We were travelling at a speed of thirteen knots. I was in charge of the afternoon watch and could see the masts on the horizon. The vessel seemed to be steering a course slightly converging on our own, but as she could have been on anyone of several recognized courses, this did not seem to be in any way peculiar. I watched her as she approached and saw nothing at all unusual. I could see one officer on the bridge and two of the crew on the poop who seemed to be sunbathing. The officer did not seem to be taking any undue interest in our vessel and was just steering a steady course.

"When she was about one and a half miles distant from us she opened fire with shrapnel, spraying our decks continuously, and she immediately steered right across our bows from port to starboard. I instructed the crew to keep in their quarters and then the vessel opened fire with shell, bringing down the wireless aerial with the first shot. She fired right into the crew's accommodation, which is in a house around the mast, and most of the injuries were caused then. Her firing was then transferred to the accommodation amidships which normally houses the Officers and Engineers. At this juncture the enemy hoisted two signals, one reading 'You should use your radio,' and this was followed immediately by another saying, 'You must not use your radio'. She had of course already brought down our wireless aerial and we hoisted the answering signal, 'We understand your signal and are obeying your instructions'. However, despite this he continued to shell us.

"The Chief Engineer then tried to get away the starboard lifeboat, but when he was lowering it the raider crossed on the starboard side and appeared to open fire deliberately on the boat with machine-guns. The men dashed for cover and got in the shelter of the deck casing and after a little while managed to get away and lower the port lifeboat containing thirty-two of the crew, leaving eighteen on board. We went up to the port for'ard lifeboat, commenced to launch it and when we had got it into the water the enemy crossed to the port side. There was only one man in the lifeboat, but we cut it adrift thinking that at least it would be someone to pick us up, and then we returned to the starboard after boat. The Chief Officer, Mr

Smart, had already managed to swing this clear and the remainder of the crew, including the gunner who appeared to be severely wounded, got aboard and we pulled directly towards the raider.

"Up to this time the raider had had no ensign flying, only the Swedish flag painted on her side, but as we were nearing her we saw the Nazi flag flying. I don't know when she hoisted it. The raider had fired at us continuously, but stopped when she saw that the last boat had left. When we drew alongside the raider she made some pretence of covering the Swedish markings on her sides. Our Master, Captain Pearce, thought it best to approach the raider and find out his intentions. The German captain ordered the wounded on board and then our captain. After they had talked he ordered everyone else on board. By this time our lifeboat was in a sinking condition. We were all lined up and searched for weapons. All our small possessions were taken away and put into envelopes with our names and addresses written on them. Then we were all made to strip and take a bath and taken before a German doctor who gave us a thorough medical inspection. I think this was to prevent any disease going on board. We went naked for two days except for towels which we wrapped round ourselves. I believe our clothing was all put through a sterilizer. At about eight o' clock we were separated from the crew and taken to another compartment farther for'ard, which was round the bulkhead by the engine-room. It was terribly hot, I should think about 105°.

"There we found the Officers and Engineers of the *British Petrol*, who told us they had been there for twenty-seven days. They told us their ship had been attacked in much the same way as ours, and shelled continuously for half an hour. The compartment contained collapsible forms and tables which we had to fold up at night and put into overhead racks. We were given one blanket each and used our life-jackets as pillows. The food we had on board was rough but there was plenty of it. Black bread was the main item, with a varying accompaniment of honey, jam, synthetic butter which looked like lard and tasted like plain grease, and cheese which came out of lead tubes. One day we had pork. The coffee was very bad, it tasted like dirty water, but we were glad of it because we were always thirsty.

15

"Captain Pearce was taken back to the *Davisian* with the Mate and the Chief Steward and the raider took all the provisions from the ship and a lot of the crew's clothing. The *British Petrol* crew had left most of their clothes on their ship and were almost naked. I think the idea was to give them the clothing from the *Davisian*. The German interpreter seemed very friendly. He had been a farmer in Kenya and was married to an Englishwoman. He told us they were soon going home, but this may have been said to mislead us.

"The *British Petrol* crew told us that the night France fell one of the German officers had come down, after celebrating, and told them that they must go home and tell their wives that they must obey the invaders when the time came. They were also told that they could listen only to the true news which came from Germany, and that all the other news they had heard was lies. They were then made to listen to some wireless propaganda from Lord Haw-Haw, but they jeered so loudly and continuously that they were not made to do so again.

"On the whole we were treated very considerately, except on one occasion when it appeared there could be some trouble. Apparently, when our Chief Wireless Operator was in one of the cabins waiting to be questioned he remarked that when the British Navy caught up with the raiders they would all be shot. This produced a message from the German commander which went something like this, 'I have noticed the difference between the two British crews and already I have had trouble with one of you. It was not necessary for me to take you out of the water; I did it for your own good because we Germans are conducting the war in our own fashion and in accordance with the wishes of our Führer. You have increased the difficulties of my ship. I do not expect gratitude from you, who are my enemies, but I will warn you that my rules must be obeyed and for any disobedience there is only one penalty – shooting.'

"Later the interpreter told us that there had been some mistake and that the German commander had investigated what had happened. I think maybe there must have been a Gestapo officer on board. The next morning we received the following typed message from the captain: 'The war between your ship and mine is now over. It was necessary for me to subdue you. I am sorry that some of your comrades have been wounded. They will be well cared for. My rules are posted up and you must acquaint yourselves thoroughly with them. For any disobedience there is only one penalty – shooting.'

"I should think that the ship's complement was about 400, and they were all young. None seemed to be over twenty-five with the exception of the senior officer and they were all naval men. The Officers wore naval uniforms with wings on their caps and the remainder wore singlets with wings on their shirts. All the crew were referred to as soldiers, then next came the sergeants and then the Commander and then the Captain.

"We were allowed on deck twice a day for about twenty minutes each morning and evening, and observed as much as we could. I noticed a garden seat on the poop hiding a four-inch gun. Immediately over our accommodation was what was obviously a six-inch gun hidden by a casing which bore foreign writing. Our prison was in the lower outward deck and we had to pass to the upper deck twice a day for exercise, and on our way we saw four full-sized mines and what appeared to be eight torpedo heads."

The *Davisian* men had been on board the raider for just three days when they heard the German crew running around with great urgency. The ship had picked up speed, to what the well-practised ears of the engine-room men among the prisoners told them was about seventeen knots. Something was in the air, for sure. And this was confirmed when one of the German sergeants came down and told them there would be some action and his men mounted a machine-gun outside the door of the prisoners' compartment. Had Ruckteschell been tagged by a British cruiser and was running for his life? If so, their lives were at stake too, because it could only be a question of time before this tin-can was caught and blown to kingdom come and the Royal Navy would have no idea that their own countrymen were on board the fleeing target.

Nothing happened for about an hour, but then the sound of gunfire began, with the staccato chatter of machine guns interspersed with the heavy, single, thumping cracks of shell-fire. The shooting stopped after about twenty minutes and the sergeant appeared again with the crews of both ships and the cardboard boxes containing their personal possessions, which he told Mr Smart to distribute. Then he took away Captain Pearce and the Chief Engineer.

The prisoners, understandably perplexed by these events and fearful of what might happen to them next, were then lined up on the upper deck. Looking over the side, they saw two boats tied up alongside the raider. One was empty, but the other contained twenty-six men. There had been no Royal Navy cruiser in pursuit of them, but the *Widder* herself had made another kill. These men were from her latest victim, the British *mv King John*. The problem from the German's point of view was that this time his prey had managed to get a brief distress signal away before her wireless aerials were brought down by a shell. And the call had been picked up by a Japanese ship, an American ship and a US Coastguard station. It was time for *Schiff 21* to make herself scarce in the wilds of the Atlantic before a posse of cruisers really did arrive on the scene. The interpreter explained that the Commander had decided to send the prisoners away in the boats, except of course Captain Pearce and the Chief Engineer, who were being kept as prisoners. The *King John*'s crew were not even coming on board their captor. He gave them a course of 218° and they climbed in, with Mr Smart taking charge of one boat and Mr Jolly the other. They pushed off, over 200 miles from the nearest landfall. Mr Jolly takes up the story again:

> "The wind was fresh, from the south-east. A heavy swell was running and we had one small square sail. In case we got carried too far north of the islands we steered as far south as we could, which was about W.S.W. We found the boat was quite well equipped, having sufficient water to allow the men three dippers a day for ten days. There were plenty of biscuits; forty-eight tins of condensed milk; a German first-aid kit containing two bottles of ersatz rum and some tinned cherries. However, after the first taste of the cherries everyone was violently sick, so, thinking that they were maybe poisoned, we didn't touch them again. On the third day out we saw a ship about five miles away. We tried to attract her attention by hoisting a blanket, but she didn't see it so we pulled it down and soaked it in oil, then set light to it and hoisted it again. However, either she still didn't see it or didn't want to see it because she sailed straight on. Everyone was disheartened after that.
>
> "At about 0300 the next morning we sighted land. It was still dark of course, and as we were wary of running onto any

reefs we decided to wait for daylight. At 0500 we sailed on and landed on the beach of what looked to be a small island. There was a small agricultural village, but as soon as the inhabitants saw us they took to their heels, with the exception of one old woman who was probably too old to run. We had with us a Yugoslav captain who understood the local dialect. He said she kept telling him it was a French leper colony, but we were not to believe this. It was an old trick that was played when people did not want you to land. However, we were not convinced and said we would return to the boat, but the Yugoslav and his men said they were not coming and we saw them set off over the hills.

"We sailed off again and as we approached a small bay about six small rowing boats surrounded us. This alarmed us a little as we knew we were near French possessions and thought we might be interned. They told us that we were at St Bartholomew and we asked them for a bearing of the nearest British island. They told us it was St Kitts, but a man flying a pilot flag said we would never make it because of the wind. A second man, whom we found out to be the Town Clerk, told us to go into port and after we had rested awhile if we still wanted to leave they would let us. We agreed to this and were met at the pier by the Mayor, who was a French gentleman and made us very welcome. I wrote out a message for the British Consul at Gustav, telling him about the three ships, but the Mayor wouldn't send it. He said he would arrange for the Governor to do that.

"They billeted us in the local school. Everyone was very poor but the inhabitants were very kind to us as far as their means permitted and gave us three mattresses. On the 16 July, about three days after we had landed, a vessel* called at the island and picked us up. I believe this had been arranged by the Admiral. We were taken to St Kitts and from there we were brought home in a passenger/cargo boat and were landed at Methil, on the Fife coast of Scotland, on Sunday 25 August."

---

* The vessel was HMS *Diomede*. She arrived at Port Gustavia at 0800 on 20 July 1940 and after the landing party had taken refreshments with the hospitable Mayor, picked up the survivors and sailed for Basseterre (St Kitts) at 1015.

Meanwhile the *Widder* was continuing on the hunt, but three weeks were to pass after she had dispatched the *King John* before Ruckteschell found another victim in 26°30'N.48°W, south-east of Bermuda, on the evening of 4 August. She was the 6,114-ton Norwegian tanker *Beaulieu*, owned by Björnstad Björn & Co. of Oslo, bound for Aruba from Ponte Delgada in the Azores. Her Third Officer was on watch. He peered into the blurred blue-blackness of the sub-tropical summer night. Was that shape on the port bow a darkened ship about half a mile away? He couldn't be sure, but just to be safe he switched on the navigation lights and put the helm hard over to avoid a collision. Instantly a deluge of shots spat from the dark shape. Machine guns, pom-poms and quick-firing small calibre armament all poured fire on to the *Beaulieu*, concentrating on her bridge, wireless office and cabin accommodation below the bridge. Tracer bullets stitched a red path across the water to illuminate the target. The Third Officer threw himself flat on the bridge and the Master, having given the order to stop engines, hurried towards his cabin to collect and destroy the ship's papers. But he never made it. He was cut down on the boat-deck, hit through the chest and legs. The assault continued for about five minutes and when the firing ceased all the officers and crew who had not been killed mustered aft and cleared away the lifeboats, one on each side.

By this time the raider had moved round to the starboard quarter. Ruckteschell switched on his searchlight and recommenced firing, this time raking the *Beaulieu* from stem to stern, and with heavier calibre shells aiming for the waterline. The merchant crew lowered their boats and pulled away as fast as they could, but the Mate and the cook were both killed. They kept pulling on their oars for a couple of hours, in the desperate hope of putting enough distance behind them to make it impossible for the raider to find them in the wide ocean. After this two hours they heard a huge explosion, followed by two lesser ones and flames lit up the dark sky as their ship exploded.

Ruckteschell had been stalking her all day, ever since a smudge of her smoke had been seen on the horizon just after the *Widder*'s morning roll call. His war diary tells the story of how he caught and killed her:

"It is a tanker with course set for Trinidad. I keep the upper edge of the funnel in sight only from the after cross-tree. An officer is aloft on permanent look-out. During the afternoon we have ascertained her course and speed. The distance is twenty sea miles. At 1200 she altered course by 25°, which threw my calculations out again, but I was *au fait* of the new situation in a few hours. [This would have been when she received orders to divert to Caripito.]

"We were to the west of her and so had the benefit of the evening sun. An hour after sunset the horizon was dark and I turned towards her and increased speed. The ship had already been made ready for battle during the day – shells laid ready, all guns and flak guns too, were ready for action, similarly the searchlights on the bridge. It was very dark. About half an hour beforehand a door must have been opened on the tanker which emitted a ray of light for a short time. The bearing confirmed our own dead-reckoning.

"Stand to! The vessel comes into view 16° to port. Faint rays of light as if from badly darkened scuttles can be seen. I look for navigation lights but can see none. The vessel must have seen us too, distance twenty-five hectometres, and switches on her navigation and masthead lights. The fact that she was sailing without lights is proof to me that she was an enemy vessel.

"I gave orders to give permission to open fire with all armament except torpedoes. The steamer was attacked with the aid of searchlights. Three short bursts of fire sufficed. The tanker is lying stopped and has set working lamps at the after-mast. I go round to her stern to find out her name in the beam of the searchlight, but there is no name to be seen. There is a boat aft at her stern with about twenty men in it. The starboard cutter is not yet in the water.

"I again bring the whole deck under fire at close range, so as to be secure against a burst of fire from the enemy from rifles or pistols – for British instructions to their ships are to hold hand weapons in readiness in case of possible attack.

"The enemy boat disappeared in the darkness and I did not see it again and also did not notice how the second one put off.

"The funnel of the tanker is painted yellow and has a large black B marked on it. [Apparently, he then fires a torpedo.] I did not really want to send off a boarding-party, for the ship is badly damaged around the bridge, and also on account of the time a search takes. But my torpedo does not explode this time. It was fired in the normal way. It turned out to be a gyro failure and endangered our own ship, which it approached at one point. I waited awhile and then go back to the tanker and sink her with demolition charges.

"If our action had been observed on the horizon during the night, an enemy vessel could have been on the spot by this time. The demolition charges set her whole stern ablaze. She does not sink for fifty-two minutes, but even then she leaves her stem above the surface. I leave her and move away to the east at thirteen knots. I make for the Azores as reported.

"This method of attack is, in my opinion the only one possible when one has no aeroplane. [All *Hilfskreuzer* were specified as carrying at least one Arado float plane, but this seems to indicate an omission in the *Widder*'s case.] True, it takes a lot of time and energy and fuel oil. True, one has possibly to take the risk of not finding out till it is dark that it is an 'innocent' vessel, with full lights and nationality markings. But there will be hardly any neutrals on these routes.

"One cannot and may not worry about boats and wounded at night, for one cannot be certain in advance when approaching them whether they are going to open fire. If a boat were to come alongside us of its own accord and ask for help I would never send it away. But the tales about us are so brutal that they would rather set out on a long sea trip than approach the warship.

"According to the Intelligence Officer, the bombardment of the tanker itself cost 4–6 dead.

"Enthusiastically as the crew viewed the great show of fireworks with tracer shots and great explosions and the blaze of oil that followed, I still had to make it clear to them why the attack had to take place at night now and why we were taking no more prisoners. I had the feeling that for the first time a sense of seriousness of war has been brought home to my men, and that was good."

Ruckteschell sped north-eastwards towards the Azores. En route, the Dutch ship *Oostplein* and the Finnish barque *Killoran* were sent to the bottom of the mid-Atlantic. At dusk on 21 August the 5,594-ton cargo-vessel *Anglo-Saxon* of London, owned by the

Nitrate Producers Steamship Co. was in 26°10'N.34°09'W. By 2020 hours it was pitch dark. The log of the Mate, who subsequently died in the gig, read as follows:

"Vessel was not sighted until she was within a mile of us. First sent four shells, 4" crashing into poop and gun platform aft. Many of crew on fo'c'sle killed. She then steamed to within three cables and raked the deck with incendiary machine-gun bullets coloured red, yellow, white and blue. Then a shell hit engine-room starboard side and main boiler burst. The bridge and wireless room were raked with pom-pom and machine-guns. Some of the crew went to the boats on the boat-deck but were mown down by machine-gun fire. The two big boats were badly damaged. Senior Wireless Operator reported wireless installations smashed, unable to send S.O.S. On reporting to Master, found him presumed shot down by machine-gun bullets in his cabin; saloon and amidships were wrecked; poop was by this time blazing and the crew were told to take to the boats. The port gig under my orders was lowered and contained seven of the crew. When the gig pulled away from the vessel the raider was lying off half a mile to port and a few minutes later fired tracer bullets into two life-rafts launched from the vessel. The vessel sank stern first and shortly disappeared altogether. Raider headed off to the eastward. Assume the Germans wanted no members of crew left alive and we were fortunate in this boat's crew escaping observation. Though the gig remained hove-to all night, no wreckage or other survivors were sighted."

"After the first salvo the steamer begins to send out distress signals, R-R-R-R," [Ruckteschell wrote in his diary.]

"But our W/T operators have a very good method of sending, with the result that, so the Wireless Officer tells me, nothing appears to have got through. Thirty seconds later there was wireless silence. The wireless traffic observed later did not give rise to any suspicious transmissions.

"The flak is in action at ranges of less than 1000 metres. It can scarcely be checked and is making such a noise that the 'cease fire' arrives late. Almost 400 rounds have been fired.

"I see by the searchlight that it is the English vessel *Anglo-Saxon*. I am about to put out a boat to have a few more details of the vessel brought in, but just when I have given the order another magazine blows up aft and she begins to burn more fiercely in other places. I revoke the order as more single explosions, probably shells, are taking place.

"I give orders to fire a torpedo, with reluctance, as we have only seven left. Torpedo fired – hit scored on No.4 hold. The smoke from the explosion is dense black and smells strongly of coal, which I presume was her cargo. Judging by her size, she must have had at least 7,000 tons cargo. What else is England exporting to the Southern states now?

"For just a short time, two lights are seen in the vicinity of the steamer – apparently from two boats which at one time keeps up a short transmission of W/T traffic which, however, cannot be read. Then no more lights or boats are seen.

"Since no distress messages of any kind were made, I do not undertake any further search operations. The distance to the Canaries is about 800 sea miles with a moderate wind, so they can be reached by the boats. I move away east on a feint course, then north. I want to keep to this longitude for the time being. There is certainly more doing here."

It may have been a mere 800 miles to the Canaries, but that was not where the gig finally made land. The little boat sailed and drifted in precisely the opposite direction, and by the time she reached the West Indies two months later, at the end of October, five of her occupants had died, leaving only two alive. But Ruckteschell was right about one thing. There was certainly more doing in that stretch of the Atlantic.

A few days later, on 25 August, he was stalking a Liverpool tanker, the 6,300-ton *Cymbeline*, but botched his run-in. He had come in too fast and was gaining on her far too rapidly. She spotted him when he was about ten miles away and warily turned away to the north. The German's skills at the game of cat-and-mouse now came into play. He turned south at speed and allowed the tanker to get right out of sight before making a long detour and getting onto the track for what he supposed to be her intended destination – Trinidad. Then he reduced speed to a five-knot crawl and waited. He was spot on. At 1800 hours on 26 August, the foremast lookout reported the tips of masts in view on a bearing of exactly 90°.

This time the mouse did not see the cat until he was only half a mile away on the port beam and was spitting a rain of fire. The *Cymbeline*'s wireless room and bridge were immediately destroyed, and she received hits in the engine-room and in several places in her hull. The onslaught went on for about twenty minutes whilst Ruckteschell positioned his ship a mere three ship's lengths away directly under the tanker's stern. Each time the crew tried to swing out their lifeboats from the boat-deck they were raked with machine-gun fire and of course they had absolutely no chance of manning their defensive stern gun, which was now directly under the muzzles of the German's own guns.

James Signey, the Third Engineer, was asleep in his cabin when he was wakened by the sound of gunfire at 2100 hours. He grabbed his trousers, patrol jacket and life-belt and rushed through the door just as the cabin was wrecked by a shell. He hurried towards the engine-room, but was driven back when part-way down the ladder by the rush of scalding steam. He went to help with the launching of the lifeboats, but the constant barrage of machine-gun bullets which chased the men from side to side as they strove to swing out first one boat then the other made it difficult even to proceed along the deck. By now the ship was bathed in the bright glare of the raider's searchlight and star shells were bursting overhead. Eventually Signey found Mr Williams, the Second Mate, who told him that they had managed to launch the starboard boat but it was badly damaged and virtually useless. The falls of the boats on the after-boat deck had been cut by the machine-gun fire and they could not be launched, but Signey and two sailors managed to heave one of the life rafts over the side. But before they could jump onto it it had been swept out of reach astern. Then a huge explosion lifted Signey clean off his feet. Ruckteschell had put a torpedo into her on the starboard side. It hit between the stoke-hold and the engine-room and exploded in one of the oil bunkers, sending a heavy shower of thick oil over everybody on the after-deck. By now the *Cymbeline* was ablaze in several places. Signey knew it was time to take his chances in the water. And within a few minutes his ship was resting on the bottom of the ocean in 27°55'N.36°01'W.

Ruckteschell heard many cries for help from the water, even as he went in to fire the torpedo and ordered some night life-buoys to be thrown over the side. He swept his searchlight across the oil-covered water and could see men clinging to bits of wreckage and the life-buoys. Then one of the lifeboats came alongside the raider with thirteen men in it. They were all drenched in mazout oil and in a state of shock. Some of them were wounded. The boat was full of water and almost sinking. He took them aboard and put out his cutters to search for more survivors. They each returned two or three times with a handful of men, until no more could be found.

For some reason, in this case Ruckteschell had reverted to the practice of picking up survivors as prisoners. To linger in the vicinity for several hours after the sinking, which was close to a recognized sea lane and had been accompanied by great leaping flames which must have been visible at night many miles distant and could easily have brought an inquisitive Royal Navy cruiser onto the scene, was putting his ship into a certain amount of danger to say the least. Nevertheless, he had saved twenty-six men from the *Cymbeline*. But that still left ten who were unaccounted for, including her Master Captain James Chadwick.*

However, he took no such merciful action when the raider sank the last victim of her only sally into the Atlantic, the neutral Greek *Antonius Chandris* at dusk on 8 September 1940 in mid-ocean WSW of the Cape Verde Islands. No provision was made for the safety of her crew and she was unable to send out any distress calls.

Schiff 21 returned to Brest on 31 October 1940 and was retired from operational duties. She was later used as a repair ship in Norway and survived the war to be taken over by the British in 1945.

But for her captain, Hellmuth von Ruckteschell, the end of hostilities did not mean complete peace. Like so many other Axis war criminals, he managed to spirit himself far beyond the clutches of his pursuers, or so he thought. He fled to China, but there he had the misfortune to require medical treatment and his presence in a Peking hospital ward was discovered. His movements were followed and eventually the Naval Staff Officer Shanghai signalled Naval Intelligence in London. Their Lordships of the Admiralty wanted to know more about this, and they wasted no words in explaining their demands. "SECRET – 27.2.46 – What is being done to apprehend von Ruckteschell?"

Back came the eventual reply, "Von Ruckteschell allowed to embark on the steamer *Marine Robin* for normal repatriation from

---

* A boat containing survivors from the *Cymbeline* was eventually picked up by ss *Yolanda* and landed at Covenas, Colombia on 16 September 1940.

China to Germany without being arrested and without due advice to Admiralty."

The reaction at the Admiralty to this apparently lackadaisical attitude can only be imagined. Telephone wires hummed peevishly and urgent orders were growled out. The result was that when the 11,750-ton three-decked *Marine Robin* berthed at Bremen on Tuesday 6 August 1946 there was a welcoming party waiting to arrest the fugitive. And there were several others on board whom the British authorities were anxious to question. It could have been the intention all along, of course, not to make an arrest in China in the knowledge that more fish could be caught in the net by waiting for the US War Shipping Administration's ship to arrive in Germany. They were all passed into the hands of the British Army of the Rhine at the Aspberg Detention Centre (code-name Tomato) on 21 August, six years to the day after Ruckteschell had blown the collier *Anglo-Saxon* to smithereens and left the seven survivors of her crew to drift 1,500 miles in the gig, five of whom were to die a horrible death in the lonely wastes of the Atlantic. Later he was transferred to a Prisoner-of-War camp near Sheffield and on 1 April 1947 he was flown to Germany to stand trial for war crimes in his home town, at Centre 24a, NW Europe War Crimes Group, Hausastrasse 8, Hamburg 13, charged with murder and destruction of merchant ships without warning and without provision of safety for their crews.

His trial began on 5 May. Defended by a Dr Zipler, he pleaded that his intention had always been to destroy tonnage, not lives. He claimed that the shooting had always stopped as soon as the victims' boats were launched. Ships' boats had not even been specifically targeted on their boat-decks, let alone in the water and that there had been no attacks with small arms or machine guns. He had not even known that the *Widder* was armed with machine guns. He had rescued survivors whenever possible and never left a sinking without first thoroughly criss-crossing the area searching for survivors. Some of these things may have been partly true in some of the cases, but Ruckteschell's pleas did not carry enough weight against the evidence presented to the Court by the Prosecution. After a two-week hearing, he was found guilty on three of the five counts against him and sentenced to ten years' imprisonment.

But Zipler was a good mouthpiece for his client, even to the extent of persuading the British to fly over the trousers, overcoat and vest that Ruckteschell had left behind in Sheffield. He appealed against the sentence and by 3 September a Brigadier Williams was writing from the Office of the Judge Advocate, British Army of the Rhine, to confirm that the ten years had been reduced to seven. And a week later that it was further reduced to three!

3

THE SEAVACUEES OF THE *CITY OF BENARES*

During 1915 the Germans made nineteen Zeppelin raids from their bases in Belgium and Holland on targets ranging from Tyneside down to Sussex. Altogether they dropped something like 32,000 lbs of bombs. 127 people were killed and 352 injured in the world's first strategic air-raids. The unwelcome distinction of being London's first ever fatal air raid casualties fell on two children, Elsie and May Leggett, of 33 Cowper Road, Stoke Newington, victims of an incendiary bomb dropped by *LZ-38* commanded by Hauptmann Linnarz on the night of 31 May. Nothing like it had ever been seen before. When raiders appeared in the sky from across the sea to bomb and terrorize the innocent non-combatants of British towns and cities, it was the first serious invasion of national privacy that the Island People had experienced for nearly 850 years.

Between the two World Wars aero-technology made giant strides. In the space of two decades the air-ship disappeared altogether as an instrument of battle and the war-aeroplane evolved from a spluttering flimsy 90 mph kite held together with wire into either a lethal 350 mph all-metal streamlined fighter or a thundering sky-juggernaut able to carry an 8,000 lb bomb load over a 2,000-mile range. By the outbreak of the Second World War Germany had built an air war-fleet of 3,200 planes – nearly twice as many as Britain and France could put into the air together.

The British Government, still mindful of the disquiet that the Zeppelin raids had caused, was fully alive to this danger. From the mid-1930s onwards it had made plans for the evacuation of up to four million people from especially vulnerable areas, mainly school children and mothers with infants, to what were thought to be safer places. For once it appeared that Great Britain was prepared, at least for something.

Following the fall of France in mid-June 1940 over 10,000 offers poured in from overseas, mainly from the Dominions and the USA, by ordinary members of the public keen to offer a safe home to British children. Immediately there was an excessive demand for the limited number of places on offer. The British Government set up a committee under Geoffrey Shakespeare, forty-seven-year old MP for Norwich and Under-Secretary of State for the Dominions, to consider how to best deal with the question.

The upshot was the establishment of the Children's Overseas Reception Board (CORB), with Shakespeare as Chairman, which opened its offices in part of the premises of travel agents Thomas Cook & Son in London's West End on 20 June. Inside, the building was crammed with parents anxious to stake their child's claim for a place, and almost 3,000 more lined the Berkeley Street pavement outside in a queue to get in. Shakespeare's main worry, which was shared by Churchill, was the danger of sea travel at that time, bearing in mind the Germans' 'unprincipled' manner of warfare and the scant availability of suitable ships.

On the evening of Sunday, 23 June 1940 Shakespeare made a broadcast on BBC radio in which he outlined the details of the plan that CORB had put together. Children between the ages of five and sixteen were to be eligible. Offers from the Dominions had now swollen to 20,000, although suitable ships to carry such numbers were in extremely short supply, owing to the pressures of war. There would be doctors, nurses and qualified guardian escorts to accompany each sailing. But Shakespeare gave no real guidance on the advisability of taking up a place if it was offered. "That is advice I cannot give," he said. "You have to weigh the danger to which your child is exposed in this country, whether by invasion or air raids, against the risk to which every ship that leaves these shores is subjected in wartime by enemy action, whether by air, submarine or mine."

Within ten days 211,000 applications had been received for one of the 20,000 places. Most of them came from grant-aided schools, which were classified as being 'working class'. CORB officially closed the list on 4 July, the day on which news came through of the sinking of the liner *Arandora Star*, torpedoed in the Atlantic. She had been sailing alone and unescorted when attacked and the loss convinced both the Government and the Admiralty that the safest form of transit by sea for the children was in convoy, with the absolutely essential provision of adequate naval escort.

"The shortage of naval vessels is the main difficulty," declared Clement Attlee, the Lord Privy Seal. "In view of the fate of the *Arandora Star* the Government cannot take the responsibility of sending shiploads of children except in convoy." Government hesitancy was causing problems on the other side of the Atlantic too. The British Ambassador in Washington, Lord Lothian, reported that the idea of giving refuge to children living under threat of war in Europe had spread rapidly throughout America and there were now upwards of half a million US homes said to be ready to take them. Lothian felt that if something positive was not done quickly interest would begin to wane. The British Government hastened to explain that the real problem was that of shortage of naval escort ships. They had long since come to the firm conclusion that children should only be transported in convoyed ships and it was vital that such convoys be adequately escorted.

The German Navy had been under strict orders from Hitler, at the outbreak of war, to observe the Prize Regulations in force at that time, but it was not long before he had begun to issue instructions which sidestepped them. Even as early as the end of September 1939, if an enemy merchant ship attempted to use its wireless when stopped by a U-boat, it was fair game to be sunk, according to Hitler's new code of conduct. Next, he gave authority to U-boat captains to sink all darkened ships, wearing whatever flag, sailing at night in waters adjacent to the British Isles and France. Then he began to extend the westward Atlantic limits within which observance of the Prize Regulations was cancelled. On 17 October 1939, he gave permission for all 'hostile', i.e. British or French, ships to be attacked without warning and in mid-November it was clarified that this included passenger liners. Hitler, it seemed, had imposed illegal unrestricted submarine warfare by stealthy stages. But the line between legal and illegal acts of war at sea had been somewhat blurred by the 1930 London Naval Treaty, to which Germany had acceded in 1936, the other signatories being Great Britain, France, the USA, Italy and Japan. The Treaty laid down that a belligerent merchant vessel must not be sunk or rendered helpless unless it had persistently refused to stop when ordered to do so, and even then not until all those on board had been put in a place of safety. And a lifeboat was not to be considered as a place of safety unless weather conditions were fair and there was a reasonable proximity to land. Importantly, an absolute priority for the rescue of survivors did not apply if it jeopardized the safety of the ship which did the sinking. This clause effectively gave freedom to submarine commanders to interpret their legal obligations in whatever way they found convenient. Moreover, it conflicted head-on with the requirements to give help to survivors and it was to provide the main nub of the argument in more than one of the war crimes trials which followed the Second World War.

But despite Hitler's unilateral re-drafting of the rules for naval warfare, the winter and spring of 1939/40 remained remarkably quiet as regards U-boat activity, although the fall of France, and the consequential access to her Atlantic ports gave the Germans fresh encouragement to go out on the hunt, now over an extended range of over 600 miles. On 31 March Winston Churchill, the First Lord of the Admiralty, made a broadcast in which he praised the convoy system. It had led, he claimed, to only one in 800 neutral ships which had depended on the protection of the Allied Navies being sunk. By early August, however, the U-boats were back in the Atlantic with a vengeance and Churchill, now Prime Minister, was singing a different tune. "The repeated severe losses in the North-West Approaches are most grievous," he wrote scathingly to the First Sea Lord, Admiral Sir Dudley Pound, "and I wish to be assured that they are being grappled with."

Shakespeare's office reiterated solemnly that the children would sail only if in convoy and adequately protected by naval escort. The parents were reassured by this statement. But the average parent is not a naval tactician, not even remotely aware of the logistical problems of fighting a sea war across an ocean. The fact was that such naval vessels as would be acting as convoy escorts, light speedy craft such as destroyers or corvettes, lacked the range of the U-boats. The escort could be provided to a transatlantic convoy only to about 17° West – about 300 miles west of the Irish coast. From that point an outward bound convoy would disperse and proceed independently, whilst the escort would meet an inward-bounder, whose time of sailing would have been carefully synchronized, to escort to its UK destination. This system may have set an example of good management of limited resources, but at the same time it signalled to any U-boats lurking in mid-Atlantic that the arrival of an inward-bound convoy was imminent. And the inward-bounders were the ones carrying the supplies vital to the Allied war effort. Parents were, of course, completely aware of the dangers which faced the sea-borne evacuees, but CORB had given them a false sense of security by failing to explain properly the 'limit of convoy' factor.

Throughout the sunlit days of August and September, 1940, whilst the Battle of Britain raged and Spitfires and Messerschmitts fought it out in the sky over the fields and orchards of the Garden of England, the U-boat war escalated in the wastes of the north Atlantic, creating even more strain for an already over-strained Royal Navy. Hitler, having apparently abandoned his plans to invade Britain, now threw everything into this new effort to bring her to her knees. On 1 August he announced a complete blockade of the British Isles to take effect three weeks later and unrestricted submarine warfare to be waged in the Atlantic east of 20° West. But simultaneously hundreds of CORB children were embarking in convoys for the Dominions and the USA and arriving safely. Had the lack of escort ships been, after all, only a myth?

*   *   *

On Thursday, 29 August the 15,000-ton Dutch liner *Volendam* sailed from Liverpool for Halifax, Nova Scotia, with 321 CORB evacuees on board among her 600 passengers. It was at 22.00 hours on the second day out, seventy miles off Bloody Foreland on the Donegal coast, that she caught a torpedo in her port side. The weather was worsening, typical Atlantic behaviour at that time of year, and *Volendam*'s British master, Captain J.F. Webster, elected to transfer his passengers to three ships that were standing by while this was still practicable. This was safely done, the only casualty being the ship's purser, who fell and was crushed between her plates and a lifeboat. *Volendam* herself remained afloat and was eventually taken in tow and beached in the Clyde estuary.

The children of the *Volendam* were all sent back home, for their relieved parents perhaps to re-consider and reflect. All, that is, except two. Ten-year-old Michael Brooker from Bourne Vale Road, Bromley, Kent, and twelve-year-old Patricia Allen from Aigburth Road, Liverpool, had both recently lost their homes in the blitz. They were delivered back to Sherwood's Lane School in Fazackerley, Liverpool, the assembly point which they had left only a few days previously, to be given priority places on the next available sailing.

33

As fate would have it, this meant that they would embark, not on the *Anselm*, the *Ceramic*, the *Hilary*, the *Ruahine*, the *Llanstephan Castle*, or any of the other merchant ships which were engaged in the overseas evacuation of children, but on the *City of Benares*.

On 9 September, two days after Hitler started the London blitz, a team of ten selected guardian-escorts for the *City of Benares* children were summoned to the Fazackerley Cottage Homes in Liverpool for briefing. There had been many thousands of applications from volunteers to perform this duty for all the 'seavacuee' sailings. After careful sifting, Marjorie Day, the fifty-three-year-old headmistress of Wycombe Abbey School, Buckinghamshire, was selected to head the team for the *City of Benares*, which also included a thirty-year-old woman doctor on special leave from Hammersmith Hospital, Betty Margaret Zeal, and a nurse, twenty-six-year-old Dorothy Smith, from the Central London Throat Hospital in Gray's Inn Road. The other female escorts were all teachers from the London area. There was forty-four-year-old Maud Hillman, an infant teacher, Mary Ann Cornish, aged forty-one, who taught music, twenty-five-year-old art teacher Sybil Gilliat-Smith, and a last-minute recruit, a part-time London ambulance driver cum LCC teacher and mother of two from New Zealand, Lillian Towns. The rest of the team was made up of three men, all with religious connections. They were Reverend William H. King, a Canadian from Ontario who had been working in Stepney, Father Rory O'Sullivan from Herne Bay, and a strapping rugby playing, motor racing Oxford divinity student, twenty-three-year-old Michael Rennie from Hampstead.

Among the children themselves, the Londoners formed the largest group, while the rest came from other ports which were taking a battering under the blitz – Sunderland, Newport, Southampton and Liverpool. The departure from home in Lilford Road, off Brixton's Coldharbour Lane, could hardly have been more dramatic for the five of the ten children of council labourer Eddie Grimmond and his wife Hannah who were eligible for the CORB scheme, i.e. between the ages of five and sixteen. On the night of 9 September their house was reduced to a pile of rubble by a direct hit. It was a miracle that none of them were hurt, thanks to their Anderson shelter, but nevertheless everything that they owned was destroyed, including the ready packed suitcases of the excited children. The five had been on the reserve list, but their new homeless predicament, Eddie argued, was such that they should now be viewed as priority cases. There had been some cancellations and the Grimmond children were given berths aboard the next sailing. And so, with only hours to spare, with only the clothes they wore on their backs, and only hours since the Germans had blown their world to smithereens, he piled into a taxi with Augusta (Gussie), 13, Violet, 10, Connie, 9, little Eddie, 8, and Lenny, 5, and took them to Euston Station where, still white-faced with shock, they boarded the train for Liverpool.

The Sunderland exodus of 7,910 children to various locations was tiny compared to London's 600,000, but it was as well organized. The civic and educational authorities were quick to assume parental responsibility for the children and a compulsory 'stiff upper lip' attitude was firmly imposed on the youngsters and their parents alike when it came to the final departure from home. One teacher was known to have told her children, "We want no tears or fuss". And they were to remember that they were "British to the backbone". At Bede School, when the time came for the *City of Benares* party to depart, parents were told not to come right up to the School to see their children off to Canada, but to wait at the bottom of the hill and wave goodbye to them from there as they marched off in crocodile file, with their gas-mask cases swinging from their shoulders, and each one correctly tagged and labelled, en route for Millfield Station. It was a classic display of organized British *sang froid*.

There were eleven children in the Sunderland party for the *Benares*. They were thirteen-year-old Edith Smith and her sister Irene, 11; Maureen Dixon, 10; Tommy and Anne Watson, 9 and 6; Dorothy Wood, 9; Eleanor Wright, 13; Billy and Peter Short, 9 and 5; and Boy Scouts George Geoffrey Crawford, 14, and Derek Leigh, aged 11. Many of them had never before been outside their home town. And despite the keen competition for one of the limited number of CORB berths, there were several who, for one reason or another, did not take up the place they had been offered. Edith Henderson, 14, had already been evacuated from her home in Kingsley Street, Sunderland, to North Cowton in Yorkshire, and was brought back home to get ready to sail to Canada. But at the last minute her mother had a premonition of disaster and changed her mind about the whole thing. So Edith and her twelve-year-old twin brother and sister Ted and Margaret, plus little sister Joan, aged nine, stayed at home. There were shenanigans at 45 Hylton Street when glass-worker's daughters Marion and Violet Gustard, aged eleven and nine, were almost ready to leave. Marion was keen to be off, along with their chums at Chester Road School, fair-haired tap-dancer Dorothy Wood and Maureen Dixon. But Violet, who had watched their mother sewing their name labels onto their clothes, was overcome with dread at the apparent finality of it all and screamed and clutched her mother's skirt so desperately that the poor woman could not bring herself to let either of them go. Marion pummelled Violet for ruining the adventure, making her cry, but she had, in fact, probably saved both their lives. And as it turned out, Dorothy Wood's little brother Lenny suddenly developed 'spots' so he was not allowed to go either.

Liverpool suffered badly at the hands of the German Air Force for the next two nights, although most of them had already experienced, first-hand, the proximity of falling bombs. They lay cramped together in the air-raid shelter at Sherwoods Lane School assembly point, Fazackerley, too excited by the adventure to sleep. At last, with everybody arrived from London, Sunderland, Newport (Mon), Southampton and Liverpool and carefully counted, they made their way by private bus to the docks, singing all the way. Unfamiliar salty, tarry, steamy, ropey aromas of ships and the sea filled their nostrils as they had their bags checked by Customs. They had only just finished their mid-morning milk and biscuit when the sirens blared again and it was a run for the dockside shelters until the 'all clear' sounded. At long last they filed up the gangway of the big drab-coloured two-funnelled ship that awaited them.

The 11,000-ton liner *City of Benares* was the proud flagship of Ellerman's City Line. She was elegant, with graceful yacht-like lines that her wartime camouflage paint did not spoil. Her Parsons turbines could thrust her along at fifteen knots, which was far in excess of the average speed of the nineteen assorted merchant vessels which would comprise convoy OB213, and to whose snail's pace she would have to restrict herself. Built to Lloyd's first-class-plus speci-fications on the Clyde only four years previously, she had been made available with her sisters *City of Simla* and *City of Paris* for evacu-ating children across the Atlantic. She was to be the commodore ship of the convoy and as such carried the sixty-year-old Admiral Edmund Mackinnon, who had emerged from a seven-year retire-ment to offer his war services. His naval staff aboard the *Benares* included signallers and gunners to man the six-inch and three-inch guns which had been mounted aft. As Commodore, Mackinnon was responsible for the convoy as a whole, whilst the *Benares* herself, with her crew of 209, which included 166 Lascars, was under command of her fifty-one-year-old master, Captain Landles Nicoll, from Fife. All convoy commodore ships, therefore, effectively had two captains. It was easy to see how overlaps in authority could cause clashes between them. The safety of the liner's passengers was clearly a matter of primary concern for Nicoll. The stocky wire-haired Scot was a close family man. He had confided his unease to his daughter. *Benares*' speed was enough to keep her safe from harm, he considered, at least from attack by a submerged U-boat, and he would have much preferred to make a fast zig-zag crossing alone, rather than be held back to little more than half-speed in a convoy. And he said he certainly would not have allowed any of his own children to be on board.

The facilities provided for the children were a feature of the ship reported in *The Times* when the *Benares* made the headlines a few weeks later. They included a play-room with paintings on the walls of characters from nursery rhymes, a full equipment of little tables and chairs and an assortment of large toys. Part of the sheltered deck on either side had been wired in for safety and there was an imposing cupboard labelled 'children's games'. Her sailing date was set for Thursday 12 September, but delay was incurred by the necessity to clear mines dropped into the Mersey by the *Luftwaffe* the previous night. One day's delay was acceptable, but any more would mean that OB213's naval escort would be late in arriving at her mid-ocean rendezvous to shepherd the next inbound convoy homewards. Such was the tightness of the scheduling. And so, perforce, the *City of Benares* sailed from Liverpool on a Friday the Thirteenth.

The *Benares*' passenger list was reduced to 191, which was some way short of the number she would normally have carried on her regular peace-time voyages on the India run. Of these, there were ninety-one adults and exactly one hundred children, ninety of whom were sailing under the CORB scheme. The remaining ten youngsters were privately booked paying passengers. The adults provided a diverse spectrum of society. Some were refugees from Germany and occupied Central Europe – publishers, authors, news editors, journalists and the like, fleeing the horrors of Nazi persecution. Some were travelling on secret missions for British and foreign Governments. Some were on assignments for the BBC. There were one or two film-makers and a playwright. Others were ordinary

Canadian or American civilians, some simply returning home to rejoin their families, some, in happiness, to be married, others, in grief, mourning sweethearts lost in the war. There was the Conservative MP for The Wrekin, Lieutenant-Colonel Baldwin-Webb, on his way to New York to raise funds for the Red Cross, and the President of the Northumberland Miners' Association, William Golightly, who was going to attend a Labour Convention in Canada.

Gussie Grimmond, exercising cockney style authority over her four younger siblings, made sure that they all sent off last-minute letters home. Ten-year-old Violet wrote, "I hope you are all right, we are all right too. We have a play-room to play in. We have life practices in case our ship got sunk. We would put lifebelts on and jump into our lifeboats."

At six o'clock in the evening of that fateful Friday the Thirteenth the *City of Benares'* crew closed all watertight doors and swung out her lifeboats. She slid down the Mersey with the excited children all waving and cheering at passing boats and ships at anchor. It had occurred to nobody, or so it would appear, to ensure any secrecy about their sailing. In Liverpool Bay and the Irish Sea most of the children felt the first effects of sea-sickness, and two of them were quarantined with suspected chicken-pox. With vessels out of the Clyde and up from Bristol, the nineteen ships of convoy OB213 assembled in the North Channel between Scotland and the Antrim coast and formed up into nine columns. As commodore ship, the *Benares* took up the centre position in the front line. With the destroyer HMS *Winchelsea* zig-zagging protectively three miles ahead of them, two Royal Navy corvettes fussing around on the wings and a Sunderland flying-boat droning overhead, OB213 set off under a sleet-laden sky at eight and a half knots to cross the Atlantic.

Winchelsea, D46, mounted two single 4-inch guns. She was old, having been first commissioned during the First World War, but she was still capable of taking her 1,100 tons through the water at twenty-five knots. She had taken part in the evacuations from the Dunkirk beaches three months earlier, but had not yet been modified to give her the extra fuel capacity to perform long-range escort duties, all the way to Nova Scotia if necessary. That was still a year away. Meantime, her range was limited. Her present fuel tanks would only carry her out to about 20 degrees west and back. OB213 was in the safe hands, and eyes and ears, of the Royal Navy. At least for a while.

Once they had begun to find their sea-legs, the CORB children found delight in exploring their luxurious ship, playing the games organized by the escorts and doing all kinds of new and exciting things. Michael Rennie had an enthusiastic attendance at his tugs o' war competitions and lassoing classes. And as for the food, every meal became a feast. To come from a world of plain strictly rationed food in war-ravaged, blacked-out Britain into an opulent existence where seemingly limitless food, especially ice-cream, was served by a smiling man wearing a blue and white uniform was like landing in paradise.

The first 300 miles, out to about 17 degrees west, were reckoned to constitute the main danger zone for U-boat attack, although recently there had been encounters with enemy submarines farther to the west. They could not expect to reach this mark until some-time during the night of Monday–Tuesday at the earliest. And there was a scare on the Sunday. Wireless warnings indicated that there were U-boats in the area, and there was a report that one of the dreaded Focke-Wulf Condor spotting planes had been seen. Hurried consultations between Mackinnon and *Winchelsea*'s captain resulted in frequent changes of course. Nothing was sighted, but nevertheless the lookouts increased their vigilance.

On the Monday Ruby Grierson, sister of the famous documentary film maker John Grierson, organized an afternoon tea-party for the children. She had been commissioned by the National Film Board of Canada to make a propaganda film of the voyage. As they munched on their tea and happily pulled their crackers, she whirred her camera, clad in her habitual beret and slacks. That night, for the first time, the children were allowed to undress for bed, although they were made to keep their cork-filled life-jacket waistcoats and clothes handy. Generally, the escorts were beginning to feel a little easier as they relaxed in the lounge that evening. They were not yet completely clear of danger, but they were at the 300-mile point. On the Tuesday morning they awoke to find that the weather had turned ugly. Heavy black clouds charged across the dull sky before a Force 5 wind. A relentless deluge of rain and sleet drove down, limiting visibility. The Atlantic had become bad-tempered and was hurling great hummocks of grey water at the *City of Benares*, making her roll unmercifully.

But the worst thing of all for them to see was that their escort had disappeared. Both Admiral Mackinnon and Captain Nicoll knew that this would happen. It was pre-planned. *Winchelsea* and the corvettes had more urgent work to perform now that OB213 was well on its way. They had to keep their rendezvous with incoming convoy HX71 from Halifax, Nova Scotia, which was carrying vital supplies of food and equipment to a hard-pressed Britain, and nurse the slow-moving heavily loaded ships through the perilous North-West Approaches. Had any of the parents of the *Benares* children been aware of this, it is unlikely that any of them would have allowed their children to sail. They had been assured that OB213 would be accompanied by a naval escort, which had been true, but the plain fact was that they had not been told the complete truth, in that such escort would be turning back after three and a half days.

Mackinnon's orders were to disperse his convoy at noon on Tuesday the 17th. That would have meant that Nicoll would then be free to pick up speed to something like his maximum fifteen knots and pound towards Halifax independently. But the Admiral did not disperse his convoy. We do not know what took place between him and Nicoll, but it is highly likely that because of the *Benares* captain's known opinions on the subject, he would have voiced them in no uncertain terms. It can only be a matter of conjecture, but Mackinnon's failure to disperse was probably influenced by the weather. He had been warned by *Winchelsea* that there was a U-boat lurking ahead, somewhere around 20 degrees west. The state of the sea rendered a submerged U-boat attack most unlikely, whilst he was confident that, given fair visibility, any surface attack could be repelled by the convoy's guns. On balance, he probably considered that there was better safety for his ship within the slow-moving convoy, rather than make a lone dash for Halifax. And so he applied the time-honoured naval principle of ignoring orders as he saw fit in the light of the circumstances of the moment.

The weather had cleared somewhat by early evening and everybody seemed happy that another day had passed safely to bring them nearer to Canada. But, unbeknown to the passengers, the *Benares*' wireless-room was still receiving U-boat warning signals from Western Approaches Command, "One probably still far out in Atlantic west of 20° W." Later in the evening, however, the wind rose again, this time to a Force 8 gale, with hailstorms and heavy rain. Many ships in the convoy found difficulty in keeping station as they were buffeted by enormous waves. And as it grew dark it seemed that there was more danger of the blacked-out ships colliding with each other than of any of them catching a German torpedo. By now the wind had risen to Force 10 and the barometer had fallen to 29.76. At nine o'clock, therefore, Mackinnon ordered zig-zagging to cease as it had become too dangerous. But still he did not disperse the convoy. It is known that he planned to order this at midnight. And that was still three hours away.

*   *   *

The handsome, extrovert thirty-year-old Kapitänleutnant Heinrich 'Ajax' Bleichrodt hailed from Berga, a little town in the picturesque Harz region west of Leipzig. He had transferred to the *Kriegsmarine* from the merchant service seven years before, in 1933, but in September 1940 had been in submarines only a bare eleven months. When he sailed from Lorient in *U-48*, first boat of the Seventh *U-Bootflotille*, on 8 September to go hunting for British merchantmen in the Atlantic, it was his first patrol as a commander. And he made an auspicious start. Catching convoy SC3 off the coast of north-west Ireland, he sank not only two merchant ships but also one of the convoy's naval escort sloops. Indeed *U-48* was destined to become the most successful U-boat of the Second World War, sinking fifty-two ships totalling 307,935 tons, and he himself would eventually be known as one of Germany's top submarine aces, with a Knight's Cross with Oak Leaves dangling from his throat.

U-48 was a VIIB type boat, built at Germaniawerft AG, Kiel in 1936–7. She displaced 753 tons and was capable of long-distance work. The extra thirty-three tons of fuel the VIIBs carried in their saddle tanks gave them a range of 2,500 nautical miles more than their predecessors the VIIAs. With the Germans now in control of the French Atlantic ports, operations well to the west of 20 degrees west were within easy scope for a VIIB. There *U-48* should find some fruitful pickings and could work in relative comfort too, well beyond the point where Royal Naval escort ships would confound her efforts. With early success already under his belt and most of the fourteen torpedoes that had been swung aboard *U-48* in Lorient still intact, 'Ajax' turned west.

Cruising on the surface about noon on Tuesday 17 September, exactly the moment at which Mackinnon's orders had been to disperse, Bleichrodt spotted from his conning-tower the lumbering

41

shapes of OB213. They were zig-zagging and making about seven knots. There was a good-sized passenger liner in the centre position of the leading line. But the German chose not to attack at that time. In fact, in one sense, Mackinnon had been right. The Atlantic was wearing such a heaving swell that a submerged attack was out of the question. So too was a daytime surface attack, which would perforce have to be conducted at long range. Outranged by the *Benares'* six-inch gun, the U-boat would have little chance of success in such conditions. Captain Nicoll, however, had not been right to have such confidence in the liner's turn of speed. A Type VIIB U-boat had a top surface speed of 17.9 knots, nearly three knots faster than that of the *City of Benares*. Even if the convoy had dispersed, and *if the weather then subsided*, then the U-boat would probably have caught the liner once she had been spotted. Therefore, for the moment, Bleichrodt held off at a discreet distance on the surface. Darkness would fall eventually. And he was a patient man. Moreover, he was about to exploit the one possible flaw in Mackinnon's probable reasoning. It would seem that the Admiral had not considered the possibility of a nighttime surface attack.

Steering a parallel course of west-south-west, he moved ahead of the *Benares*, leaving her on his starboard quarter, but keeping her in sight. To him the liner was a legitimate target for attack without warning. She was sailing in convoy, which presumed that she was resisting 'stop and search', and furthermore she was armed with two guns. These two factors disqualified her from the protective rules of any convention, treaty or agreement as far as he was concerned. Nothwithstanding these considerations, his battle instructions were quite definite. 'Fighting methods will never fail to be used merely because some international law forbids them.' He had no doubts that it was his clear duty to sink her.

At ten o'clock exactly Bleichrodt saw his moment. A layer of cloud had just passed over the moon, leaving the silhouette of the *City of Benares* bathed in light. She was at a perfect angle in his sights. A pair of torpedoes left the bow tubes of *U-48* and sped on their way towards the unsuspecting liner.

*   *   *

As the evening wore on the adult passengers aboard the *Benares* grew more relaxed. To them every minute that passed meant that they could breathe that little bit more easily. Here, 600 miles out in the Atlantic, surely they were safe. Three of the escorts, Mary Cornish, Sybil Gilliat-Smith and Marjorie Day, chatted over their after-dinner coffee in the lounge and then went up on deck for some fresh air before turning in. It was still raining, but there was a fleeting moon, with some sparse stars filtering through the thick shelves of inky cloud. They could just make out the muffled shapes of the unlit convoy stretching away into the distance behind, whilst ahead of them the bows of the *Benares* ploughed confidently into a dark nothingness. It seemed eerily quiet too, but for the drumbeat thud of the engines.

The children under their care all seemed to be glowing with health, thanks to good food and plenty of fresh sea air. The expected bouts of home-sickness had come and gone, at least for the time being, and most of them were turning out to be good sailors. The younger ones were now all sleeping peacefully. One or two of the teenagers were reading in their bunks. The women were entitled to congratulate themselves on a good job done so far.

*   *   *

But Bleichrodt had fluffed his shot. He had miscalculated his angles. Both torpedoes missed their target and tore unseen past the unaware lookouts on the *City of Benares*. The German calmly made a slight adjustment to his course and one minute later a third torpedo was streaking through the water. This time he had made no mistake. It struck the portside after-part of the liner with a mighty explosion which shook her to her ribs. In her after cabins, several of the CORB children were hurled from their bunks. Wooden panelling and furniture were reduced to splinters, glasswork was shattered into shards and jets of water gushed from split pipework. Most of the electric lighting flickered dimly, then died. Passageways were blocked with debris, the air was filled with choking dust and the Atlantic Ocean was pouring in through a gaping hole in the side of Number Five Hold.

Mary Cornish had decided to make a final check on the children's' cabins. She had just started along the passageway on C deck when the torpedo exploded. Suddenly she found herself staring into a huge black hole where the bathroom had been, with tons of water falling into it. Quickly recovering her senses after the initial shock, she knew

43

she must get to her group of children and get them safely into the boats. Tearing aside the splintered partitioning which now blocked the passageway, she managed to squeeze herself through, to find her colleague Lillian Towns on the other side. With soothing words to the frightened youngsters, together they ushered their charges on deck. Already the liner was well down by the stern and people were starting to get into the lifeboats. But then the emergency lighting came on and Mary went to go below again to check that nobody was still in the cabins, but she was stopped by one of the ship's officers. He ordered her into the nearest lifeboat, but it wasn't the one with Mrs Towns and the girls in it.

Fourteen-year-old Liverpool girl Beth Cummings had nearly fallen asleep, but suddenly she sat bolt upright in her bunk, startled by the explosion. Blinking herself wide awake and shouting to her cabin-mates, fellow Merseysiders Joan Irving and Betty Unwin, she tried to turn on the lights to look for her clothes and life-jacket. But nothing happened. In the darkness she stepped out of bed to find her feet in water from the broken bathroom pipes. As a confident teenager thrust into a new and strange group of peers, Beth had struck up an instant friendship with fifteen-year-old Londoner Bess Walder, who was in the next cabin. Bess found her way out jammed with shattered woodwork and wrecked furniture. Somebody outside in the corridor, she never knew who it was, reached into the narrow gap and a pair of strong arms pulled her through.

Billy Short, the nine-year-old from Sunderland and his twelve-year-old cabin-mate Derek Capel from Hanworth, Middlesex, both had five-year-old brothers on board. But at that time both Peter Short and Alan Capel were laid low with chicken-pox and had been carted off into quarantine quarters. Billy and Derek also found themselves trapped in their cabin. The door had become hopelessly jammed within its twisted frame. They too were up to their ankles in water and a fitted wardrobe had fallen away from its fastenings onto them. The wardrobe provided their salvation. In falling, it had created a slender gap in the bulkhead. Using all their juvenile strength, they managed to rip it away from its remaining fixtures and winkled themselves through the hole into the passageway. There they could hear somebody in the next cabin beating on the door, also trapped. Somehow they all managed to push and pull on both sides of the door until it opened. Inside was their escort, Father Rory

44

O'Sullivan. "Come on, lads," said O'Sullivan. "We've got to get ourselves to Boat 12, quickly."

The *City of Benares* was settling fast, stern first, and listing. There was clearly no way of saving her. On the bridge Captain Nicoll rang down to the engine-room. "We're up to our waists in water," came the report. "Right, get everybody out and go to your boat stations," said Nicoll. Then he turned and gave the order, "Lower the boats to the embarkation deck. Prepare to abandon ship." Orderly lines of children marched across the embarkation deck, each to stand and wait patiently at their allotted lifeboat station. Chief escort Marjorie Day went to each group in turn to check all were present and correct, just as if she were making a final check after a school visit to Madame Tussaud's, except that here she found that one boy had been killed and one of Mary Cornish's little girls was missing. Desperately anxious, Mary climbed out of Boat 10. This might be her last chance to find the child and she knew she must take it. This time nobody stopped her from going below, but when she returned, empty-handed, she found that Boat 10 had already been lowered and the Chief Officer, Joe Hetherington, ordered her into Boat 12, in which were several small boys and Lascar seamen.

Beth Cummings and Bess Walder half-carried, half-dragged Joan Irving, who had been laid low with sea-sickness since leaving the Mersey, towards Boat 5. This was on the starboard side and was going to be difficult to lower because of the liner's portside list, which made it hard for the girls to keep their feet. Then came a moment which was poignant to recall. They found themselves in company with several tiny children, five and six years old, whose faces were all the more touching for their innocent unawareness of danger. And then a girl's voice piped up. "We'll be picked up, like we were before. You'll see." It was Patricia Allen, who had survived the torpedoing of the *Volendam* less than three weeks before.

It was a forty foot drop from the promenade deck to the water. The lifeboats swung sickeningly from their davits. It was a difficult task for the boat crews to control the falls as the now wallowing *Benares* heaved and lurched on the waves. Fall ropes became snarled, causing pulley-blocks to jam and many boats, battered by the towering waves while still in mid-air, were already half-full with sea water before they were fully lowered. Worse still, many of them came down 'end up'. Sybil Gilliat-Smith's boat was one of these. It was coming down in a series of jerks when suddenly one of the falls

45

seized, throwing the boat lopsided. The screaming occupants, which included all five Grimmond children, were catapulted headlong into the foam far below, never to be seen again. In other boats terrified people, some shrieking and others dumb with terror, tried to keep their balance by clutching desperately at anything around them, and in their panic that often included each other. Dozens drowned within the space of a few minutes. The MP, Lieutenant-Colonel Baldwin-Webb, had stayed on deck to help people find boat-stations, checking life-jackets, and generally making himself useful. Now he stood, hesitantly, poised at the rail looking down at the chaos below him in the sea. All the boats had gone. So had the rafts. He launched himself into mid-air, but his dive turned into a belly-flop and he hit the water far below with a sickening slap. He was not seen again.

Some of the boats crashed repeatedly against the sides of the liner, caught by the swinging backwash. And in the narrow gap between the looming hull and the helpless lifeboats swirled a treacherous current of rapids. A small boy popped to the surface of this boiling tiderace. It was little Louis Walder, Bess's ten-year-old brother. Sunderland Boy Scout George Crawford leaned from his boat to fish him out, but he could not reach. Bravely, he leaned out farther and just managed to haul the lad to safety, in process of losing his own balance and he toppled in headfirst. Strong as he was, George could not swim against the current and was swept away. Meantime, escort Michael Rennie, a powerful swimmer, was diving into the water from Boat 11, time and again, to haul a youngster to safety. Fifteen of them had been in No. 11 and they had been tossed all together into the water at one fell swoop, like a handful of angler's ground bait. Rennie was urged to slow down by his companions, who pointed out that everybody had a life-jacket and would be rescued in good time. But he feared that his boys, who were being tossed back and forth like corks on the water, would be crushed between the pitching boats and he doggedly refused to rest. Thanks to his unstinting devotion to duty, thirteen of them were brought back from the brink of death.

The shouts and screams, the distress flares soaring from the doomed liner into the night sky, the dancing phosphorescence of the bobbing life-jackets spangling the water, the forlorn shapes of the life-boats and the now distinctly upturned bows of the *City of Benares* herself pricked out in silhouette by an occasional gleam of moonlight from between the dark clouds all combined to create a scene from Hell. And then, suddenly, all was bathed in bright light. It was a searchlight from a ship. "They've come to rescue us!" cried one elderly lady, but she was mistaken. It was the searchlight of *U-48*. 'Ajax' Bleichrodt was inspecting his handiwork. *Benares* was clearly sinking. There was no point in expending more torpedoes or shells on her. And he had already sunk another member of the convoy, the freighter *Marina*. He turned away, his night's work done.

In Boat 5 Beth Cummings and Bess Walder sat up to their waists in water. Only the buoyancy tanks were keeping them afloat. The girls tried to perch on the gunwales, but it was hard to keep their balance as the swamped boat rolled and pitched. Most of the children and Lascars who had occupied it at first had been thrown or fallen into the sea to drown. And then a heavy wave caught No. 5 and she turned over completely, to lie on the heaving surface like a giant turtle. Everybody was thrown into the water. Beth felt herself sinking. She was sure that she was about to die. But then she began to rise and, with her lungs at bursting point, she floated to the surface, gasping and choking. She could not swim, but she proved that one can learn very quickly if faced with death. She flailed her arms and legs as hard as she could and made it back to the boat, where she found her friend Bess with her body barely out of the water, clinging to the upturned hull. Bess had been given swimming lessons by her father and knew well what happened when you fell into deep water. If you could hold your breath you came up again, and on seaside holidays she had confidently jumped off many a harbour wall to prove it. This time, however, when she came back to the surface she was in mid-Atlantic. It was dark and her eyes took a minute or so to adjust. There was a girl looking at her from the other side of the keel. It was her friend Beth. Shouting above the groaning of the wind, they told each other to hang on. Help would surely arrive shortly.

❖   ❖   ❖

The *Benares*' Radio Officer, Alistair Fairweather, and his deputy, Canadian John Lazarus, had wasted no time in transmitting distress signals giving their position, 56°43' North 21°15' West. In fact it was less than five minutes after the torpedo struck, at six minutes past ten to be precise, when their call was acknowledged by the shore station at Lyness, in the Orkneys. And it was only another twenty-three minutes later that the C.-in-C. Western Approaches was taking action. HMS *Winchelsea* had left the convoy twenty-two hours earlier and was still probably the nearest Navy ship to the scene. But she was engaged on a mission of top priority – escorting the vital inbound convoy HX71 safely home. The next nearest was the escort for the outbound OB214, which was 300 miles astern of OB213. The escort leader was the destroyer HMS *Hurricane*, H06, commanded by Lieutenant-Commander Hugh Crofton-Simms. Western Approaches signalled *Hurricane*, "Proceed with utmost despatch to position 56.43N 21.15W, where survivors are reported in boats."

Simms read the decoded signal at six minutes past midnight. "We'll do our best," he said grimly, mindful that the terrible weather in the Atlantic would hinder progress. The 1,880-ton destroyer had been ordered by Brazil as the *Japarua* and was being built at Vickers Armstrong on the Tyne when war broke out. She was taken over by the Royal Navy and given the name *Hurricane*. Her two Parsons steam turbines produced some 34,000 hp, and with a top speed pushing 36 knots she could really motor. But Crofton-Simms knew that he risked severe damage to her if he attempted anything like that speed in these conditions. Half-speed would be about all that was prudent, but even if the weather subsided, allowing him to put on more knots, he would be unable to get there before early afternoon the next day. He shaped a course of 286 degrees and *Hurricane* swung off to face a long battering from the fury of the Atlantic.

*　　*　　*

By morning the lifeboats and rafts had drifted apart, although many could still see each other between the squalls of hail and sleet. Odd bits of flotsam drifted about. The beautiful rocking horse from the playroom of the *Benares* nodded its head on the waves. Many people had died during the night, either from drowning or hypothermia and exhaustion. Dead bodies were put over the side, although in some boats there were no survivors left to perform this grisly task. Daylight brought a little sunshine and those with enough energy left began to search the boats' lockers for food. The lucky ones found tins of condensed milk, corned beef and biscuits. Some even found rum and blankets. But none found fresh water, and some found nothing – their boat's provisions had been lost overboard and were now at the bottom of the ocean.

Clutching the keel of Boat 5 with Beth and Bess were two Lascars. One was clearly delirious, rolling his eyes and muttering to himself. The other had lashed himself to the rudder and sat bolt upright, seemingly oblivious to the deluge of spray which cascaded over him every few seconds. But he had been dead for several hours. The girls now found it hard to speak. Their throats, mouths and lips were so dried out by the salt that they could barely manage to croak. Their hands were frozen, but they hung on defiantly. By now they felt no pain. And they had begun to hallucinate, imagining huge icebergs on a collision course with their boat and fearsome sea-creatures emerging from the depths.

Another boat found itself sailing through a sea of planks. It was the *Marina*'s deck cargo of timber, which had floated off when she sank. What a Godsend! The drenched and shivering occupants of the life-boat managed to haul up three of the big baulks and placed them athwartships over the gunwales. This made a high and comparatively dry platform on which to sit or a shelter to crawl under when it rained.

In Boat 11 Michael Rennie tried to urge his lads into a sing-song, but they could not sing for shivering. Most of them were sitting up to their chests in sea-water. If only the "no undressing for bed" rule had been kept up, things might not have been so bad. Rennie, with the *Benares*' barman, bean-pole Glaswegian Jimmy Proudfoot, tried to comfort them with assurances that help was on the way, but the youngsters' faces were set with cold and shock. There was little that mere words could do for them now. Proudfoot produced a bottle of whisky which he had thoughtfully purloined from the bar, and passed it round. Each took a cautious swig and for a while it restored their spirits. But only for a while. During the night Proudfoot had noticed that Rennie's eyes had taken on a fixed and glassy look. He was clearly exhausted from his rescue marathon and looked close to unconsciousness. Proudfoot hoped that a few hours' 'rest' through the night would allow his companion to recuperate. But it was not to be. Rennie, who had become a hero to the lads in his charge, began chattering in a strange gobbledegook and soon afterwards, when he had grown quiet, they saw that he had died.

On one of the rafts Chief Officer Joe Hetherington and the purser, John Anderson, were crouched behind the corpse of escort Maud

Hillman. They had fished her alive from the water, and now in death she was repaying them with a little shelter from the chill wind. Then Hetherington, who stood six feet four and had clambered shakily to his feet, shouted, "I saw a ship!" Anderson got to his feet and together they stared at the horizon. But there was nothing.

At 0810 hours that morning the weather had abated sufficiently for Crofton-Simms to think it safe to increase speed to twenty-seven knots. The sea was still choppy and *Hurricane* hurtled forward at well over thirty miles an hour. Simms consulted with Lieutenant Pat Fletcher, his navigation officer. They decided to head for a point some thirty miles E.N.E. of the sinking, in which direction they concluded that the wind would have carried the boats, and start their sweep from there. They reached it at 1330 and every member of the ship's company who could be spared was assigned to lookout duty.

Three-quarters of an hour later, a sail was spotted. It was one of the *Marina*'s lifeboats. It had picked up five of the *Benares*' survivors, including Marguerite Bech and two of her children, eleven-year-old Sonia and Derek, who was nine. But their fourteen-year-old sister Barbara was still missing. Nets were slung over the side and those who were able clambered up on to the deck of the destroyer. Those who had not the strength to climb were pulled up by the strong hands of *Hurricane*'s sailors, and all were ushered below to be given warm clothing and hot drinks. *Benares* passenger Eric Davis, a BBC man, who had been on his way to Malaya on an assignment, looked at the glass of Navy rum in his hand and then at eight-year-old Brixton boy Jack Keeley. The youngster was all in, but he had faced his ordeal like a man and he deserved to be treated like one. Davis poured half his rum into the lad's hot milk. Jack's eyes widened. "I say," he said, "I say, thanks very much."

Hurricane steamed on, west-south-west, sounding her siren in long blasts. An hour later she came across a group of four rafts. Two miles farther on there was a lifeboat. Then another. And another. And another. In Boat 4 was the missing Barbara Bech. In the now dead Michael Rennie's Boat 11 only two of the fifteen boys that he had given his life for had survived. In some of the boats there was nobody at all.

Beth and Bess saw *Hurricane* steaming towards them. They were worried that she would miss them altogether, being low in the water clutching the shell of the overturned boat. And they were unable to shout, nor even wave, because their hands had somehow become locked desperately to the lifeboat's hull. But then they saw that the destroyer had stopped. It was close enough for them to read its pennant number. It was H06, but the sea had knocked off some of the white paint and it appeared as 106. It had seen them. Beth saw a whaler being lowered, and its big oars swinging in and out of the water as the sailors pulled towards them, but then she passed out. Bess had gripped the keel so determinedly and for so long that her cold fingers were set, as if glued to it. "Come on, darling, let go," said a man's voice. It was the whaler's coxswain, Leading Seaman Albert Gorman, who literally had to prise her fingers back to free her hands. The next thing they knew was that they were surrounded by *Hurricane*'s lustily cheering sailors and they were being carried below. They could not swallow the hot soup that was offered them because their mouths were too swollen. Instead, they sipped glucose drinks and rum. Then it was hot baths that were agonizing as the circulation flowed back into their frozen limbs.

It was seven o'clock in the evening when the last boat in sight was rescued. On board the destroyer the tireless Surgeon-Lieutenant Peter Collinson worked non-stop to tend the exhausted survivors, some of whom were injured, while others had become comatose. One boy, chicken-pox sufferer Alan Capel, had survived the terrors of the sinking only to die aboard *Hurricane* the minute he was rescued. Some of the boats contained nothing but dead women and children and even the war-toughened destroyermen were affected by such sights. As they toiled with the rescues many cried unashamedly, cursing Hitler and all things German.

Crofton-Simms had combed and quartered an area of four square miles thoroughly and systematically. But as yet unseen, way out on the rim of the search box, were two men and a delirious woman on a raft. They were Chief Officer Joe Hetherington and Purser John Anderson, who was still clasping the safe-custody bag, and a German-Jewish passenger who had been fleeing from the horrors of the Fatherland. Between themselves, the men had quietly agreed that they could not endure another night exposed to the elements and if they were not seen and picked up they would simply slide into the water once darkness fell, leaving the woman to her fate. The light was fading fast and *Hurricane*, with her hooter blaring, was making her final sweep when she spotted them. As the ship drew alongside her bow-wave washed the German woman into the sea. An AB and a Lieutenant dived from the destroyer's deck and somehow managed to get a bowline around her. The young officer was George Dudley Pound, son of the Chief of Naval Staff himself.

With eighteen women, fifteen children and eighty-two men from the *Marina* and the *City of Benares* on board, *Hurricane* swung towards Gourock and home at twenty knots. Next morning, in bright Atlantic sunshine, her crew gathered on the quarter-deck for the burial service of Alan Capel and two of his shipmates who had died during the night, ten-year-old Londoners Derek Carr and Terence Holmes. They had fallen asleep, as Collinson had hoped, to recuperate, but had never woken up. As the bodies slid from under the Union Jacks into the ocean, many of the watching sailors were overcome. Their red-hot anger of the previous day seemed to have evolved into a tight-lipped fury. "Pity the poor Hun who meets *Hurricane*," wrote Crofton-Simms.

Bess Walder was sure that her brother Louis had perished and was dreading having to give the news to her parents. There was nothing she could have done to save him, but all the same she was the eldest and she had promised to look after him. She lay there, filled with a sick feeling that, somehow, she was responsible. But in fact *Hurricane* had picked him up before she and Beth were found. It was only when Louis was being shown round the destroyer's engine-room that he recognized a familiar dressing-gown hanging up to dry near the boilers with the other survivors' clothing. "That's my sister's!" he shouted. Crofton-Simms himself took Louis to the cabin where Bess was in bed, recuperating from her ordeal. Her big sister instincts took over immediately. "Where have you *been*?" she scolded.

At home all announcements of the sinking were censored until the families had been informed. Brown envelopes containing the usual words of official sympathy were delivered to the fifty-nine homes around the country affected by the tragedy on 20 September, one week after the *City of Benares* had sailed from the Mersey. The news brought unimaginable scenes of grief. All five Grimmond children drowned. Thirty-one Middlesex children, including seven pupils from one Wembley school alone, all lost. In Sunderland they learned that Eleanor Wright was their only survivor. Beth Cummings was the only one from Liverpool. And not one of the twelve Welsh children ever came home.

Griefstricken, Eddie Grimmond left his job with the council. "I'm going back to the King's Royal Rifle Corps," he announced, "and

I hope to get a front line job. I've got to find some way to get back at the Nazis." He would never get over the loss of his children.

From Great Britain, Canada, Australia and all around the civilized world came outraged and horrified condemnation of Hitler. "Of all the brutalities that have earned Nazism the execration of the civilized world," snarled *The Times*, "none will stay longer graven upon the records than the sinking of the children's ship the *City of Benares*." "Hitler and all his gang of murderers must be hung on the lampposts of Berlin when we have won the war," wrote a grimly vengeful *Sunderland Echo* correspondent. In griefstricken Newport, the Director of Education, Dr Oates, told the *South Wales Argus* that it was "an act of wanton and barbarous cruelty which will be condemned by all right-thinking and right-feeling people throughout the world." In America there were fresh calls for the USA to forget its policy of neutrality and a Gallup Poll concluded that most Americans were now in favour of such action. In Germany Goebbels, the Master Liar, followed the same line that he had taken when the *Athenia* had been sunk on the first day of the war. He blamed Winston Churchill, accusing him of slyly arranging the sinking himself in an attempt to bring the USA into the conflict on the side of the British. The irony was that Churchill had never been in favour of evacuee sailings at all.

On Monday, 23 September *The Times* announced the names of the CORB dead:

Joan Foster, 10, of Bournemouth; Paul Shearing, 12, of Bournemouth.
John Spencer-Davies, 9; Rosemary Spencer-Davies, 15; Leonard
Grimmond, 5; Violet Grimmond, 10; Constance Grimmond, 9; Edward
Grimmond, 8; Augusta Grimmond, 13; Joyce Keeley, 6, all of Brixton.
John Pugh, 13; Donald Pugh, 11; Charles Pugh, 12; Ailsa Murphy, 10;
James Spencer, 5; Joan Spencer, 9; Joan Irving, 15; Gordon Walsh, 10;
Betty Unwin, 12; Philip Mollard, 6, all of Liverpool.
Enid Butlin, 12, of Hillingdon, Middlesex; Audrey Muncey, 13, of
London, W.12; Edna Beesley, 10 and Phyllis Beesley, 12, of London
N.21; Bruce Hillyard, 11, and Jeffrey Hillyard, 8, of Wembley,
Middlesex; Sheila Chase, 14, and Michael Chase, 12, of Twickenham,
Middlesex; Derek Car, 10, and Beryl Car, 8, of Southall, Middlesex;
Pauline Crawley, 11, and Sheila Crawley, 8, of Edgware, Middlesex;
Derek Goodfellow, 13, and Christopher Goodfellow, 8, of Wembley,
Middlesex; Robert Baker, 12, and Kathleen Barrett, 12, of Southall,

Middlesex; Barbara Fairhead, 10, of Teddington, Middlesex; Cynthia Dadds, 14, of Twickenham, Middlesex; Terence Holmes, 10, of Wembley, Middlesex; Beryl Myatt, 9, of Hillingdon, Middlesex; William Moon, 10, of North Wembley, Middlesex; Robin Miller, 8, of Southall, Middlesex; Marion Thome, 7, of Wembley, Middlesex; Dorothy Nolan, 12, and Patricia Nolan, 8, of Southall, Middlesex; Colenso Rodda, 6, of Uxbridge, Middlesex; Kenneth Sparks, 13, and Audrey Mansfield, 8, both of Wembley, Middlesex.

Dorothy Wood, 9; Peter Short, 5; William Short, 9; Ann Watson, 6; Thomas Watson, 9; Maureen Dixon, 10; Derek Leigh, 11; Edith Smith, 13; Irene Smith, 10, and George Geoffrey Crawford, 13, all of Sunderland.

Anthony Taylor, 6 and June Taylor, 9, of London, S.E.5.

Harry Steele, 11, of Eastleigh, Southampton; Derek Capel, 12, and Alan Capel, 5, of Hanworth, Middlesex; Patricia Harrington, 8, and James Harrington, 7, of Alperton, Middlesex; Henry Smoolovich, 10, of Wembley, Middlesex; Howard Clayton, 11, of Kenton, Middlesex; Peter Willis (known as Lloyd), 12, of London, S.W.1. Leighton Ryman, 9; Lewis Came, 11; Margaret Lloyd, 14; Nesta Lloyd, 12, all of Cardiff. John Pemberton, 10; Anita Rees, 14; William Rees, 12; Rita Moss, 8; Marion Moss, 10; Aileen Moss, 12; Roger Poole, 11, all of Newport (Mon). Michael Brooker, 10, of Bromley, Kent and Patricia Allen, 12, of Liverpool.

Doctor and Nurse – Doctor Margaret Zeal, 30, of Hammersmith Hospital, Miss Dorothy Smith, 26, hospital nurse, of Central London Throat Hospital.

Escorts – Miss Mary Cornish, 41, of London, W.l; Miss Sybil Gilliat-Smith, 25, of London, S.W.10; Mrs Maud Hillman, 44, of London, W.12; Rev. William King, 28, of London, E.1; Father Roderick Sullivan, 32, of Herne Bay, Kent, and Mr Michael Rennie, 21, of Hampstead, London, N.W.ll.

But *The Times* had been premature with its obituaries, because far out on the Atlantic there still bobbed a lifeboat with forty-six people in it, including six children. It was Boat 12. Boat 12 had been on the lee-side of the sinking liner and it was the farthest aft. This meant that it had had a relatively smooth lowering and had been launched safely. So it had not been swamped with water like so many of the others. But, paradoxically, this turned out to have been the reason why it had not been found by *Hurricane*. As a dry boat, No. 12 sat much higher on the surface than those half-full of seawater. This presented a much larger area of freeboard to the wind, and so she had drifted faster and farther than her sisters throughout the night. And she had wandered way outside *Hurricane*'s search-box.

Fourth Officer Ronnie Cooper, a level-headed twenty-two-year-old from Dundee, was in charge of Boat 12 and it was largely due to his professional care and refusal to be rushed that she had been launched without mishap. With him were naval ratings Johnny Mayhew and Harry Peard, merchant navy cadet Douglas Critchley, steward George Purvis, and thirty-two Lascar seamen; two escorts, Father Rory O'Sullivan and Mary Cornish, and six boys; Derek Capel, twelve, and Billy Short, nine, neither of whom yet knew that they had lost their younger brothers Alan and Peter, Kenneth Sparks, thirteen, from Wembley, Howard Clayton from Kenton, Middlesex, Freddie Steels from Eastleigh, Southampton, and Paul Shearing from Bournemouth, all eleven years old. The forty-sixth person was a fare-paying passenger, Bohdan Nagorski, a Polish shipping executive with the Gdynia-America Line, who was immaculately clad in a Homburg hat, kid gloves and overcoat.

During the first night they had met up with one of the *Marina*'s boats, which had her master, Captain Paine, in command. They had kept company until dawn, but by then Paine had decided that, because of his limited supply of water and the good sailing ability of his boat, his best plan was to make for Ireland, 650 miles distant, as rapidly as possible. He thought that, with luck, it would take a week. And so, at 8.30 next morning, he bade them farewell.

In Boat 12 Cooper set about checking his resources. He found ten and a half gallons of water, which meant less than three pints per person, plus some tins of condensed milk, corned beef, sardines and salmon. And, of course, the traditional rock-hard ship's biscuits. He organized the seating, placing the escorts and children, with Nagorski in the bows, where Purvis had rigged up a small tarpaulin shelter; midships were the Lascars and in the stern sat the European crew. He was mindful of the fact that the Lascars outnumbered the Europeans by six to one, and whilst they seemed placid enough at the moment there was always the possibility that they could change under stress. It was prudent to keep a careful eye on them.

From the start space was a major problem. It was almost impossible to move without treading on somebody. And how to sleep in such cramped conditions? The best they could do was to try to ignore the hard edges of Boat 12's woodwork, lean against each other and take turns to shelter from the chill under the little canvas awning in the bows. Most of the boys wore only their pyjamas and cumbersome cork life-jackets, and Mary Cornish had on a silk blouse, thin skirt and a jacket. Very quickly they all became numb with cold. Row after row of white-maned 'race horses' tore across the grey seascape. Stinging spindrift lashed their faces. Boat 12 bucked and reared uncontrollably, as helpless as a straw in the wind. It had no oars to complement its sail, but a system known as Fleming gear, which consisted of a series of vertical handles, like outsize beer pumps, along its length. The theory was that when these were rocked back and forth by the occupants the motion would drive a shaft, which was connected to a propeller. In practice it gave them little hope of ever reaching Ireland, but it did serve some purpose. It helped Cooper keep her head to the sea at times when it looked like she might broach. And it did help the operators to keep warm.

Father O'Sullivan had been suffering from the effects of a feverish chill even before the sinking. Barefoot, he had urged Derek and Billy and his other boys into Boat 12, even carrying one of them who was still half-asleep. And now he was overcome with sea-sickness, too. He lay shivering in his pyjamas in the bottom of the pitching boat, among the damp legs and feet of those around him, quite unable to be of any help. It fell to Mary Cornish to take over the care of the six lads. She knew that it would be vital to keep their minds occupied. But with what? She found herself to be quite a skilful story-teller, and invented a serial, straight out of her head, about Captain Bulldog Drummond, a contemporary hero of boyhood fiction. They listened, enraptured, until the end of each twice-daily instalment. Then there were games of I-Spy and Animal, Vegetable, Mineral. And community singing, with "There'll always be an England", "Run, Rabbit, Run" and "Ten Green Bottles". But it was the times in between that were the worst, when all fell quiet, except for the moaning of the wind, the slapping of the waves against the hull and the occasional piping squeal of a sea-bird.

Cooper had imposed strict rationing, particularly of water, from the outset. It meant two small 'dippers' per person each day. And as early as the middle of the second day thirst began to torment them. He issued everybody with a tin of condensed milk with a small hole punched in it, to suck as and when. Normally, this would be heaven to any small boy, but the sweetened goo only made them thirstier. A day or so later, when there was a heavy shower of rain and hail, they managed to collect quite a puddle in the bight of the sail, but the canvas was heavily impregnated with salt and their catch was no good to drink. Most meals consisted of a biscuit and a sardine or a sliver of corned beef. But the dryness of the boys' mouths and the hardness of the biscuits made chewing difficult, and more often than not, after each meal Mary found herself holding several large fragments of biscuit for safe-keeping.

When it came to sanitary arrangements there was little scope for privacy, which for Mary, as the only woman on board, was a particular problem. Nevertheless, it was no time for prudishness and what had to be done had to be done. A bucket was selected for her to use, and whenever she called for it from her place in the bows, it was passed down by the smiling Lascars to the 'memsahib', and everybody courteously averted their gaze. But as time wore on and their bodies had but little waste to pass, these occasions became less frequent.

The naval gunner, Harry Peard from Bristol, sometimes came for'ard to visit the lads when he was off-duty at the tiller. He was a 'hard as nails' sailor of the old school and a firm believer in self-discipline. His salty opinions and outspoken manner were somewhat abrasive, at first, to Mary's comparatively genteel ear. But he was good for the boys' morale. "What do you escorts think you're here for?" he inquired on one occasion, shooting an accusing look at them, "This boy ain't got no blanket on. He's cold, poor little bastard. Come on, son, let's tuck it under like this. That's the way. Somebody should be keepin' an eye on these kids." And every day, if the sea was not too rough, he would undress and jump over the side for a swim. "Why do you go swimmin' so much, mister?" one lad enquired. "Well, I want to keep in practice, see, 'case we get torpedoed again." "Water? You want water?" he was heard to say to a croaking boy who was complaining of thirst, "Course you do, we all do. But you just forget about it, see? You'll have plenty of water when we're picked up, and that won't be long now. Water? Huh! Is that all you're worried about?"

On the fifth day Purvis promised them all a special Sunday treat. It was a slice of tinned peach. Their dipperful of water, plus a little peach juice, swirled around in an empty condensed milk tin, slid down their parched throats in slow relished sips, soft and cool. Every last sense of the heavenly taste was licked from cracked lips by a searching tongue. And that fifth afternoon brought drama too. First they sighted smoke. Then, a little later, the clear outline of a ship. Mary Cornish had donated her petticoat for use as a distress signal, and it was excitedly run up to the mast-head, to flap incongruously on the breeze. The ship was coming towards them, for sure. Obviously, it had seen them. The boys all jumped up, waving and shouting and singing. Naval signalman Johnny Mayhew got ready with his flags. Soon their ordeal would be over. But then, before their horrified unbelieving eyes, the steamer turned away slowly, until they could see the creamy wake churning from her screws. She gradually grew smaller again and eventually disappeared. Then the heavens opened and another violent storm erupted. It was their worst moment, without doubt.

But Harry Peard was not downhearted. "What's the matter now? That ship shows we've reached the sea-lanes, see? There'll be plenty more ships tomorrow." His attitude was infectious. Mary found herself using similar tactics. Hearing a forlorn whimper from under a blanket, she said, "Don't you realize you're a real hero ? Bulldog Drummond is only a pretend one. But you're a *real* one, on a real life adventure. What any boy in England wouldn't give to change places with you. And real heroes don't *snivel*." It worked. The whimpering ceased right away.

Tuesday came. They had been in Boat 12 for a week. All were growing weaker. They had scarcely eaten anything for three days and the water had nearly all gone. Cooper had decided that he must halve the daily ration next day. Muscles ached with cramp, hair was stiff with salt and eyes were puffed and bloodshot through lack of proper sleep. Mary Cornish was finding it hard to maintain the Bulldog Drummond serial, not from any lack of ideas for the plot, but because her swollen tongue made it difficult to speak. Several of the Lascars were barely conscious and lay groaning in the bottom of the boat. That evening Cooper passed the word down that some of the fitter Lascars were, at last, growing restive. The escorts had used a hatchet to open tinned food. Now they kept it handy, just in case.

It was Kenneth Sparks who spotted it first. Suddenly he pointed at a dot in the sky and shouted, "Look! It's a plane!" And sure enough it was. It was a Sunderland flying-boat of 10 Squadron, Royal Australian Air Force, skippered by Squadron-Leader W. Garing, on its way to rendezvous with incoming convoy HX73. It circled low, with a helmeted figure waving from the cockpit window. Garing had only barely enough fuel for his role as convoy escort and he dared not alight on the water. In the cheering waving boat, naval 'bunting tosser' Johnny Mayhew was flinging out a message in semaphore, but the aircraft was travelling too fast to read more than the words "City of . . ." But that was enough. The *Western Mail* reported on 28 September that Garing had said that he saw a figure in the boat dressed in what looked like Boy Scout's uniform sending semaphore, and he was full of praise for "a boy's knowledge of signals". The plane flashed by lamp that it would send help quickly and then droned away into the distance. It was just after one o'clock on the afternoon of 25 September. They had been adrift for nearly eight days. Surely they would make it now?

Garing returned to the outbound convoy he had just left and passed on the news to his replacement, Flight-Lieutenant 'Doughie' Baker, in Sunderland P9624 of 210 Squadron. And it was only an hour after Kenneth Sparks had first spied the R.A.A.F. aircraft that Baker's plane, too, was flying low over the lifeboat and the 'boy scout' Mayhew was tossing his arms around again with well-practised semaphore. Baker could not put the aircraft down on the water because conditions were too rough. But he knew that there were British warships less than forty miles away with the convoy. He dropped food and cigarettes in a parachute bag, together with a smoke float with instructions to set it off when a ship appeared.

Minutes later the destroyer HMS *Anthony*, H40, peeled away from the convoy to head towards the lifeboat. The Sunderland returned to circle over the boat, its crew taking photographs, and Baker did not leave the scene until 1630, when he was satisfied that Boat 12 was safely made fast to the side of the warship.

Grinning sailors lifted the boys on board the *Anthony*. There was over half a case of condensed milk left over, despite their desperate thirst. It was simply too sweet and too thick for their swollen throats to swallow. But now each one clutched a tin, as a present for Mum. Mary Cornish needed help to climb aboard. They carried her to the Engineer Officer's cabin, where she collapsed into an arm-chair. A sailor named Stoker Potts brought her a tray of bread and honey and some tea. She had an agonizing wait while the tea cooled, before she could drink it, because her throat was too sore to take anything hot. But when at last she put the cup to her lips, to drink with normal size swallows for the first time in days, it was bliss.

The boys were accommodated in the wardroom, where they consumed jugful after jugful of orange juice, and slept on the leather-topped locker seats. Billy Short's bed was underneath a padlocked cabinet full of real revolvers hanging on the bulkhead.

Potts, who had been detailed to look after Mary Cornish, brought her a toothbrush, some hot water and pyjamas. But when she went to brush her teeth she found them encrusted with a hard coating of salt. And, strangely, she found that she had forgotten how to undress and needed to concentrate hard to make her fingers undo the buttons. She laid flat out on the Engineer's bunk, which was a luxury in itself, but she could not sleep. She called out to be taken to check that her boys were all right, but the Engineer came to the door and with a smile said, "Don't worry. You've handed over to the Navy now."

In the morning there was a shout and suddenly the cabin was full of excited little boys who had come to see how Auntie was. They were dressed in an assortment of naval sea-jerseys that reached their ankles and long white sea-boot stockings with heels that came halfway up their legs. It was remarkable how their young spirits had revived so quickly. Then they stampeded out again. They were on a real-life fighting destroyer and they wanted to see as much of it as possible. This was truly a real adventure, not like Bulldog Drummond. And by the time *Anthony* had steamed up the Clyde to berth at Gourock at 1930 on the evening of 26 September nearly all of them had resolved to join the Navy when they grew up, just like the boys who had come home in *Hurricane*. The amazing thing was that so many of them did just that.

O'Sullivan and eleven-year-old Paul Shearing, who had been confined to *Anthony*'s sick-bay, were taken to hospital, while the others were bussed to a Gourock hotel for the night. Next day came a civic reception in Glasgow and appearances for the newsreel cameras. And a profusion of gifts awaited them. Mary and the boys were each given a gold lapel pin and a blue leather-bound copy of 'Songs from Robert Burns'. The Lord Provost explained that the gold pins entitled the wearers to a free meal with the City Fathers at any time. And the boys were each presented with a kilt and taken to see a wartime Rangers v. Celtic football match.

For some reason Billy Short did not get a kilt and he never has called on the Glasgow City Fathers for the free meal to which he has been entitled these sixty years. Nor did he join the Navy when he grew up. Instead, he helped build three new minesweepers in the Sunderland shipyards.

With the six boys and two escorts from Boat 12 saved, the final tally of lives lost from the CORB party was seventy-seven children out of ninety and six of the ten escorts. Geoffrey Shakespeare said, "I am full of horror and indignation that a German captain could be found to torpedo a ship over 600 miles from land in such tempestuous conditions." He disembarked thirty children from the *City of Simla* and cancelled the sailing of 270 more on the *City of Paris*. It spelt the end of the CORB scheme. But the memory of that awful night in 1940, when as mere children they all came so close to death in mid-Atlantic, has lived with the survivors of the *City of Benares* for the rest of their lives. They have had frequent re-unions, and a 'final' one, the sixtieth, took place in 2000. And on 17 September 2000 a memorial service, organized by the Roker Volunteer Life Brigade, was held in Sunderland Minster for the nine local children who lost their lives sixty years before. Violet Stoker (née Gustard) would have been there to remember her childhood friends Dorothy Wood and Maureen Dixon, but was prevented doing so by a sad and ironic occurrence. Her sister Marion, who as an eleven-year-old had pummelled her for causing the tearful farewell scene which led to neither of them sailing on the *Benares*, lay dying. Instead of going to the service Violet spent the time at the bedside of her sister. Marion died the next day.

It was not the end of *Hurricane*'s involvement with the rescue of those on Ellerman's City Line ships. In 1943, not long before she was sunk herself on the Christmas Eve of that year, she raced to the assistance of the *City of Nagpur*, which was being used as a troop transport, when it was torpedoed in the Atlantic.

After sinking the *Benares* and the *Marina* on 18 September, Bleichrodt shadowed the ill-fated convoy HX72 with four other U-boats. No fewer than eleven of the heavily laden inbound ships were sunk and two more were damaged on 21 September, and four days later U-48 was safely back at Lorient. Bleichrodt left her in December 1940 and she was taken over again by her original captain, Kapitänleutnant Herbert Schultze. In contrast to her record as the most successful of the Second World War U-boats, her end was ignominious. In company with many of her sisters who survived the ferocious anti-U-boat onslaught waged by the Allied destroyers and aircraft in the later stages of the war, and with Nazi Germany overwhelmed but defiant in its death throes, she was scuttled on 3 May 1945 off Neustadt.

The saga of the *City of Benares* provided a round of useful ammunition for the accusers of U-boat chief Admiral Karl Dönitz when he was charged with war crimes. But the main core of the case against him was yet to be enacted. It arose from the orders he issued to U-boat captains following the dramatic sinking of another British liner – the *Laconia*.

4

THE *LACONIA* AFFAIR

The 20,000-ton ex-Cunarder *Laconia* prepared to weigh anchor in the swelteringly hot Gulf of Suez on 12 August 1942, bound for home via the Cape of Good Hope, crammed with a motley selection of passengers – returning service personnel, some of them wounded, several dozen British civilian officials and their wives and children, who rushed about shouting to each other excitedly, two hundred brassy women, who, it later turned out, were prostitutes who had been rounded up in various Middle Eastern towns as suspected spies, 1,800 wretched but noisy Italian prisoners of war from the Libyan campaign, dressed in shabby thin green cotton uniforms and their fixed bayoneted British soldier guards. Not one of those on board can have realized that they were embarking on a voyage that would eventually result in Admiral Dönitz facing ten years' incarceration for war crimes.

Laconia, built on Tyneside by Swan Hunter in 1922, had been taken over by the Admiralty at the outbreak of war and converted into a troop carrier. They had given her two 4.7 inch guns, four quick-firing Bofors and fitted her with anti-mine paravanes. Given some half-decent coal in her bunkers, she could shake herself up to sixteen and a half knots, which it was hoped would be enough to keep her clear of torpedo attack by U-boats as she entered the danger zones.

All the same, her captain, Captain Rudolph Sharp, CBE, RD, RNR, had misgivings. Coming from a long line of Cunard Line seafarers, Sharp's blood was laced with plenty of the proverbial salt, which often seems to bestow an uncanny sixth sense in those who possess it. And Sharp had more reason than most to be uneasy. He had already seen catastrophe at first hand in this war. In fact it had turned out to be the biggest single British shipping disaster of the war. The 16,250-ton liner *Lancastria*, with Sharp in command, had lain off St Nazaire on 17 June 1940, shortly after Dunkirk, waiting to sail with over 5,000 servicemen on board, when she was bombed by Dornier DO17s. Over 3,000 lost their lives and Sharp had had to face a four-hour swim for his life. Nor was that all. As he would have well known, regardless of any of the sailor's traditional superstition, the previous bearer of his new ship's name had been unlucky. The old 18,000-ton Cunarder *Laconia* had been charging through a blizzard, Liverpool bound, when at 10.30 pm on the evening of Sunday, 25 February 1917 she was torpedoed and sunk by a U-boat 160 miles west-nor'-west of the Fastnet, with the loss of twelve lives. It was, perhaps, therefore not surprising that on taking over command of the present *Laconia* Sharp had written to his wife, "This ship is not much to my liking."

Under a full moon she slid down the Red Sea, flat as a mirror, with nearly three thousand souls on board. Although she was now out of range of attack from Axis aircraft, *Laconia* was badly overloaded, and Sharp knew it. With only thirty-two lifeboats, and poorly provisioned ones at that, forty large rafts and several small ones, there would be little chance of evacuating everybody to safety if she received a serious hit, particularly as many of them were badly wounded men, besides women, children and the Italian prisoners.

And it was very hot, at 110°F in the shade. For the prisoners, battened down in the stuffy sweaty holds and sleeping in hammocks so close together that they touched their neighbours, the heat was insufferable, broken only by twice daily one hour exercise periods on the upper deck and early morning ablutions under cold showers from suspended buckets topped up by sea water hoses.

After stopping at Aden, the next port of call was Mombasa for fuel, 1,300 miles down the East African coast. Mombasa was an important wartime British naval base, crowded with war-weary ships, big and small, with all their associated paraphernalia. As the *Laconia* berthed, the usual dockside commotion that accompanies the arrival of any big ship broke out and the passengers and off-duty crew crowded the gangways, anxious to get ashore for the few hours' leave which was to end, strictly, at midnight. Here, the local police came aboard and the two hundred prostitutes were hustled down onto the quay, after a careful roll call, and loaded into lorries to be taken away into internment camps. It was a move which saved their lives.

Replenished with fuel and supplies, the big liner sailed the next day, 22 August, and made her way down the coral-lined channel towards the open sea and her next stop – Durban. The *Laconia* stopped for three days at Durban and Sharp allowed the prisoners to stretch their legs on the quayside, under close guard. Some youthful RAF officers under a Wing Commander Blackburn came aboard, having been transferred, to their disgust, from the liner *Stratheden*, bound for Halifax, Nova Scotia. Along with them was a civilian Rolls Royce engineer, a Spitfire engine specialist named R.S. 'Jock' Miller, a Merchant Navy engineer named Sime, a gigantic and irrepressibly cheerful Scottish artillery officer called Ben Coutts who had had the complete bridge as well as most of the rest of his nose blown away by shrapnel at Tobruk, and several other ex-*Stratheden* passengers. Among these was the beautiful and vivacious Lady Grizel Wolfe Murray, pregnant wife of a Lieutenant-Colonel in the Black Watch. Lady Grizel, daughter of the Earl of Glasgow, had been working as a nurse in Alexandria, until, with Rommel's guns advancing to within range of the town, her husband had decided that she should go home to have their baby in safety. With her was her friend, Sister Doris 'Freckles' Hawkins, a nursing missionary who was taking a fourteen-month-old baby, Sally Readman, home out of danger for her parents, who were actively engaged in wartime activities in Palestine. There was also a Major Creedon and a Mrs Davidson with her teenage daughter Molly. And a hundred and three Polish soldiers embarked to take over the guarding of the prisoners. These were part of a division which had been formed four months earlier in northern Persia and had arrived in Durban in June in the *Mauretania*.

Once south of Durban they came within range of attack from U-boats, besides the danger of hitting one of the mines that the enemy had planted in large areas around the Cape, especially off Cape Town, which was to be the *Laconia*'s last port of call. Leaving the Cape, where a contingent of a couple of dozen RAF personnel joined the ship, security tightened even more. Sharp took to sleeping and taking his meals in the chart-room, so as to be instantly ready to deal personally with any emergency. Frequent boat-drills were ordered, although some of the passengers failed to take them very seriously. The darkening of the ship at nightfall was met with extra thoroughness and strict radio silence was observed.

By now, in the way of all long liner voyages whether during time of peace or war, little sub-communities had developed among the passengers. Regular groups assembled for card schools or dancing; furtive couples met in corners and cabins, intoxicated by the illicit passion of their shipboard affairs, and gangs of children played hide-and-seek. As for the Polish guards, watching with fixed bayonets over their Italian charges cooped up below, they realized that the 1,800 suntanned but thin p.o.ws could, if the notion took them, quite easily make a concerted rush and take over the ship. Eighteen hundred against one hundred and three. It was a particularly uncomfortable thought, particularly as they had each been given only one round of ammunition for their rifles. If the need to defend themselves arose, the bayonets alone would have to suffice.

The liner zig-zagged her way northwards through a choppy Atlantic, belching smoke into the clear sky as her furnaces consumed the mountain of steam coal that lay piled in her bunkers. The weather grew warmer again as they drew nearer to the equator and, taking the air on the upper deck, all the while with life-belts close at hand, hundreds of pairs of eyes cast frequent uneasy glances at the waves. Was that the wake of a periscope or the top of a conning-tower, or a school of porpoises, or simply a fleeting shadow on the water? Somehow, although shipboard life continued in an apparently normal fashion, an uneasy unspoken sense of danger prevailed, setting everybody's mind into an instinctive state of constant semi-alertness.

*　　*　　*

U-156 was on her third mission in the year since she had been commissioned at Kiel. Her commander, Korvettenkapitän Werner Hartenstein, a thirty-two-year-old with a Goebbels-like face and a duelling scar across his left cheek, was popular with his volunteer crew. By now the operations which they had carried out in the course of that year had forged them into a close-knit team, each man, whether officer or rating, being confident in the ability of his fellows.

August 1942 found *U-156* at Lorient, preparing to join Admiral Karl Dönitz's *Eisbär* 'Polar Bear' group. The flotilla left various French Atlantic ports on 16 and 17 August to comb the ocean for whatever Allied merchant shipping they could find. It was on the morning of 12 September, five degrees south of the equator, having already sunk the freighters *Clan MacWhirter* and *Willimantic*, that

Hartenstein found some more prey. The sea was as white as a bowl of cream under the glaring tropical sun. The horizon was almost invisible through the dazzling intensity of the pale light which blurred the line between sky and water.

At 0937, the port after lookout shouted, "Smoke, bearing 230!" In the conning-tower, binoculars were swung onto the bearing. Sure enough, there was a faint smudge of distant smoke, barely discernible through the haze. The lookout had done his job well; it had been the old coal-burning furnaces of the *Laconia* which had betrayed her presence to him.

Hartenstein needed to investigate. Was it in fact smoke, or would it turn out to be merely some low-lying cloud? It would not be the first time that he had been disappointed in that way. He ordered speed to increase to sixteen knots and *U-156*'s 2,500 horse-power twin diesels hummed in response.

Within an hour, they were able to see that there was in fact a large ship and she was steaming fast, probably at around fifteen knots, on a forty degree zig-zag. She looked like an armed merchant cruiser, with her after-mounted 4.7" gun. Hartenstein kept his distance. He wanted to attack on the surface, as Dönitz had instructed his captains to do whenever possible. With her low conning-tower, the U-boat would not be seen by the big ship's lookouts at this range, but, conversely, the submarine would always be able to see her giant victim. Now was not the time to attack. He would wait for nightfall before moving close in to sink her.

Laconia zig-zagged on her way innocently. In fact, Sharp had received a signal from the Admiralty at 0115 on the morning of the 10th. Deciphered, it read, "Alter course, September 11th, two hours after sunset," and gave details of the new course that he should set. This took her farther away from the African coast and plumb into the middle of the gap between Brazil and West Africa. It was on this track that she was now being stalked by her unseen killer. Evening came and the sudden tropical darkness fell. Dinner finished and the dancing, card playing and love-making began. The soft wail of the blues rose from the dance-floor as the passengers gathered into their habitual groups for yet another mid-ocean night of uneasy pleasure. The sea was still calm.

Buckingham, the senior Third Officer, was about to pay a promised social call on a Fleet Air Arm officer and his wife, who were being repatriated after a serious bout of Malta fever. He had actually raised his hand to knock on their cabin door when the ship suddenly shook and a huge explosion erupted like thunder from below. The door vanished, its wooden panelling shattered into slivers, the lights flickered and dimmed, and the passageway, its linoleum, now buckled and twisted beneath his feet, filled with dust and eye-stinging smoke. Buckingham looked inside the cabin and saw his would-be hosts clinging together in shock. He was dazed for a second or so, but his training soon brought him to his senses. "Lifebelts!" he rapped out, "Get to your boat stations! Leave everything and hurry!"

He made his way to the bridge, where he knew he would be needed. The ship now seemed strangely silent except for the determined hiss of escaping steam from her many fractured pipes. Her engines had stopped and she had taken on a distinct list to starboard. Buckingham came up the ladder into the wheelhouse just as another mighty roar filled the air as a second torpedo buried its nose into her side. Then the alarm hooters groaned into the mid-Atlantic quietness with their mournful sound.

'Freckles' Hawkins, with another woman's baby in her care, found herself to be strangely calm. In her book, *Atlantic Torpedo*, written when she arrived home after a terrible ordeal, she says,

"I came up after dinner to look at Sally. She was asleep; beside her all was ready in case of emergency. I went into Mary's [Lady Grizel's] cabin and we sat talking about submarines and torpedoes. Suddenly there was a shattering explosion . . . the first torpedo had struck. I fled to Sally, wrapped her up in her woollies, picked up her shipwreck bag and as I turned to leave the second torpedo struck, flinging us across the corridor. Just ahead of me was Mary and we made our way upstairs together, carried on by a surging wave of people. Then the lights went out. It was very difficult going with my precious burden as I stumbled over fallen doors and shattered glass to our lifeboat station. There we waited for what seemed an age.

"In the pitch-darkness, with a heavy sea running, it was very difficult to swing out some of the lifeboats owing to the ship's list. And the second torpedo had apparently burst among the prisoners, understandably causing tremendous panic and chaos, trapped below as they were. They rushed their hopelessly outnumbered Polish guards, streamed on deck and

68

stormed the lifeboats or leapt into the sea. Then we were told that our lifeboat had been swept away. We wondered what to do. Sally had never cried once, despite the noise and turmoil. Then we saw Squadron Leader Wells. He took us from boat station to boat station, but all the boats were either already overfull or jammed in their davits. It was forty-five minutes after the torpedoes had struck that we saw a boat in the water, still alongside the ship. A young Fleet Air Arm officer offered to carry Sally. He tucked her into the back of his greatcoat, tied a blanket around his waist and carried her, papoose fashion down a swinging rope ladder and into the boat, which was tossing like a cork. Mary and I followed quickly. The lifeboat was crammed with men, women and children. It was leaking badly and kept crashing against the side of the ship. Just as Sally was passed over to me, the boat filled completely and capsized, flinging us all into the water. I did not hear her cry even then and I am sure that God took her immediately to Himself without suffering. I never saw her again."

The *Laconia* was listing more and more with every minute. The swarms of passengers making for the upper decks were met with equally determined throngs of people trying to go down to their cabins to look for things to take with them. One of the Polish guards, Roman Haupel, said that in their frenzy to break out of the hold the Italians were trampling all over each other. Some were even killing each other. Even so, only about a quarter of the 1,800 was to survive the sinking.

Mrs Davidson and her daughter Molly had been sitting in the lounge chatting. Now they held on to each other firmly as they tried to make their way through the mêlée to their boat station. The moon had now vanished behind clouds. It was totally dark. They were borne along on the human tide towards B deck. People were shouting each other's names, anxious not to be separated from friends and families in the jostling mass. An Army officer nearby noticed that Mrs Davidson was wearing only a thin silk evening dress. He insisted on giving her his coat, helped her to put on her lifebelt over it and disappeared into the crowd.

Major Creedon, a friend of the Davidsons, had been watching a game of bridge in the after-lounge. When the first explosion occurred, he quietly went to his cabin, picked up his sheepskin coat and a few other knick-knacks, slung his camera over his shoulder and went up towards A deck. Molly Davidson spotted him on the way and called out to him. He joined them and immediately set about trying to find them a place in a boat.

Ex-farm manager and race-horse stable boy, the towering Scot Ben Coutts, now a Captain in the Surrey and Sussex Yeomanry, was in the sick-bay. Always self-conscious of his size twelve feet, for which he had suffered a never-to-be-forgotten rebuttal from a certain lassie at a Borders country dance in his youth, he had had a pair of 'winkle-picker' shoes made in Alexandria in the hope that they would disguise this embarrassment. Instead, they had resulted in a painful ingrowing toenail which needed removal. He had decided that the middle of the South Atlantic, with a lengthy cruise still ahead, would be a convenient place and time to perform the operation. Now the ship was sinking and the noseless Coutts was faced with the added handicap of having his foot swathed in bandages.

Still wearing his pyjamas, he put on his greatcoat, loaded his revolver and put it in his pocket. Then he took his haversack, containing a water bottle, some whisky and his medical records, and elbowed his way out of the sick-bay through the crowd. Coutts' bridge and deck-games partner, Jock Miller, had been reading in the lounge when the first torpedo struck. He went quietly to his cabin to collect some belongings and some dried fruit, raisins and figs which he had bought at Cape Town. Emerging from the cabin, he caught sight of Coutts, hobbling along, dragging his bad foot and clutching two bottles of Johnny Walker which he had taken the opportunity to appropriate as he passed through the bar. Nobody had objected to this, especially the barman himself, who was busy stuffing his pockets with notes from the till.

"What a business!" said Miller, matter-of-factly, as if he were commenting on the weather. "It is that," agreed Coutts stolidly. And with that they fixed their life-belts and made their way up onto A deck. Things seemed quieter at the after end of the ship. They found a raft there and heaved it over the side into the mass of screaming people, upturned boats and general debris in the water. Then they swarmed for what seemed miles down a rope ladder and climbed aboard it. It was clear that the *Laconia* would not stay afloat for much longer and it was touch-and-go as to whether they could hack through the rope with which they had fastened the raft to the liner's hand-rail before she went down and took the raft with her. They managed to free themselves in time and set off to swim as far as possible away from the ship to avoid being sucked down, towing the raft behind them. They turned to see the huge shape of the stricken ship, its stern towering high into the night sky like a block of flats as she put her nose down and prepared to die. Coutts said that it occurred to him that there was something obscene about an old lady showing her propellers in public in such an uninhibited fashion. Then, quite quickly, with an enormous rumbling groan, she was gone.

Despite his desperate predicament, he chuckled to himself that the Army doctors had prescribed frequent douches in saline solution for the hole that was once his nose. And now it was being bathed by the whole Atlantic Ocean!

Laconia crew member, cockney Tony Chawe, said that the thing that was to haunt him for years afterwards was the sound of the pitiful cries and screams throughout the night from the watery darkness all around him as he bobbed on the waves. One of the Italians, Bruno Beltrami, shuddered as he felt the rough skin of a shark brushing against his leg like a piece of sandpaper. He looked down into the water and, despite the darkness, was relieved to see that the big fish already had a body in its jaws.

*   *   *

Early evening and the low shape of the submarine merged into the contours of the waves in the failing light. Hartenstein had tried to rest on his bunk behind the curtain which formed the door of his pigeon-hole of a cabin. But sleep was difficult as he thought about the unknown ship that he was about to destroy. And the voice of Heinz the cook, singing loudly and cheerfully as he prepared their evening meal, did little to help him relax. During the day they had overhauled the steamer, which was now over on their port quarter. Hartenstein sent the hands to supper at six o'clock, although they had already eaten but a short while before. This raised excitement as they leaned over their plates of potato soup. They all knew that a meal always preceded a call to Action Stations.

"They'll be having dinner on that yacht over there, too," said one of the sailors with a grin. "And soon we will start them dancing."

By eight o'clock the sun had disappeared towards Brazil and night had fallen like a curtain. The unsuspecting steamer's lights had been blacked out and the crew of *U-156* were waiting at their stations in patient anticipation of what was to come. At seven minutes past, the sub's klaxon gave its grating rasp. "Stand by, tubes One and Three." Hartenstein checked his target through his Zeiss again. "Ready. Tube One. Fire!"

"Guten appetit, meine Herren," he muttered grimly, not yet knowing the scale of the tragedy that he had triggered off.

The U-boat's wireless operator had heard the distress calls going out from the *Laconia* on two wavelengths, repeating her position over and over again. He had tried to jam them, but it was too late. This placed Hartenstein in a dilemma. On the one hand, he needed to find the liner's Captain, if he was still alive, among the thousands of survivors who were now scattered around in boats, on rafts, planks and doors or bobbing in life-belts in the water itself. On the other, he knew that if he hung around there would soon be swarms of Allied rescue planes and ships on the scene. And they would be after his blood.

"Let's go in closer," he said to Polchau, his chief engineer, "but not too near."

At walking pace *U-156* crept quietly among the boats and rafts. At that stage the *Laconia* had not yet sunk. She just lay there, with her bows peering into the depths of the ocean, issuing great clouds of steam from her sides and billowing black smoke from her tall single funnel. Her decks still were crowded with hysterical people. And they were mostly civilians!

Suddenly the Germans heard cries of "Aiuto! Aiuto!" They came from two men in the water, clutching a large crate which had once contained oranges. Aiuto?

"That's Italian," exclaimed Mannesmann, the U-boat's first lieutenant. The two men were pulled aboard for questioning and Hartenstein was appalled when they explained that he had sunk a ship containing not only hundreds of women and children, but also 1,800 men who were on his own side. His dilemma was intensified.

A Second World War submarine was a relatively small craft. Hartenstein could rescue only a very few of this mass of people, and that at great risk to one of the Führer's U-boats. Yet, how could he leave any of them to such a horrible fate? Especially as whole families of hungry barracuda were seen to be gathering around.

"Shall I radio the Admiral for orders?" enquired Mannesmann.

72

"No, I have decided that we must rescue as many as possible," replied Hartenstein. By early dawn, *U-56* was crammed with about ninety British and Italian survivors. Many of them were missing chunks of flesh torn from legs and buttocks by sharks as cleanly as scoops from a tub of ice-cream, or in the case of the Italians, were nursing wounds from the jabbing bayonets of their Polish guards.

*   *   *

In the luxurious block of flats overlooking Paris's Bois de Boulogne which served as the Headquarters of the German U-boat Command, Admiral Karl Dönitz was asleep in his sparsely furnished apartment. It had been a tiring day, preparing for a Berlin meeting with Grand Admiral Raeder. Suddenly, towards midnight, the telephone rang. A signal had been received from Hartenstein. "Sunk British *Laconia* – unfortunately with 1,500 (sic) Italian prisoners. 90 rescued so far."

Fifty years old, tall and slim, with blue eyes, large ears and a straight gash for a mouth which gave him a permanently determined look, Dönitz was himself a veteran First World War U-boat commander. He got up, dressed and took the sheet of paper to his desk, where he sat thinking in the dark. 1,500 Italian prisoners! Shipwrecked by one of his own submarines. This would do little for the already delicate relations between Hitler and the Duce. But what about Hartenstein? *U-156* was in a precarious position, lingering at the scene of the sinking. He liked Hartenstein, seeing him as a man of character who knew his own mind and was not afraid to speak it. Should he order him to abandon the survivors and sail away? He wrestled with the problem as the night drew on, trying to imagine the scene thousands of miles away in the South Atlantic. He could almost hear the screams of those in the water. And of course, there would be sharks. There were always sharks. He could picture the desperate faces, the overturned boats and the bloated corpses. All these thoughts must have raced through in his brain. At 0330 he came to his decision. Hartenstein needed help, quickly.

Dönitz took up his signal pad and wrote, "Schacht, Würdemann, Wilamowitz, head for Hartenstein at full speed. Square 7721." Then he went back to his bed to try to sleep.

Thirty-three-year-old Harro Schacht commanded *U-507*. He had taken her into the Gulf of Mexico to sink oil-tankers and had then proceeded south, along the coast of the Guianas and on past Brazil, intending to cross the ocean towards Freetown to lie in wait for Allied convoys up from the Cape. At 2015 on the evening of the 12th Schacht had received Hartenstein's radio message that he had sunk the *Laconia*. It was five and a half hours later when Dönitz's order arrived. Schacht replied immediately, "Am making for point of torpedoing 750 miles distant at fifteen knots. Can be there in two days. Schacht."

U-506, commanded by Leutnant Würdemann was *U-507*'s sister. The two had operated together in the Gulf of Mexico and then parted company off north-eastern Brazil. Schacht had sailed south while Würdemann had intended to move up to the eastern seaboard of America to hunt off New York. He was farther away from the *Laconia* than Schacht, but nevertheless, when he was brought Dönitz's signal by Wireless Operator Rüter, he turned the boat around, rapped out orders for extra hammocks to be slung in all available spaces, the wardroom to be cleared to accommodate rescued survivors, and ordered full speed ahead.

Wilamowitz-Möllendorf, in *U-459*, made a considered decision to disregard Dönitz's order. Being well over twice the size of her sisters in the *Eisbär* Group, and much slower, she was the farthest away of the three, somewhere off the Cape Verde Islands. He decided that he was not in a position to provide much help for several days, and in any case, as the squadron's *Milchkuh*, he was carrying essential fuel-oil to replenish the tanks of the others at a rendezvous planned for 2 September, without which Operation Polar Bear could not continue. To waste several tons of this on a futile journey would be foolish. At a steady eight knots, the big U-boat continued on her original course.

Reassured by the news that the Admiral had ordered the other three subs to assist him, Hartenstein was further placated by the wireless operator's assurances that he could hear other vessels exchanging messages in code. They could not be far away. This meant, surely, that he could quietly slide away with a clear conscience and leave the British to rescue their own. The worrying factor was that *U-156* now had 193 extra people crammed into her. Would she be able to dive safely under such a load if she were attacked? The ever-reliable Polchau assured him that she could. "Good. We'll do a practice dive," answered Hartenstein. It worked perfectly, but while they were dived it occurred to Hartenstein that, if any trouble had flared up between the British and Italian survivors, it could have meant death for them all. When they were safely back on the surface, he took up his microphone. "Attention! Attention! Commander speaking. You are all shipwrecked without distinction of nationality and we shall treat you all alike. I shall not tolerate any dispute between you, and if any should occur you will be punished severely and without distinction."

Meanwhile, at U-boat Command in Paris, Dönitz had had more inspiration. "It's mostly Italians that are being rescued," he said to Hessler, his Chief of Operations and son-in-law. "I'm going to inform Admiral Parona at Bordeaux what's happened. He has some submarines near Freetown. Let him send some help, too." As he continued gazing at the map of the Atlantic another idea occurred to him. What about the remnants of the Vichy French Fleet still cooped up in Dakar where the British Royal Navy had pounded them into almost complete destruction in 1940? But would *les matelots* be prepared to go to the rescue of the shipwrecked? Of course they would. They were sailors too, weren't they?

The wires hummed and buzzed urgently over the next half-hour as the Italian and Vichy governments were informed of the situation and their assistance requested.

Hartenstein, too, had had ideas. At 0400 he sent out a general radio message, *en clair*, on 600 metres and 25 metres. "If any ship will assist the wrecked *Laconia* crew, I will not attack her, provided I am not attacked by ship or aircraft. I have picked up 193 men. 4°52' south, 11° west. German submarine." Meanwhile, in the hellish scene in the water, the barracuda were fighting over the floating corpses.

Hessler was furious when he learned of Hartenstein's signal, sent purely on his own initiative without any higher approval. It was tantamount to calling a truce with the enemy and, besides, the British would not venture any ships into the area. They would strongly suspect a trap. His staff officer colleague, Godt, agreed, and urged Dönitz to call off the salvage operation immediately.

The moment was interrupted by the ringing of the telephone from Berlin. It was Admiral Fricke, speaking for Grand Admiral Raeder. Hitler, Fricke announced, was displeased with the *Laconia* situation. The Führer had ordered that they should take no risks whatsoever with the U-boats. And Berlin had already urged the Vichy Government to dispatch French ships to the area at full speed.

75

Sunday the 13th was a day of torment for the hundreds of *Laconia* survivors still awaiting rescue. By midday the equatorial sun had reached searing heat. Arms, faces, shoulders were blistering agonizingly. And there were stinging purple jelly-fish to torture those still in the water. Everybody was desperately hungry and thirsty. Nurse Hawkins was lucky enough to get a piece of an orange that somebody had spotted floating by. She chewed on the peel for hours, thinking of her family at home. They would surely be in church on that Sunday morning, praying for her safe home-coming. During the morning her heart had been in her mouth when she saw the U-boat that had sunk them approaching at slow speed. It stopped about half a mile away. There had been many stories of German cruelty and she feared a hail of machine-gun bullets. But none came. In fact, the Germans were rescuing people by throwing them life-lines and pulling them on board.

They had joined their raft to another by means of a rope and now the two had nine people on them, including two RAF officers and an Italian. Seeing the submarine's rescue operation, the two officers quickly jumped into the water, with lines around them, and set off to swim towards the sub, towing the rafts behind them. But it was laboriously slow work and just as they were nearly within hailing distance the U-boat moved off. Exhausted, they spent the rest of the day drifting aimlessly.

The sun was almost below the horizon and they were getting ready to spend another uncomfortable night when *U-156* headed straight for them and they suddenly found themselves looking up at the faces of the German sailors who were tossing life-lines to them. And to her delight, when taken to the sub's little wardroom for some food and to get dry clothes, she found her friend Lady Grizel, who had been picked up just five minutes earlier. The Germans were most respectful and kind, and gave the women soothing cold cream for their sunburn.

Buckingham had spent the night with a corpse which was floating face down in the water. It had helped to keep him afloat and to conserve some of his strength. He was grateful to it. It looked like a man of about forty and from his clothes it seemed that he was one of the crew of the *Laconia*. Whoever it was, Buckingham felt that they had formed a kind of kinship in the course of their common ordeal. But then he caught a glimpse of the drowned man's face, with its bulging eyes and swollen lips, and he was aghast. Instinctively, he felt the urge to get away from the disgusting object.

One last time, he used the body as a support to raise himself a little in the water, as he had done many times during the past hours, to enable him to look around for help. There was something there for sure, but it was far away. It wasn't a ship. Too small. He couldn't quite make it out. But soon he had drifted a little nearer and he could see that it was, in fact, the heads of two men. And they were in a boat.

He gave the corpse a farewell shove and set off to swim towards them. It was hard going because he was weak and the sea was choppy. It took him a full hour to reach it, having to stop for frequent rests to regain his breath on the way. But it was crammed with people. So much so that they were all standing up, with those on the outside linking arms to form a safety cordon to prevent anybody from falling overboard. He could see that it was hopeless to try to board. " Any more boats around here?" he asked. "One over there, quite a way. But watch out for sharks," said a man, indicating eastwards with his arm. Buckingham saw that it was Purslow, the *Laconia*'s doctor. There was no other option but to swim on towards the other boat and hope that the sharks had had their fill.

It meant another hour of exertion and by the time the other boat came in sight he was extremely tired. After a day and a half in the water and two hours hard swimming, it was all he could do to grab the oar that was reached out to him and to haul himself over the gunwales to flop, deadbeat, into the bottom of the boat. He found that he had joined fourteen Italians and a solitary RAF officer and that the boat was quite well equipped. It even had a compass, a good set of sails and rigging. But they were a good 500 miles from land, probably about a month's sail, with luck, and they weren't going to make it on a handful of Horlicks tablets, some biscuits and a couple of gallons of fresh water.

By the time Buckingham had recovered sufficiently to sit up and talk to his new companions, Purslow's boat had drifted into sight, as well as a couple of others which seemed to have room. They elected to stay close together. It seemed safer. Several of the survivors in Purslow's dangerously overcrowded boat were transferred to the newcomers and everybody was a little more comfortable. At night it was agreed that Buckingham's boat would show a hurricane lamp at its masthead and they would all keep station on it. The little flotilla now carried eighty-six Italians and three British.

In another boat about a mile away, nearly having lost her dentures as she was hauled in, Dorothy Davidson tried to doze, wrapped in a blanket, propped against the knees of the man holding the tiller. But she couldn't sleep. Where was Molly, she asked herself repeatedly. Then the U-boat came and twenty of the boat's Italian occupants were taken on board. The resonant voice of the German captain still echoed in her head. It sounded sincere. "I am sorry for you, but your ship was armed as an auxiliary cruiser. You will surely be rescued, because some wireless messages were sent. I shall not attack rescue ships."

Coutts and Miller had abandoned their raft and managed to get themselves into a boat with seven other British and six Italians. But it was leaking badly and all fifteen of them were obliged to take their turn in baling her out with buckets. Towards evening the U-boat they had seen touring the other boats throughout the day came near to them and stopped. Whether or not it was the one which had sunk them they did not know. An officer appeared in the conning-tower. "Any wounded on board?" he shouted. "No," came the answer.

"Right, you'll be rescued from Ascension Island or Dakar. I have done the necessary."

As the submarine moved off Miller spotted a large raft drifting empty. They managed to catch it and tied it to their boat's stern. It might come in useful in an emergency. During the night the boats all somehow drifted apart and when dawn came each was only visible to the others as a mere dot in the distance.

With his pale Scottish skin, Coutts was beginning to suffer badly from sunburn. There was no protection whatsoever in the boat from the powerful rays except for a little corner beneath the sail. And his foot was hurting. Nevertheless, he kept up his usual cheerful patter, bringing smiles to the faces of the Italians, even though they did not understand a word of it.

The water was now ankle deep in the bottom of the boat. It would surely sink within the next few hours. The British officers, using much charm, managed to persuade the Italians to go over onto the raft to lighten the boat's burden. One lost his head on the way over and tumbled into the waves crying "Mamma mia". They never saw him again. And in the morning, cold and stiff after another damp and chilly night, they found that there was now no sign of any of the other boats. They were completely alone in the middle of the Atlantic. And there was only one Italian left on the raft.

*   *   *

The Italian submarine *Capellini* had sailed from Bordeaux on 13 August. Her captain, Tenente-Comandante Marco Revedin, had been ordered to proceed on a mission which would take him into the mid-Atlantic at its narrowest point, between Brazil and West Africa, hopefully to find rich pickings among the Allied merchant shipping coming up from the River Plate and from the Cape of Good Hope.

On 13 September, just after 0800, the submarine's wireless blipped. "Betasom (the Italian code word for Bordeaux) to *Capellini*. Make urgently for sub-square 0971*. Other units heading same zone."

This meant he should proceed at best possible speed towards a point to the north-east of Ascension Island. Why? He shrugged his shoulders and told himself he would find out soon enough. Meantime, he increased speed to twelve knots. It made for an uncomfortable ride on the surface, because the ocean was in one of its choppy moods and the *Capellini*'s design made her ride high in the water. Nevertheless, they ploughed on.

During the afternoon and evening and throughout the following day more signals came in from Bordeaux, changing and counter-manding details of the rendezvous point, recognition signals to be used and so on. The top brass were clearly indecisive about the whole thing.

By ten minutes past midnight on the morning of the 15th Revedin was exhausted by the sheer volume of wireless traffic. He knew now the purpose of his mission. It was going to be heavy work, this rescue operation. He handed over the bridge to Di Siervo, his First Lieutenant, and flopped onto his bunk to try to sleep.

The weather in Dakar was hot and clammy on the morning of Sunday 13 September. The heavy air had made every living thing seem to be listless and without energy as the sun blazed down. The

---

* The Axis Navies used a grid system of numbered squares to identify positions. These were broken down into smaller sub-squares for accuracy. The numbers were changed frequently for the sake of security.

Vichy French naval Commander-in-Chief, Admiral Collinet, sat in his office dealing with a backlog of paperwork. The port was quiet, too quiet even for a Sunday morning. The Admiral did not like it when it was quiet like this. It always seemed to him that it was probably just a lull, after which the storm of war would resume worse than before, bringing more startling surprises with it. Indeed, the strange situation which the French Fleet now found itself in, having largely been destroyed in 1940 by its would-be Allies, the British Navy, was discomfiting in itself. Across the river sat a garrison of Germans, with whom there was an uneasy armistice, watching the French ships in the harbour like a family of cheetahs with a herd of wildebeest in their sights. Seawards, there was always the British. Was a squadron of battle-cruisers steaming towards Dakar at this very moment, hell-bent on destroying some more French warships in case they became useful to Germany? One o'clock came and Collinet was just on his way to lunch when a signal arrived from Vichy. He was charged with the task of arranging for the rescue of the *Laconia* shipwrecked.

His nearest ship to the scene of the wreck at that moment was the escort frigate *Dumont-d'Urville*, at anchor off the port of Cotonou, 1,250 miles along the coast of West Africa in Dahomey. The 2,000-ton ship could make sixteen knots and carried enough guns, including several anti-aircraft weapons, to be able to look after herself. He signalled her captain, Commander Françis Madelin, to sail immediately to rendezvous with the German U-boats. But the clammy atmospheric conditions that day distorted the message. It was indecipherable. All Madelin could do, having himself received earlier orders to maintain strict radio silence, was to wait in the hope of a repeat from Collinet. In the evening, at 1930, another message came through from Dakar announcing yet another change of rendezvous, but it was as garbled as the first. It was not until the following morning, at 0800 on the 14th, that Madelin was aware of the *Laconia* sinking. From the two unreadable signals he had assumed that something urgent was afoot, but had had absolutely no idea as to what it was until a re-transmission of the Admiral's orders arrived from the base commander at Cotonou. A whole day and night had been lost doing nothing but listening to the roar of the surf on the beach. Madelin took on supplies for the 1,000-mile trip, discharged to shore the sailors in the *Dumont-d'Urville*'s sick-bay, weighed anchor and at 1700 hours set off at fourteen knots to meet the Germans.

In Dakar Collinet realized that Madelin would not be able to take on board all the survivors from the *Laconia*. He would need to send more ships to help. There was the *Annamite*, another escort vessel. She was faster than *Dumont-d'Urville*, but tiny, at 650 tons. At that moment she was shepherding a small convoy to Conakry in French Guinea. The officer of the watch brought Collinet's signal to her Breton captain, Lieutenant-Commander Quémard, as he walked on his bridge, binoculars slung around his neck, watching his sailors going about their work. Quémard bore little love for the British, but orders are orders. The Breton took his little convoy into French territorial waters at twelve knots, which was as fast as it could steam, then turned his bows towards Ascension Island at full speed.

Two small ships and a submarine were now thrashing their way into the ocean. The rescue mission was on at last. But it wasn't enough, by far, to save the number of shipwrecked people they were likely to find. The Italians, with 1,800 lives at stake, had cause for the most concern. Pressure on the French Admiralty to give "as generous consideration as possible to the German request relative to the saving of the Italian prisoners" was exerted from Turin, the HQ of the Italian Armistice Commission. The plea was heard, with the result that the 7,600-ton six-inch cruiser *Gloire* was placed under sailing orders. With a range of 6,500 miles at 15 knots, the cruiser would be easily able to conduct a protracted search in mid-Atlantic without any worries about fuel. Admiral Longaud, in command of the Dakar cruiser squadron, was not too pleased to receive orders to detach one of his ships from his superior, Collinet. Co-operation with the Germans, and the resultant presence of Italian ex-p.o.ws on his ship, could well lead to an attack on the *Gloire* itself by the British.

Reluctantly, Longaud summoned Graziani, captain of the *Gloire*, aboard his flagship *Georges-Leygues* on the afternoon of 14 September. "I have a delicate task for you, *mon ami*," said the Admiral, going on to explain about the *Laconia* situation. "How soon can you sail?" "In four hours, sir," came the reply.

"Right. But remember that you are on what is strictly a humanitarian operation. You are dispatched simply to rescue the largest possible number of survivors, and will make no distinction of nationality among them. On no account will you open fire unless attacked. At twenty knots, you can be there in forty-eight hours. Good luck."

Graziani snapped his crew into action. On the beach a bathing party from *Gloire*'s crew of 540 suddenly noticed that black smoke was swirling from her funnel and that a recall flag was fluttering from her yard-arm. The officer in charge of the party, Sub-Lieutenant Vivier, summoned their launch and within minutes they were heading towards the cruiser. On board, parties of matelots hustled and bustled about as equipment was checked, extra stores taken on, awnings taken down and boats hauled in. At 2100 hours the *Gloire* sailed south. With her twin shafts humming, she quickly picked up speed to twenty-one knots as she buffeted her way through a strong Atlantic gale.

*   *   *

Würdemann, in *U-506*, was the first of the Germans to arrive on the rescue scene. He brought his boat alongside *U-156* with a flourish and shouted to Hartenstein, "Sorry I couldn't make it sooner!" He took half of Hartenstein's passengers and the two boats separated to go in search of more shipwrecked people. Some they found in waterlogged life-boats, many of them already corpses, others unconscious and frozen stiff. Those who were alive were lifted on board, rubbed down with towels to restore their circulation and given hot drinks. Then the submariners repaired the cracks in the lifeboats as best they could and took them in tow to accommodate more survivors to await the racing Vichy rescue ships.

By mid-evening, Hartenstein had filled the last boat in the little chain that he was towing and just before midnight radioed to his Commander-in-Chief, "4°46' south by 11°50' west. Last boat found 9.50 pm Hove to. 11.24 pm."

U-507, bustling along at fifteen knots, sighted a small sail on the afternoon of the 15th. It was one of Buckingham's little group of four lifeboats, carrying thirty-five Italians, twenty British and four Poles. There had clearly been much ill-feeling among them, particularly between the Poles and Italians, and Schacht was careful to keep them apart. Understandably, the British contingent was apprehensive at boarding a U-boat, but were soon reassured by plates of hot soup, bars of chocolate, soap and cold cream for their sunburn.

Guided by Buckingham's intelligent guesswork, Schacht steered a course to take him closer to the spot of the *Laconia* sinking. They found more survivors. And another boat. At 5.55 pm Schacht radioed Dönitz, "One hundred and fifty-three survivors on board."

In Paris Dönitz and his team of officers gazed anxiously at the big Atlantic wall-map. They had done everything possible to get help to Hartenstein, but now the fate of the survivors depended entirely on the French. To add to their disquiet, another telephone call came in during the night from the Führer. It was a repeat of his earlier order that no risks whatsoever must be taken with the U-boats. Yet, under the Admiral's orders, there were the submarines, in a group, sitting in the middle of the Atlantic, far from home and the enemy knew exactly their position. In fact, even the *Gloire* was already being shadowed by a Sunderland flying boat.

Hartenstein, exhausted now, sat perched in the conning-tower of *U-156* and swung his Zeiss along the horizon for signs of the French ships. He had lingered at this spot to save over four hundred people from the *Laconia*, but now the realization of the danger that he was in from attack by Allied forces made him extremely anxious.

At 11.25 am the lookout reported a large four-engined aircraft. Soon its throbbing hum was audible. Hartenstein ordered a large white sheet, six feet square, which had already been embroidered with a big red cross, to be spread over the for'ard gun. Everybody on the U-boat's casing lay down, and the people in the four lifeboats in tow gazed up and waited. The plane came in low and circled over the sub. It was an American Liberator.

Hartenstein signalled in Morse, in English, "Have British ship-wrecked on board. Is there a rescue plane?" But there was no reply.

Even a second message, transmitted as dictated by one of the British officers, "R.A.F. Officer calling from German submarine. *Laconia* survivors on board, women and children," received no answer. The plane droned off towards the south-west. On board the U-boat dozens of pairs of eyes watched it disappear from view, re-assured by the knowledge that they had now been spotted by friends. At 12.32 pm the sound of engines was heard again. It was another Liberator. It dived to about 250 feet over the submarine. But suddenly the bright smiling faces looking up at the aircraft gave vent to shrieks of terror. Two bombs were actually falling from the open hatches in the plane's belly! They splashed into the sea and the Liberator wheeled, banking low as it turned to make a second attack run.

The cries of alarm were now joined by roars of anger and a torrent of abuse in English, Italian, Polish and German. The aeroplane came back over the boat, dropping two more bombs. They missed the sub, but one of the lifeboats, crammed with people, received a direct hit and another was overturned. A tower of white water erupted from the spot where the lifeboat had been and fragments of wood cartwheeled into the blue sky.

"Keep calm!" ordered Hartenstein, as yet two more bombs, the plane's last, emerged from the hatches. "Hard a-port" One of the bombs hit the water near the U-boat with hardly a splash. But it was a depth-charge and after a few seconds it exploded directly under the control room. A mountain of water enshrouded the submarine, which shuddered and rocked under the impact. Below, screaming women and children, struck with terror, rushed towards the ladder to try to reach the comparative safety of the upper casing. Mannesmann pushed his way through the crowd to report the damage to his captain. The control room and forward compartments were taking in water, the batteries were giving off deadly chlorine gas, the periscopes were jammed, the wireless was out of action and the sounding gear was damaged. Meantime, the Liberator was circling the area, apparently calmly checking on the effects of its handiwork.

Hartenstein had not permitted the deck-guns of U-156 to fire a single shot at the plane, but now he realized he should have destroyed it. How much longer would it be before more Allied aircraft appeared in the sky, guided to the spot by the Liberator? Or even destroyers? He needed to dive to safety and make his boat ready to fight if necessary. He made a quick decision and ordered all his passengers over the side and into the sea, to swim towards the lifeboats. Most of them took it quite calmly, as if they understood the German's dilemma.

'Freckles' Hawkins and Lady Grizel found themselves in shark-infested water again. There was a heavy sea running and it was hard going, especially for the six-months pregnant Lady Grizel. Nevertheless, helped by the gallant Squadron Leader Wells, they made it to the nearest lifeboat, utterly exhausted after almost an hour's swim. The thirty-foot boat then carried sixty-eight people, of which they were the only two women.

Within an hour Hartenstein's technical crew had repaired the damage well enough to make a test dive. He stayed submerged for eight hours, surfacing into a fine and calm Atlantic night. Steering westwards, he wirelessed Dönitz at 2304 hours, "From Hartenstein.

1. Bess (*right*) and Beth sail again on Liverpool Bay – 59 years later.

2. Safely aboard HMS *Anthony*, left to right Kenneth Sparks, Derek Capel, Freddie Steele, Billy Short and Howard Clayton.

3. Louis Walder and John Baker aboard HMS *Hurricane*.

4. The rescue of Boat 12 – Billy Short on far left in bows.

5. Mary Cornish.

6. *(Left)* Kapitänleutnant Viktor Oehrn, sinker of the *Sheaf Mead* and the *Severn Leigh* *(photo: U-Boot-Archiv – Cuxhaven)*.

7. *(below left)* Lady Grizel Wolfe-Murray.

8. *(below right)* Ben Coutts, complete with rebuilt nose – farming again in 1954.

9. In the dock at the *Peleus* trial, *left to right* Eck, Hoffman, Weisspfennig, Lenz and Schwender.

10. Commander Dudley W. 'Mush' Morton U.S.N. *(US Navy photo)*.

11. Fisherman Wilfred Allen who was killed on the *Noreen Mary*
(*by kind permission of Dennis Allen*).

12. The trawler *Kate Lewis* before her name was changed to *Noreen Mary*.

13. The trawler *Kingston Diamond*, formerly *Lady Madeleine*, which rescued the two survivors from the *Noreen Mary*.

14. Eric Halfhide *(left)*, a survivor of *Rakuyo Maru,* meets up again with Norman Hunter, ex-crew member of USS *Sealion II (by kind permission of Eric Halfhide).*

15. Oil-covered survivors from *Rakuyo Maru* on their raft *(US Navy photo).*

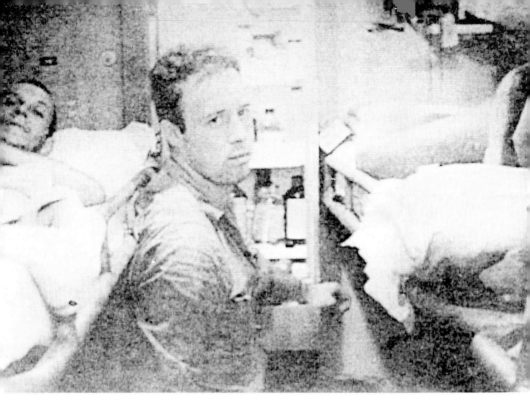

16. Pharmacist's Mate Roy Williams with *Rakuyo* survivors in *Sealion's* sick-bay *(US Navy photo)*.

17. Sketch-plan of *Lisbon Maru*, by Ashley Aslet after a drawing by Sergeant S.J. Chin of the C.I.C.

NO 1 — 俘虜 P.O.W
COTTON
MANGANESE ORE
COPPER
TUNGSTEN
LEAD
ALUMINIUM
BISMUTH

バラスト BALLAST 300 TON

NO 2 — 俘虜 P.O.W / 俘虜 P.O.W

NO 3 — 俘虜 P.O.W / 俘虜 P.O.W / 俘虜 P.O.W

将校室 OFFICER'S MESS
兵室 TROOP'S MESS

NO 4 — 俘虜 P.O.W

諜備庫房 AUXILIARY COAL STORES

機關室 ENGINE ROOM

水槽室 WATER TANK

NO 5 — 糧秣 RATION ROOM / 兵室 TROOP'S QUARTERS

機房 SCRAP IRON

NO 6 — 兵室 TROOP'S QUARTERS
バラスト BALLAST 200 TONS

NO 7 — 兵室 TROOP'S QUARTERS
5" SHELLS
LEAD
LEATHER
COTTON
GOLD DUST
SALTED PIGS HIDE
バラスト BALLAST 200 TONS

搭載地 PORT OF EMBARKATION	揚陸地 DESTINATION	丸乾 合計
九龍 KOWLOON		合計 TOTAL
大阪 OSAKA		1643 6Z TONS AND CUBIC METRE
東京 TOKYO		32.809 TONS
合計 TOTAL		1676466 TONS AND CUBIC METRE

18. Miers with *Torbay* crew at Buckingham Palace, July 1942.

19. Prisoners of War on their way to Shamshuipo Camp, Hong Kong, 30 December 1941.

20. The Japanese hell-ship *Lisbon Maru.*

21. Kapitänleutnant Erich Topp, whose *U-552* sank the freighter *David H. Atwater (photo: U-Boat-Archiv – Cuxhaven)*.

22. Korvettenkapitän Ottoheinrich Junker, who sank the *m.v. Tulagi* in the Indian Ocean *(photo: U-Boot-Archiv – Cuxhaven)*.

23. Grossadmiral Karl Doenitz *(photo: U-Boot-Archiv – Cuxhaven).*

24. Kapitänleutnant Heinrich Bleichrodt, sinker of the *City of Benares (photo: U-Boot-Archiv – Cuxhaven).*

25. Another raftload rescued by the *Pampanito* (US Navy photo).

American Liberator bombed us five times at low level in good visibility, while we had four full boats in tow, in spite of large Red Cross flag, four metres square on bridge. Am discontinuing help: all men overboard: am moving away to the west. Repairing damage."

From U-boat Command came the reply at 0145 hours on 17 September, "To Hartenstein. Take no further part in salvage operation. Report state of fuel supply, torpedoes, provisions, and operational readiness as soon as possible." Later that day, no doubt aware that he had incurred the displeasure of the Führer for having risked three U-boats, Dönitz issued the order which was to result in a charge of war crimes against him three and a half years later:

1. *No attempt of any kind must be made at rescuing members of ships sunk, and this includes picking up persons in the water and putting them into lifeboats, righting capsized lifeboats and handing over food and water. Rescue runs counter to the rudimentary demands of warfare for the destruction of enemy ships and crews.*
2. *Orders for bringing in captains and chief engineers still apply.*
3. *Rescue the shipwrecked only if their statements will be of importance to your boat.*
4. *Be harsh, having in mind that the enemy takes no regard of women and children in his bombing attacks on German cities.*

*   *   *

Ben Coutts and Jock Miller, cold and wet, watched the sun come up from their lurching raft. It was a pleasant surprise to find themselves not far from one of the *Laconia*'s lifeboats, with Second Officer Rose in charge of nine British and six Italians on board. The boat was leaking badly and had no provisions. There was so much water in it that it was impossible to lie down to sleep, but for Coutts and Miller it was as a luxury liner compared to their raft. For the noseless Coutts, it also meant relative safety, because for him there had been a special danger. If he had become submerged, even for a short while, he would almost certainly have drowned in 'saline solution'. After three days and nights of hard baling and permanent wetness, they met up with another lifeboat. This one was in far better condition and had several of the sunken liner's officers in it, together with fifty-five people. By transferring some of the Italians among them to the leaking boat, room was made for the damp Britishers to come on board. Salvation arrived on the fifth day after the sinking in the shape of the graceful lines of the *Gloire*, which had already found seven lifeboats and thereby rescued several hundred people.

The lifeboat heaved and pitched on the ocean swell alongside the big cruiser and the survivors grabbed at the scrambling nets tossed to them by the French matelots. Those who were able to climbed up them, but Coutts, with his legs badly swollen by long exposure to sun and sea-water, was unable to make it. He said afterwards that he would never forget the kindness of those smiling and cheerful French sailors who hauled him up, still in his silk pyjamas, and gave him coffee and brandy. Their officers seemed to be of a different breed, however, and Coutts got the distinct impression that they were all pro-Nazi to a man, especially the one who kicked him up the backside as he was crawling on his hands and knees towards the toilet. This view was vindicated on arrival in Casablanca, when, as the British contingent went ashore down the gangway to the cheers of the *matelots*, the French officers turned their backs.

The three U-boats had spent much time, all the while placing themselves in greater danger from air attack, in rounding up lifeboats and rafts, and rescuing people from the water itself. Scouser Edward Johnson said that after the initial relief to find that he was not, after all, to be machine-gunned in the water, he watched the submarines acting for all the world like mother hens looking for their chicks and keeping them together to await the French cruiser.

Dorothy Davidson's lifeboat was one of eight taken in tow by *U-507*, to be taken to the rendezvous point to meet up with the *Gloire*. The women and children were taken aboard the submarine, where they were treated with much courtesy and kindness by Schacht's crew, even to the point of escorting them around the boat in order to prevent them being molested by the Italians! Dorothy was relieved to find her daughter Molly already on board the cruiser, having been picked up by the little escort vessel *Annamite*.

Also among the eight lifeboats was Buckingham's. He was mystified how Schacht knew that he was an officer, as he wore no badges of rank. The fact was, the German captain *did* know, which meant that poor Buckingham was to finish up in a prisoner-of-war camp rather than be repatriated.

For Sister Hawkins and Lady Grizel the worst of their ordeal was to come. Their lifeboat was one of two who had drifted so far away from the others that the 'mother hens' did not find them. The days passed by in depressing monotony. And the nights were chilly and wet, even though they were in the tropics. The women huddled together for warmth, but the cold Atlantic wind cut right through their thin clothing. The lifeboat's limited provisions, especially of water, were strictly rationed by Geoffrey Purslow, who had been the liner's doctor. Soon their thirst reached a state of torment. Parched tongues hung out to catch the few drops of rain that sometimes fell in the early mornings. Saliva dried up, making it difficult even to swallow the few mouthfuls of food that Purslow issued twice a day. Pores closed up, so that they did not sweat at all, despite the searing equatorial noon-day heat. They all became delirious, unable to sleep properly, but dozed fitfully, dreaming of cool drinks and ice cream. Rotted by the sun and sea water, their clothes were soon no better than tattered rags. Bodies broke out in sores and Purslow, having no medical supplies, was reduced to opening septic areas to drain the pus with a pen-knife cleansed in sea water, aided by Doris Hawkins. Some just faded away and died. One was Billy Henderson, the *Laconia*'s Fourth Engineer. He had selflessly taken on far more than his share of pumping and always stood the longest watches at night. Often, in the mornings, he would be found still at his post, blue with cold, until one morning the women found that he was no longer breathing.

Lady Grizel, too, was one of those who simply faded away. Characteristically, she maintained her cheerfulness to the end, sharing many a private joke with her friend 'Freckles', although she must have carried in her heart a deep sadness for her family waiting at home and for her unborn child. On 25 September she seemed to realize that her end was near and thanked her friend for looking after her, saying, "We've had lots of fun". Her last words seem to have been a repeating of her home address, before falling asleep. 'Freckles' sat with her arms around her all through the night and it was at six in the morning that her breathing stopped. She had never woken again. Doctor Purslow held a little burial service as they lowered her into the water. And they tried to sing Abide with Me with croaking voices.

As the days wore on, life drained away from more and more of their number as they succumbed to the torture of hunger, thirst and illness. Even the Doctor himself had become acutely affected by blood poisoning, despite efforts by 'Freckles' to drain the septic gatherings with a razor-blade. One morning, after about nineteen days adrift, she awoke to hear voices. It was Purslow, talking to her. He said, "I cannot help any more, and I am now a source of danger to you all. It is better that I should go. Good-bye." With that, he heaved himself backwards over the side and the water closed over him. "Greater love hath no man than that he lay down his life for his friends," she was to write later in *Atlantic Torpedo*.

Royal Navy rating Harold 'Geordie' Gibson recalled years later how the dwindling water supply dramatically affected their views on the value of life. He said that he watched the eyes of the dying. They knew that their time was about to come and they seemed to say that they would be grateful for relief from the torture of hunger and thirst. And rather than waste precious water on somebody who would clearly be dead by the next day Gibson confessed that the survivors tipped them quietly over the side, still just alive. The indelible memory of that awful scene never left him. "I'll never forget that look in their eyes," he said, choking back tears in his own.

In the early dawn of Thursday, 8 October Geordie Gibson was at the tiller. He thought he could see some strange things sticking up from the water in the distance. As they drew nearer, he saw that they were trees! Trees and hills. Eyes smarted with tears of relief. They were five miles off the coast of Liberia, sixty-five miles south of Monrovia.

It took the best part of a day to make the final short distance to the shore and night had fallen when the boat crept through the surf and gently crunched onto a palm-fringed shingle beach near a village of thatched huts to be met by a crowd of locals carrying torches. All day long they had watched the tiny boat slowly approaching, borne along only by the strength of the tide, but had not expected to find a living soul on board. A tall man, obviously their chieftain, came forward, flung his long arms around one of the survivors and announced, "Thank God you safe."

They had travelled over 700 miles in their open boat. Just sixteen of them had made it out of the original sixty-eight.

The other stray lifeboat was to spend over a month drifting in the Atlantic before it found itself in the middle of an Allied convoy. Squadron-Leader Wells and fifty other people had crammed into it, but gradually they died, a few every day. At first it was the urine- and sea-water drinkers who succumbed. By 21 October there were only four left – all naval ratings. They had managed to survive by catching fish and had had the good fortune to get a fall of rain during the last days. One of the four, A.V. 'Tiny' Large, said that when the ships were spotted, an impromptu service was held in the lifeboat to give thanks for their deliverance. "Of course," he went on wryly, "we were all profoundly religious by that time."

Altogether 1,621 out of the 2,732 souls who had been on board the stricken *Laconia* perished. But that bare statistic did not signify the end of the story. Exactly which Air Force had it been whose plane had bombed the *U-156* while the German submarine was carrying out its plainly obvious rescue mission? Was it an RAF Liberator, or was it an American? That question would come to be debated at length. Various accounts offer differing opinions as to the nationality of the Liberator. The Americans operated a base on Ascension Island with B-24s, and the RAF also had B-24s based on Freetown, flying frequent anti-submarine sorties over the area. Statements by Dönitz and other German naval personnel seem to suggest that in their opinion the plane was British, and official US research, although inconclusive, appeared to lean in the same direction. On the other hand, United States Air Force historical records did indicate that a B-24, based on Ascension, did attack a U-boat about 130 miles NNE of the Island on 16 September 1942. The question of the identity of the culprit remained one of controversy for many years after the war. Neither its pilot nor any of its crew ever came forward until the late 1990s when a TV documentary film revealed their identities. On Ascension Island, USAF captain Robert Richardson heard news of the sinking over the radio from Freetown early in the morning of 13 September. He decided to fly off to take a look and see if he could help. He found *U-156*, but was unable to do anything to assist. His B-25 was not a long-range aircraft and he was obliged to return to base for fuel. Next day a B-24 flew in for minor repairs. The B-24 Liberator *was* a long-range plane and as soon as the mechanics had sorted out the problem its pilot, Harten, took off to find the U-boat. He saw the people crowded onto the boat's upper casing and the big red-crossed sheet spread out wide. But, like Richardson, there was little he could do other than drop some containers of fresh water. He radioed base for instructions while he circled overhead. The reply came, tersely, "Sink the sub".

In a war one must always beware of enemy duplicity. It was possible that the apparently compassionate *U-156* was nothing more than a decoy. Richardson justified the American action by saying,

"We were at war with Dönitz. Nobody had told us anything about Hartenstein's message. We knew nothing of this until after the war. I consulted with my deputy, Colonel Ronan, and we came to the conclusion that our clear duty was to sink the enemy."

None of the three German submarines engaged in the rescue work, or their chivalrous captains, survived to the end of the war. All of them fell victim to bombs from Allied aircraft. *U-156* herself was sighted by a US Navy Catalina about 325 miles east of Barbados on 8 March 1943. Lieutenant Dryden brought the flying-boat down through the clouds to catch the submarine completely by surprise. Some of her crew were even sunbathing on the upper casing. From no more than about 100 feet Dryden dropped four Torpex bombs. *U-156* broke into three parts which all sank immediately. The Americans dropped a life-raft and food to the eleven men they counted in the water. Some of the Germans were seen to climb aboard the raft, but no more was ever seen of them, despite a lengthy search.

Public comment by the *Laconia*'s survivors is unanimous in its glowing gratitude for the kindness shown to them by those German sailors, giving the lie to much of the wartime propaganda that distorted the minds of whole nations. As for Admiral Karl Dönitz, the controversy over the order that he issued following the *Laconia* affair, forbidding U-boat commanders to place their vessels in danger by lingering to rescue survivors from ships they had sunk, was to hound him all the way to the dock at Nuremberg in January 1946.

In the loss of the *Laconia* itself, the British had failed to do exactly what the Japanese failed to do throughout the war with their hell-ships, of which more later, and which omission resulted in the deaths of thousands of helpless POWs. They had simply failed to mark the ship as a POW carrier and to arrange safe passage with the enemy. This fact seems to have been overlooked by most historians.

It would be uncharitable to close the *Laconia* chapter without a sympathetic thought for the unfortunate Captain Rudolph Sharp. Although he had displayed all the qualities of a good sea-captain, a total of 5,109 lives were lost in two ships under his command, including his own. It is an unkind statistic.

5

THE SECOND PATROL OF HMS *TORBAY*

When HM submarine *Torbay* was commissioned at Chatham in late 1940 the war was not going at all well for the British in the Mediterranean and Middle East. The Afrika Korps, under Rommel, was pouring into the Western Desert to cancel out Wavell's defeat of the Italians and would soon be at the gates of Egypt to threaten the Suez Canal. Malta, within easy range of enemy bombers flying from Sicily and the southern mainland of Italy, was the only red speck on the map between the eastern extremities of the Mediterranean and Gibraltar. The little island stood, bravely isolated, in the knowledge that it was fixed in the sights of the Axis as a prime target for capture. Even Gibraltar itself seemed to be in danger from a plan of Hitler's to advance from the south of France down through Spain and take it.

Torbay's captain, Lieutenant-Commander Anthony Cecil Capel 'Crap' Miers, was born at Inverness on 11 November 1906, the younger son of a captain in the Cameron Highlanders. He joined the Navy as a cadet at HMS *Thunderer* in 1924 and entered the submarine service in April 1929 soon after his promotion to Sub-Lieutenant. The outbreak of war in 1939 found him in battleships, on the staff of the C-in-C Home Fleet, but he returned to submarines the following year to commission the newly built *Torbay*.

For *Torbay* the desperate situation in the Mediterranean was to form the backdrop to her activities in the not-too-distant future. On 21 March 1941, at 0100 hours, Miers was given fifteen hours' notice to sail from Holy Loch on the Clyde for the Bay of Biscay to form part of an 'Iron Ring' of British ships engaged in bottling up the German battle-cruisers *Scharnhorst* and *Gneisenau* in their lair at Brest. With half his crew on five days' leave after an uneventful trip to Halifax, Nova Scotia, and back as escort to an inbound convoy, Miers was obliged to assemble a scratch crew from the depot ship. Even then, he could not find a ship's cook, so an able seaman was 'pressganged' into the job. The 'Iron Ring' idea seems to have worked, although when it was eventually removed by the necessity for the patrolling subs to re-victual, re-fuel and refit, the two big German ships did eventually make their famous dash up the Channel in February 1942.

Meantime, *Torbay* had received fresh orders: "Your services are urgently required in the Mediterranean. Proceed to Gibraltar." She arrived there on 13 April 1941, after having been at sea for twenty-two days, to be given a short respite before sailing for Alexandria at the other end of the Med on 22 April. The 2,000-mile trip took her nearly three weeks, including a fourteen-knot nighttime dash on the surface through the dangerous Narrows between Sicily and the jutting point of Tunisia at Cap Bon.

As they approached Alexandria on the surface in bright moonlight during the night of 12/13 May, the officer of the watch, Lieutenant Paul Chapman, reported a group of ships standing to the north-east. Big heavy ships. Miers joined Chapman on the bridge and made ready to fire torpedoes. *Torbay* was in a perfect position from which to mount an attack. Fortunately for Miers, however, it was realized just in time that the battleships were British. The easily recognizable burly silhouettes of the *Queen Elizabeth* class, so different from those of their streamlined Italian equivalents, had saved many lives. And Miers' bacon.

This incident immediately gave rise to another which served to endear their captain to the crew of *Torbay*. He stood them down from 'action stations' and fired a pyrotechnic grenade to identify his boat as friendly to the inner screen of destroyers. But there were no warm words of welcome in response. Instead came a stream of Oerlikon fire from the nearest destroyer, HMS *Kingston*, which was very close. Miers stepped up to the side of his conning-tower, faced the destroyer's bridge and roared with a well-modulated bellow, "Don't be a cunt!", with which the firing ceased instantly.

Miers' career was dotted with several similar anecdotes which bore out his character as a man who was courageously outspoken, sometimes too much so, and with a temper which was a little too quick on occasions. But most times he got away with it, perhaps because of his honesty and ability to take a liberal dose of self-criticism. His hot-headed streak had once led to him being dismissed from his ship, the fishery protection vessel *Dart*, in 1933. He had lost his cool on the football field and threatened to strike a rating. The matter would have been forgotten but for the fact that Miers voluntarily reported himself to his superiors, with unavoidable results. And when taking command of *Torbay* he objected to the motto she had been given – *Je maintiendrai* – I will persevere – which was the same as that of William of Orange who landed at Torbay in 1688. It did not sound positive enough for Miers' liking and he succeeded in persuading the Admiralty to change it to – *Penetrabo* – I will get through.

After arriving safely in Alexandria, *Torbay* sailed on her first Aegean patrol on 28 May 1941. The situation in the eastern Mediterranean at that time can only be described as dire from the British viewpoint. Crete had just fallen and three cruisers and six destroyers had been sunk in the Battle of Crete, including Mountbatten's famous *Kelly*. Moreover, two battleships and the one aircraft-carrier on station had all been damaged and were away for essential repairs in South Africa and the USA. By the time *Torbay* returned to Alex on 16 June she had sunk or destroyed two tankers, a schooner, three caïques and an Axis destroyer, mainly in the area south of the entrance to the Dardanelles. She had also survived the experience of being depth-charged, twenty-one times to be exact, a careful tally of which was kept on a blackboard by the Chief Stoker. And Miers was on his way to becoming one of the most famous submarine 'aces' of the war.

It was on her next patrol, however, on which *Torbay* sailed on 28 June, that events occurred which were to enshroud both the boat and her captain in controversy. Hitler had just attacked the Soviet Union and some pessimists were already envisaging him sweeping through the Caucasus and down through Asia Minor and Palestine to take Suez 'by the back door'. Although beefed up by having the Russians now on their side (at least for the duration), the fortunes of the Allies had not seen much general improvement over the past month. Indeed, the war-tension in the Middle East and eastern Mediterranean theatres had heightened.

Miers had managed to arrange the transfer of two 'folboteers' from the SBS to his ship's company. These canoeists could provide a valuable service, especially when the boat was working off a beach or within an enemy harbour or indeed on any clandestine individual operation which required absolute silence and stealth. The canvas canoes, or folbots, were simple wooden-framed affairs, propelled by double-ended paddles. They were shipped in sections and taken out via the submarine's forward hatches to be assembled on the upper casing before launch. Their most famous wartime story is, of course, that of Royal Marines Major Blondie Hasler's 'Cockleshell Heroes'. Many folboteers were indeed primarily Royal Marines, but Miers' two men were soldiers, Corporals Jim Sherwood and George Bremner of the Gordon Highlanders. They were to play a major role in the ensuing drama.

Five days out of Alex *Torbay*'s lookouts spotted two enemy merchant ships, escorted by two destroyers in the Zea Channel, between Kea and the Greek mainland. Miers fired six torpedoes, three at each of the merchantmen. One of them, the *Città di Tripoli*, blew up with a tremendous explosion and sank, but the other ship, warned by the fate of her companion, managed to avoid the 'tin fish' just in time by altering course. Two days later, on 4 July, they encountered a caique and a schooner, both carrying German troops, to the south-east of Doro Island. *Torbay*'s First Lieutenant, Paul Chapman, wrote later in his book *The Submarine Torbay*, "The troops were not allowed to escape: everything and everybody was destroyed by one sort of gunfire or another." These actions were to bring heavy criticism onto the head of Miers from several quarters.

By the following evening *Torbay* was off the island of Mykonos and sighted an Italian submarine, the *Jantina*, which was a sitting duck. She too blew up when she caught at least two of the six torpedoes Miers fired at her from a range of less than a mile. This sinking gave Paul Chapman some bitter satisfaction. Only nine months before, his brother Patrick had been lost in the submarine HMS *Rainbow* in the Gulf of Taranto when she was sunk by the Italians. Ironically, Miers himself had been First Lieutenant of *Rainbow* back in 1933.

After sinking a schooner in the Kithera Channel north-west of Crete on 8 July, *Torbay* was getting low on torpedoes and ammunition, and would soon be obliged to return to base. But first there was to be the so-called Battle of the Caïques. Again it would turn out to be controversial. On the afternoon of 9 July, between the islands of Kithera and Antikithera a troop-carrying flotilla of four caiques and a schooner were seen heading for Cape Malea in the Peloponnese. They were carrying petrol and ammunition and about seventy-five German soldiers going on leave from Crete. When they became aware of the submarine's presence, they scattered. Miers destroyed or disabled all four of the vessels with his 4-inch gun and Lewis and Bren gunfire, but the fifth managed to escape. As *Torbay* drew near to one of the still floating caiques, its German captain, Ehlebracht, together with several of his crew and some of the soldiers, jumped into the sea. Being low on ammunition, Miers sent a boarding-party on board to blow it up and a voice shouted from it, "Captain is Greek. We surrender." The remaining crew and soldiers all raised their hands in surrender.

Now right alongside, with the demolition team about to board, one of the folboteers, Bremner, who was on the upper casing and about to lead the boarding-party, was covering his shipmates with his tommy-gun when he caught sight of a man on the caique about to throw a grenade. So he shot him. Then another man was seen pointing a rifle from behind the wheelhouse and Lieutenant David Verschoyle-Campbell, the navigating officer, shot him too. And then, in Chapman's words, "we shot the lot".

Ehlebracht's version of events was somewhat different and far more descriptive. He said that while the explosive charges were being laid in the caïque Bremner tried to take seven of the surrendered Germans on board *Torbay* as prisoners, whereupon Miers shouted angrily that submarines did not take prisoners and would not allow them to be taken below. The SBS man therefore went to look for a float or a raft on which to put these men, but could not find one. Then he disappeared below. Ehlebracht, still in the water, then saw the men still aboard the caïque ordered into a rubber dinghy which was produced from somewhere, with which Miers' log agrees. However, what is not known for certain is whether the Germans still on the upper casing of the submarine went with them.

When Bremner reappeared he asked what had happened to the seven Germans he had brought on board. He was informed that they had been shot in the water. Ehlebracht's version was that he had seen two men killed and two more wounded by gunfire whilst they were in the dinghy, and then the submarine circled the men swimming in the water, spraying them with machine-gun fire. He said it went round twice and eight more men were killed. Then it made off to chase the fifth caïque which was escaping in the distance. The German captain and some of the other survivors clung to floating timbers from the caïque until they were rescued.

Torbay sank the tanker *Strombo* with her last four torpedoes on the way back to Alexandria. On her second patrol she had sunk one Italian patrol boat, one tanker, one freighter and eight caiques. And the Chief Stoker's blackboard showed eighty-one more chalk-marks.

Miers made no attempt to conceal what had happened in his patrol reports:

Friday 4 July.
0447   Dived in position 089° Doro Island 9.2 miles and patrolled in the centre of the approach to the channel.
0615   Sighted and chased large caiques (about 100 tons) on direct course from the Doro Channel to Lemnos and well filled with troops and stores.
0659   Surfaced in position 084° Doro Island 8.5 miles and engaged caique which looked to contain petrol and was soon burning fiercely.
0716   Dived when it was obvious the caique must sink, but remained in vicinity. The caique heeled over until the masts were only just clear of the water, but the fire was extinguished and the survivors (about 30) clambered back and huddled on the gunwale.
0943   Just when it seemed that a few practice projectiles might profitably be fired to finish her off, the caique sank and *there being no boat serviceable the occupants were soon drowned.* (author's italics)
1425   In position 139° Doro Island 6.4 miles, sighted schooner wearing the Nazi colours approaching the channel from the northeast and heading straight for the submarine. The position was uncomfortably close to the land but it was felt that the German flag could not go unpunished, hence gun action was ordered. The schooner was well filled with troops and stores and was of about 60 tons.
1450   Surfaced and sank the enemy *using both Lewis guns to destroy the boats and personnel in order to ensure a quick success in view of the proximity of land.* (author's italics)
1502   Dived and resumed patrol.

Wednesday 9 July.
0220   In position 100° Cape Malea 24 miles, steering 240° sighted caique on the horizon in very good visibility, course about 320°. Turned to close, keeping end-on. Whilst so doing sighted three more

caiques each about two miles apart, all steering approximately the same course and obviously having started off from Crete.

Having only 11 rounds of H.E., 17 of S.A.P. and 9 rounds of practice ammunition remaining, decided to bring them to in turn with one well aimed round of H.E, clear the decks with Lewis gun, go alongside and blow them up with T.N.T. Charges.

0319   The caique, which was wearing the German flag, fired a single red Very light as a recognition signal.

0320   In position 126° Cape Malea 22 miles, opened fire as arranged with Lewis gun and H.E. Such a blazing fire was started in the enemy caique that it was not possible to go alongside. Lewis gun was continued until the occupants had all been either killed or forced to abandon ship and she was left to burn. The caique, which was about 100 tons, obviously contained troops and stores (including petrol).

0337   Set course to engage second caique.

0357   Opened fire on second caique whose crew took to the water whilst those remaining on board made signals of surrender, shouting, "Captain is Greek.". The submarine was put alongside, the berthing party on the casing being accompanied and covered by one of the embarked soldiers (folboteers) with a "tommy gun" with which he shot an obviously German soldier as he was *about to hurl a grenade.* (author's italics)

After a brief pretence at being Greek, the whole party when addressed in German by the Navigating Officer, replied in German that they were Germans. They were all forced to launch and jump into a large rubber float (which was the only form of lifeboat) and the demolition charge was then laid and fired. The Navigating Officer, (who was fortunate to use his pistol first against a lurking German who was *about to fire a rifle at point-blank range*) (author's italics), reported that the caique was filled with ammunition, oil and petrol. She was of about 100 tons, was fitted with a spark W/T transmitter, wore the German flag and had L V painted on her side.

0427   Submarine cast off and with the Lewis gun *accounted for the soldiers in the rubber raft to prevent them regaining their ship* and then set off in search of Number Three, course 300°. (author's italics).

0435   Charge fired and started a fierce blaze which continued until the ship sank, with the cargo of ammunition exploding at frequent intervals.

0445   Sighted the third, a very large auxiliary schooner of about 300 tons, making for Antikithera at a good 10 knots. Chased at full speed but did not come up with her until 0530 by which time it was daylight and boarding was out of the question.

0530   In position 068° Piri Island (Kithera Channel) 11.5 miles, opened fire on enemy schooner which fortunately was filled with petrol and explosives and was very quickly ablaze from stem to stern, with loud intermittent explosions.

0612   In position 064° Piri Island 12 miles, sighted fourth and last of the convoy bearing south and also apparently heading west. Turned south-west to intercept.

0624   . . . decided to abandon the chase on the fourth caique. The destruction of the three vessels had cost only 9 rounds apart from the T.N.T and Lewis gun ammunition.

The rest of the day, 9 July, was spent in evading the patrols of German Dornier and Italian Ghibli, Macchi and Caproni aircraft who were bent on sinking *Torbay*. Miers was forced to dive no fewer than eight times to avoid being seen. At last, in failing light, he surfaced at 2148 and proceeded towards the moon so as to present the narrowest possible silhouette. Soon afterwards orders were received to intercept the Italian tanker *Strombo* and he hurried towards the Zea Channel. It was important to reach it before dawn.

There were no complaints about the 4th and 9th July shootings either from Admiral Cunningham or from other senior officers based in the Middle East. From the submarine depot ship HMS *Medway*, the Captain (S) wrote in his report to the Commander-in-Chief, Mediterranean dated 1 August 1941, " *Torbay*'s war patrol off the Dardanelles had marked success. Two tankers, four caïques, and maybe an Italian destroyer sunk. Characterised by determination and an offensive spirit which is invaluable. Her next patrol in the west and south-west Aegean was carried out with the same fearless and determined manner. A transport, a large tanker and an Italian submarine torpedoed and sunk, plus two schooners and five caïques carrying German troops and stores sunk by gunfire. The morale of *Torbay* is extremely high and I attribute this entirely to the leadership and force of character of her commanding officer,

Lieutenant-Commander A.C.C. Miers." To this glowing accolade the C-in-C, Admiral Cunningham, added in his report of 18 August, "I fully concur . This officer is full of the offensive spirit and has done splendid work in the short time he has been in the Mediterranean. The success of this patrol was no accident. It was a well planned operation." Nevertheless, there were some deeply furrowed brows in the Admiralty in London, where there was concern that the incident could spark off another spate of German reprisals.

Admiral Sir Max Horton, Admiral (Submarines), reporting to their Lordships on 25 September 1941, wrote,

"Ref: SM 4051. Docket M 013843/41 SECRET.
As far as I am aware the enemy has not, up to now, made a habit of firing on personnel in the water, rafts or open boats, even when they were members of the fighting services. Since the incidents in *Torbay*'s report, he may now feel justified in doing so.'

Regardless of the wisdom, or otherwise, of Horton's conclusions, it seems that he was a little out of touch with events. Clearly he had no knowledge of, or had forgotten about, the fate of the sailors of the *Severn Leigh*, machine-gunned in the water by Oehrn's submariners in 1940. But his sense of foreboding was accurate. There was indeed more to come.

In the end, after a round of rumbling debate at the Admiralty, the reply came back, dated 14 November 1941: "Their Lordships are satisfied that Commanding Officers of submarines can be trusted to follow the dictates of humanity and the traditions of the service and it is unnecessary to promulgate general rules which may give the impression that they [the Commanding Officers] are not in the habit of so doing."

The official conclusion was that "commanding officers should act as they see fit, according to the circumstances in which they find themselves". Privately, Miers received a strong letter from their Lordships instructing him to desist with such tactics on future patrols.

Nearly half a century later, however, in 1989, the official naval historian, Captain Stephen Roskill, said in an interview with broadcaster and author Ludovic Kennedy, "It was a submarine atrocity.

It was disgraceful." According to Roskill, *Torbay* had encountered several caiques, each of about 100 tons, which were known to be carrying German troops, ammunition and fuel. Miers had surfaced and in the ensuing skirmish two of the Germans were killed. The rest, seven men from an Alpine regiment, had been forced into a rubber dinghy whilst the British sailors prepared demolition charges on board the caique. As the submarine pulled away, Miers ordered one of his folboteers to shoot the survivors in the dinghy with his Lewis gun. The man refused, as did the First Lieutenant (Paul Chapman), Roskill said, but eventually a seaman obeyed the order and all seven Germans were killed.

Clearly, Roskill's version of events bears no comparison with that of Chapman, whose book appeared shortly after the publication of the Roskill/Kennedy interview. According to Kennedy, Roskill made no mention of any Germans reneging on their surrender and he had Bremner, who according to Chapman fired the first shots, actually refusing Miers' orders to do so. And then he stated, quite categorically, that *Chapman himself also refused to fire*. Chapman makes no mention of this whatsoever, which surely he would have been likely to do if it were true, out of a natural desire to absolve himself from any potential stains of guilt. On the contrary, he admits that "we shot the lot," taking pains to use the first person plural. And Chapman's story does not include any Germans being forced into a rubber dinghy. Not unnaturally, he took the opportunity to make some comment when preparing the final manuscript for his book:

> "In 1989, when this book had been virtually completed, a story burst in the national and some local press and radio. It was to the effect that *Torbay*'s actions, on the 4th and 9th July 1941, amounted to war crimes. We know who inspired the story, but we do not know why. The writer' s opinion, for what it may be worth, is that there is more of a resemblance to a publicity stunt than to an unburdening of conscience. He who inspired the story was in home waters on the date in question, and had known of the matter for some years . . . the Germans were trying to use arms after calling surrender. Bremner and Verschoyle-Campbell shot one each for that reason. The Germans did seek to decamp in a large rubber boat not unlike that used by *Torbay*. The sea was calm, and they would probably have made it to Antikithera."

As regards the question of not taking prisoners, he explains that the war in the Eastern Mediterranean was, at that time, going through an especially vicious phase following the fall of Crete. The troops aboard the caïques were men of the German 11th Air Corps, Goering's pets, and nearly all fanatical Nazis and former members of the Hitler *Jugend*. It is most unlikely that soldiers such as these would have been unarmed whilst in a theatre of war, but even if they were the question remained, as Chapman put it, "Who would contemplate having such a bunch at large in a submarine where there is no secure place to put them?"

The high point of Miers' and his crew's war was yet to come. Patrolling off Corfu Island on 3 March 1942, he sighted a large convoy, escorted by three destroyers, making for Corfu Harbour. This harbour is, effectively, the channel between Corfu and the Greek mainland. Narrowed by dangerous shoals, its southern entrance is only about two and a half miles wide. *Torbay* tagged along behind the convoy, following it right into the harbour channel. Needing to recharge his batteries, Miers trimmed down, so that only his conning-tower was visible above the water in the moonlight. At 2200 a signal was received recalling *Torbay* to Alexandria. In a typical display of the 'Nelson touch', Miers remarked, "I am relieved to find that this signal does not conflict with our present operation." At 0100, he took *Torbay* slowly towards the anchorage, but he could see no sign of the convoy. He waited until dawn. It was a long and dangerous wait, and it ended in disappointment. Daylight revealed that the convoy had either sailed again or not even stopped at all the previous evening. The only ships in the anchorage were two large 5,000-ton transports and a destroyer.

Firing a spread of three torpedoes, he sank the transports but missed the destroyer. Turning to make her escape to the open sea, *Torbay* shuddered and lurched under the crunching rumble of very heavy depth-charge attacks. Miers and his men had spent seventeen hours, hardly daring to breathe, in closely patrolled waters and the Chief Stoker had put another forty crosses on his blackboard. Miers admitted that he always suffered acute stress when being depth-charged and never ceased to be reassured by the coolness of his crew in such situations. It amazed him that they stayed so calm and seemed almost to treat it as a sort of game, even to the extent of keeping a scoreboard.

Torbay's spine-tingling escapade in Corfu Harbour earned Miers the Victoria Cross. Like many a captain before him, he expressed regret that the award could not be bestowed on the whole ship's company. Nevertheless, the investiture at Buckingham Palace on 28 July 1942 was an extraordinary one. King George VI presented Miers with his VC; the DSO went to his engineer officer Lieutenant (E) Hugh Kidd, DSC; Lieutenants Paul Chapman and David Verschoyle-Campbell earned bars to their DSCs and twenty-four members of *Torbay*'s lower deck were awarded DSMs or bars to their DSMs.

ss *PELEUS* – A GREEK TRAGEDY IN THE ATLANTIC

If the mere issuing of the *Laconia* order did not, in itself, spell guilt for Admiral Karl Dönitz, it was the carrying out of it in practice, in several cases, which sealed his fate on charges of Conspiracy, Crimes against Peace and War Crimes at Nuremberg in January 1946.

The *Peleus* was a 4695-ton steamer, a work-worn sea-tramp, typical of her breed. She had ploughed many thousands of sea-miles through the oceans of the world, humping many a varied cargo since her builders, William Gray & Co. Ltd. had sent her down the West Hartlepool slipways in 1928. Owned by the Nereus Steam Navigation Co. of Greece, she was chartered by the British Ministry of War Transport in 1938. Her master was Greek-born Minas Mavris, with a crew of thirty-four officers and seamen composed of a whole hatful of different nationalities – British, Greek, Chinese, Egyptian, Polish, Russian, Chilean and one from Aden.

March 1944 found her in mid-Atlantic, heading for the River Plate in ballast out of Freetown. On the evening of the 13th she was just south of the equator, at 00°20' S by 09°30' W, barely a good day's steaming from the spot where the carcass of the *Laconia* now rested in its ocean grave. At about six o'clock two bubbling streaks were seen heading towards her port beam. Antonios Liossis, the Chief Officer, was on watch on the bridge. As per usual practice, he swung *Peleus*'s bows towards the speeding torpedoes in an effort to narrow their target, but it was too late. Both of them hit the freighter full on and she sank within two minutes with a huge hole in her side.

She had been tagged by *Unterseeboot 852*, commanded by Kapitänleutnant Heinz Eck, on its first patrol out of Kiel, from where it had sailed three months earlier, on 18 January 1944.

What happened next was to land Eck and four members of his

crew, Leutnant-zur-See August Hoffmann, Marine-Oberstabsarzt Walter Weisspfennig (the sub's medical officer), Kapitänleutnant (engineer officer) Hans Richard Lenz and Matrosen-Gefreiter (petty officer) Wolfgang Schwender in the dock on charges of war crimes in Hamburg on Wednesday, 17 October 1945. All pleaded Not Guilty.

It was alleged that these men had machine-gunned helpless survivors from the *Peleus* and thrown grenades at them as they clung to rafts and pieces of wreckage. There had been no time for them to lower any lifeboats. There had been only four survivors from the steamer's company of thirty-five; Chief Officer Liossis, Rocco Said, a greaser, Dimitrios Argiros, an able seaman, and the Third Officer Agis Kefalas, who died before they were rescued.

Affidavits had been sworn by Liossis, Said and Argiros before South African Naval officers and at the Admiralty in London. Outside the court-room the autumn drizzle fell from a dull sky as a Colonel Halse rose to read their statements for the prosecution.

"I, Antonios Cosmos Liossis, of 46 Princes Square, London, W2, make oath and swear as follows: I was born at Kilas in Greece on 7th November 1906 and am a Greek citizen. I first went to sea in 1923. I escaped from Greece after the German occupation on 16th July 1943 and joined SS *Peleus* at Suez as Chief Officer. *Peleus* sailed for the UK, thence to Canada and back to London. She then loaded at Immingham for Algiers and the River Plate, calling at Gibraltar and Freetown. She sailed from Freetown on 8th March 1944. On 13th March, I was on watch and at about 1920 I saw the tracks of two torpedoes approaching on the port beam. I ordered the helmsman to comb their tracks but they could not be avoided. I do not remember anything more until I found myself in the water. I swam for a bit until I found some wreckage to which I clung. Whilst I was hanging on to a hatch-cover I heard someone whistling. I found that it was a sailor named Dimitrios Kostantinidis, who said that he had nothing to cling to so he joined me. We made for a raft which we could see in the distance. Shortly afterwards the submarine surfaced and proceeded slowly with two men on the forward deck who were shouting to find out the name of the ship. The submarine passed us and we then got onto the raft where we found a

Russian sailor whose name was Pierre Neuman. Then we found another raft. The Russian got onto it and was joined by three men who were hanging on to bits of wood in the water. They were Agis Kefalas, the Third Officer, Stavros Sogias, a greaser and a Chinaman. The submarine came back and hailed the Third Officer's raft. He was ordered to go aboard the submarine and he subsequently told me that they had asked him the name of our ship, where she was bound and from what port and also asked questions about convoy routine, the number of warships in Freetown and whether there were any aircraft-carriers. They kept a lifebuoy which the Third Officer handed them, then told him to go back to his raft and assured him that help would be coming next day. The submarine left. I could see most of the rest of our crew in the water, clinging to rafts and wreckage, shouting and blowing whistles. We lashed two rafts together and soon the submarine re-appeared and hailed us to go nearer. As we approached the submarine suddenly opened fire with a machine-gun. We all ducked, but I could hear cries of pain from Kostantinidis who was hit by bullets in several places. The rafts were riddled with bullet holes but did not sink because they had buoyancy tanks. The Germans also threw hand-grenades at us, one of which wounded me. The submarine crew were shining their signalling lamp to see if everyone was finished off, but I lay very quiet and as my back was covered in blood, I think they decided I was dead. The submarine made its way to the floating wreckage and kept on firing big bursts from their machine-guns. Just before dawn the submarine went away and I found that Kostantinidis was dead. I was joined by the Third Officer who had fallen from his raft into the sea and had been hanging onto mine. He was very badly wounded in the right arm from bullets. As many sharks had gathered round the wreckage and we did not want to see Kostantinidis eaten, we waited until nightfall to throw him overboard. We were both in great pain, but we found some drugs and medicines and collected biscuits and water and made an awning to shield us from the sun. On the fourth day after the sinking, we sighted a raft with Rocco Said and Argiros on it and on the eighth day they were near enough to transfer to our raft, abandoning theirs. Twenty-five days after the sinking, the Third Officer died of his wounds.

We had made a sail and were using an oar for a rudder and made for the coast of West Africa. On 20th April, we sighted a Portuguese steamer, s.s. *Alexandre Silva* who fortunately saw us and picked us up. We were given good care and seven days later reached the port of Lobito."

Rocco Said's affidavit affirmed similar events. He said that the submarine machine-gunned the men in the water and began ramming the wreckage of the rafts. Men in the water threw up their hands and sank. The rafts capsized. At about four o'clock the following afternoon Said found another raft on which was a dead Chinese fireman. He had injuries to his face and chest that could only have been caused by the explosion of a grenade. Eventually, he came across Liossis' raft and helped to nurse the dying Third Officer, Kefalas, who passed away from gangrene and yellow fever 25 days later.

Said was about to recount a story told to him by Kefalas just before he died, when there was an objection by Major Lermon, for the Defence, on the grounds that it was third-hand evidence. Nevertheless, after conferring, the Judge Advocate announced that the Court had decided to hear it.

Immediately after the sinking, Kefalas had said, he got onto a raft together with one of the Russian sailors, Liossis and Kostantinidis. The submarine came alongside and called Kefalas and the Russian on board for interrogation. Among other things, the Germans wanted to know the name of the ship and retained a lifebuoy with her name on it, presumably as proof of the sinking. The two men were returned to the raft and were on it when a grenade was thrown. The blast broke the Third Officer's arm, and both Liossis and Kostantinidis were wounded. The latter died of these wounds on 15 March and was buried at sea.

Able Seaman Argiros' story followed very similar lines, with the additional evidence that he had experienced a strong smell of gas, so much so that he splashed sea-water in his face to avoid it affecting his breathing. (The prosecution later confirmed that it had no intention of accusing the Germans of gassing the helpless seamen in the water. The smell probably arose from the explosion of the torpedo, which was quite usual.)

Various *U-852* crew members were then called by Colonel Halse. Some of these men were only identified to the Court by their initials.

J.C., a petty officer, testified that he was on the bridge when machine-pistols were brought up and he saw Hoffmann and Weisspfennig fire them at some rafts and wreckage in the sea to starboard. But he was unable to see whether anybody was on the rafts because of the darkness. Engineer Lieutenant Woldemar Rauft said he came onto the bridge, where he found Eck, Lenz, Hoffmann and Schwender. The latter fired a few shots somewhere into the sea but Lenz snatched the machine-pistol away from him forcibly, and started to fire it himself, apparently at large pieces of timber floating in the water. He had also seen Hoffmann fire some shots. The witness said that he had heard no orders from Eck with regard to the shooting before it happened.

The navigating officer, Obersteuermann H.H., said that he came up to the bridge from the control-room and saw the *Peleus* sinking. He saw Mauser pistols and hand-grenades being brought up, as ordered by Eck, and he heard shooting shortly afterwards, although he did not know who was doing the firing. He heard the captain ordering the ramming of the rafts, although this witness, too, was unable to see if there were any men on them. Wilhelm Schmitz, a *Mechanikershauptegefreiter* (leading mechanic), swore that he was below when he received orders to send up small arms – hand-grenades, pistols and light machine guns. Of the grenades, he sent up five, but received only two back afterwards. The number of rounds of ammunition for the guns was not checked out or in. *Sanitätsobergefreiter* (leading sick berth attendant) Werner Hameister saw the weapons being brought up and heard the firing, but it was too dark to see what their targets were. He said that he had treated Hoffmann for burns and for splinters in his hand and that the officer had told him they had occurred when he threw a grenade.

A voluntary statement made by Lenz on 3 June 1944 whilst under interrogation at a British Prisoner of War Camp was then read to the Court:

> "I heard that the captain had decided to eliminate all traces of the sinking. I assumed that it was intended to kill all survivors, and went to the captain and told him that I was not in agreement with this order. He replied that he was determined to do it. I then went below and later heard the sound of gunfire from above. The boat circled the area for some time, with several

bursts of fire audible and with the noise of minor collisions. Later I went up on the bridge myself. It was quite dark. I saw Schwender with a machine-pistol in his hand, pointing it at various pieces of wreckage. A shape resembling a human form had been reported seen from the bridge, clinging to a piece of wreckage, although I could not see it. Schwender was about to fire the gun, when I took it from him and fired it myself in the general direction indicated. I did this because I considered that Schwender, long known to me as one of the most unsatisfactory ratings in our boat, was not worthy to carry out this order. I did not agree with the order, but since it was an order I realized that it had to be carried out. I fired two or three bursts, but do not know whether I hit anything owing to the darkness. When *U-852* was scuttled on 3rd May 1944, I was brought to England as a prisoner of war. I make this statement voluntarily and of my own free will."

After sinking the *Peleus*, Eck had run south, where he caught and sank another British merchantman, the 5277-ton *Dahomian* on 1 April 1944 off Cape Town. Then he turned into the Indian Ocean and moved northwards up the coast of East Africa, presumably intending to attack traffic in the vicinity of the British bases at Mombasa and Aden. But his progress was being monitored by the British. On 2 May the German was located 100 miles south-east of Cape Guardafui by an RAF Wellington bomber of 621 Squadron (Flying Officer H.R. Mitchell) on patrol out of Aden. Eck dived, but he was unable to avoid being damaged by the depth-charges which straddled the submarine and was forced to resurface where he came under renewed attack from Wellingtons of 8 and 621 Squadrons. Next day, such serious damage was inflicted on *U-852* by Flying Officer J.R. Forrester of 8 Squadron that Eck was obliged to beach her at Ras Mabber, near Bender Beila, Somaliland. He set scuttling charges in her bow and stern, and she was effectively destroyed. Seven German sailors had been killed by the attacks and Eck, together with fifty-eight of his crew, was captured by the Somaliland Camel Corps and a naval landing party. Unfortunately for Eck, he omitted to destroy his log before scuttling his boat. It transpired to be a fatal oversight.

The wreck of *U-852*, lying in the shallows on the Somali coast about 100 miles from the tip of the horn of Africa, was a source of valuable information for the Allies. A salvage team was sent up from HMS *Tana*, Kilindini Dockyard, Mombasa, under Commander Fox- Pitt. The party was composed of men from HM Submarine *Osiris*, HMS *Sennen* and HM Tug *Prudent* from Aden. It was dangerous work.* Bad weather had stirred up the sandy bottom, reducing underwater visibility to almost zero. And there was always the danger that there could be unexploded depth-charges buried in the sand. Fox-Pitt decided that much time could be saved if they lived 'local' rather than repeatedly sail to and from Kilindini. He set up camp on the beach, which was accessed by breeches buoy, and that was where he and his men lived while the work was going on, sustained by a diet of corned beef, biscuits and tea.

They brought up the confidential ship's papers with call signs etc., a minefield chart, the ship's wiring and piping diagrams, periscope, two torpedoes, echo sounders, an AA gun and some radar units. They were obliged to leave the radar fittings and containers because they were made of some kind of aluminium alloy which gave off noxious fumes when the cutting torch was applied to them. But their most fateful discovery, from the point of view of the defendants at Hamburg, was the U-boat's log, which Eck had so negligently failed to destroy. Entries therein which pinpointed the date and position of the *U-852* when she torpedoed and sunk a ship were shown to coincide with the affidavits of the *Peleus* survivors.

At the Hamburg Trial the Court listened to the Prosecution argument that, as the U-boat's commanding officer, it was Eck who was ultimately accountable for the actions of his crew. He had already made a statement saying, "Neither before sailing nor on passage did I receive orders to shoot or otherwise eliminate survivors on any vessel or ship that I might sink." This, the prosecution submitted, precluded any suggestion that he was acting on orders from higher authority, even from the *Befehlshaber der U-boote* himself (the

---

* The salvage team was rewarded for their dedicated work undertaken in perilous conditions. Commander Fox-Pitt and Lieutenant-Commander F. Thornton were awarded OBEs, Lieutenant M. Wilson the MBE and Engine-Room Artificer F. Scotney, C/MX 504891 (*Tana*) the BEM. Several were mentioned in dispatches – Lieutenant C. Atkinson (*Prudent*), Lieutenant J. Bisset-Clayton, RNZNVR (*Tana*), Sub-lieutenant S. Butler (*Prudent*), Shipwright Fourth Class J. French, C/MX118903, (*Tana*) Stoker Petty Officer W. Morgan, D/KX 88644, (*Osiris*), Leading Stoker A. Berkshire, P/KX 138412 (*Osiris*), Stoker R. Daley, D/SKX 968, (*Osiris*).

Commander in Chief of the U-boat arm Dönitz). The fact that *U-852* had remained in the area for five hours after the *Peleus* had sunk, and in darkness, rather than make away at high speed to distance herself from the scene in case of attack from Allied rescue ships, which would have been the correct thing to have done "according to the text-book", served only to underline his guilt.

A Dr Todsen opened for Eck's defence, saying that he did not wish to delve too deeply into detail, as the prosecution had done. The general case of the defence would be that the submarine's captain had acted not out of cruel spite, but purely from a desire to eradicate all traces of the sinking. Eck had found himself in a very special situation. Here there was a need to consider a complex area of International Law, which would be dealt with by his colleague Professor Wegner. The Professor rose, and expounded at great length on this side of things, liberally sprinkling his speech with Latin tags and references to cases of legal precedent. The main thrust of his address, however, was to make the point that it had long been held under International Law that "an individual, forming part of a public force and acting under authority of his own government is not to be held answerable as a private trespasser or malefactor . . . and that the responsibility, if any, rests with his government." He went on to explain that superior command as excluding personal responsibility had also been recognized in the treatment of prisoners of war since the Convention of 1929.

Examined by Todsen, Eck explained that the area between Freetown and Ascension was particularly dangerous for U-boats at that time, because of heavy Allied air traffic. In fact, four of *U-852*'s own sister boats, *847*, *848*, *849* and *850*, had all been lost there recently. After the sinking, he had seen several rafts, barrels and planks and the like floating in the water, and knew that these would indicate to an aeroplane that there was a submarine in the vicinity. He admitted giving the order to bring the guns on the bridge, intending to attempt to destroy this evidence. He was also concerned that the rafts may have been equipped with modern signalling apparatus, which had become well-known. He had seen no people on either the rafts or the wreckage. (This may be thought strange, because he had testified earlier that he had sent Kefalas back onto his raft!) Gunfire had failed to sink any wreckage or rafts, so he had tried to do so with grenades and ramming. He admitted that destruction of the rafts and wreckage would also mean that any survivors

110

would die. Finally, he said that he knew of the attack on Hartenstein's *U-156* after he had rescued survivors from the *Laconia* rather than consider first the safety of his own boat.

Colonel Halse asked Eck what orders he had received from the *Befehlshaber der U-boote* before sailing on patrol. The German replied that he had been instructed that it was forbidden to take on board survivors from ships because the U-boat would be endangered through such action. The exceptions to this were the ships' masters, first officers, navigators or pilots, who should be rescued if possible for interrogation. He denied that machine-pistols had been used to fire at survivors.

On behalf of the defendants Hoffmann, Weisspfennig and Schwender, a Doctor Pabst said that none of them wished to shoot at human beings. They acted on orders, not realizing that those orders involved a crime. In fact, refusal to carry out those orders would have placed their own lives in danger. (The Court had heard earlier that it was within Eck's power to have had them shot for such refusal. Nevertheless, Weisspfennig, being a medical officer, would have been entitled to refuse to bear arms.)

Lenz described to the Court how he had questioned Eck's decision to shoot at the wreckage, how the captain had been determined, nevertheless, to do so and how he, Lenz, had taken the machine-pistol from Schwender's hands and fired it himself.

In his closing speech Colonel Halse referred to the case of the *Llandovery Castle*. "In the very country where we are sitting," he said, "the Supreme Court of the German Reich had decided that it was a war crime to kill the survivors of ships."

The hearing was well into its fourth day, Saturday 20 October 1945, when the Judge Advocate, Major A. Melford-Stevenson, KC, came to do his summing up. The five accused sat in a row in the long wooden dock. A newcomer to the room may have remarked how young and fresh-faced they all appeared. The twenty-two-year-old Hoffmann, in particular, seemed barely old enough to shave. How could such mere boys have ever manned a U-boat, let alone carried out the callous crimes of which they were accused? Now they all sat with lowered eyes, clearly frightened, awaiting their fate.

It had not been proven, by any means, that, whilst there may have been some ambiguity in Eck's orders from the B.d.U, the fact was that they did not include any explicit instruction to *kill* survivors of sunken ships, but merely that they should not be rescued.

All the accused were found guilty as charged and their lawyers immediately entered pleas of mitigation on their behalf. The Court retired again at twenty-five minutes to five to consider their sentences. It was back within the hour.

Eck, Hoffmann and Weisspfennig were all sentenced to death by shooting, the sentence being carried out on Lüneburg Heath on 30 November 1945. Lenz was given life imprisonment, and Schwender fifteen years. It was the only case of capital punishment being awarded for war crimes committed by submarine crews in the Second World War.

7

THE YANKS GIVE NO QUARTER

In his essay "How we felt about the War" written shortly after the end of the Second World War, Pulitzer Prize winning American historian Allan Nevins took the view that "probably in all our history, no foe has been so detested as were the Japanese". Most commentators agreed with him, and furthermore they also agreed with each other as to the reasons for the detestation. It was simple. The Japanese behaviour had been both outlandishly ruthless and fanatically savage to a degree which was completely beyond the pale of warfare as the 'white man' knew it. This hate, then, had some of its roots in racialism and religion. The Japanese had been committing unspeakable atrocities for years in their war against the Chinese. But China was a long way from both Madison Avenue and Fleet Street, and, anyway, were not the Chinese also of the same race, more or less, as the Japanese? These were things that could be put to the back of the Euro-American mind without too much strain on the conscience. But the infamous and treacherous Japanese attacks on Pearl Harbor and Kota Bharu brought things much closer to home, and the Old Testament principle of an eye for an eye flared up with a vengeance in hearts on the Allied side.

It took a mere six hours after the Japanese attack on Pearl Harbour on 7 December 1941 for the USA to renounce the 1930 London Submarine Agreement. That very same day the order went out from Washington, "Execute unrestricted air and submarine warfare against Japan". Indeed, the whole American population soon became so enraged against the Japanese, including their own Japanese-Americans, that the national mentality could almost be described as genocidal. Admiral William Halsey, future commander in the South Pacific, vowed that by the end of the war Japanese

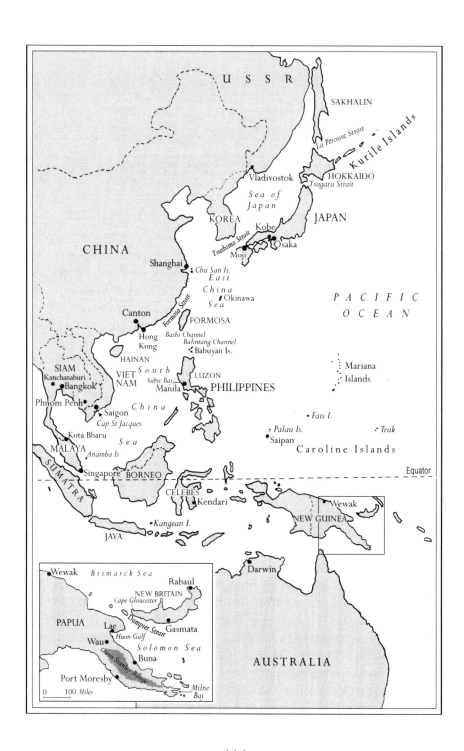

would be spoken only in hell, and the US Marines adopted the unofficial slogan, "Remember Pearl Harbor – keep 'em dying".

The tit-for-tat spiral of accusations grew apace. The difference was that, although many of the stories about outrage by the Allies were nothing more than highly imaginative rumours, (for instance it was said in Japan that in order to qualify as a US Marine you had to murder your parents), on the Japanese side they were not only equally outlandish and perverse – but true. That is not to say that the Americans were entirely innocent of atrocity. A favourite hobby among the GIs and Marines seems to have been the collection of gold teeth and Japanese ears as trophies, even from the living, and the carving of bones and skulls (after boiling off the flesh and hair) as ornaments to send home. One man carved a letter opener from a Japanese shin-bone and sent it to President Roosevelt as a trophy. It was tactfully refused.

At sea US sailors were not averse to sinking hospital ships, firing at survivors in the water and shooting at helpless enemy pilots as they descended by parachute. In late 1943 one young sailor recorded in his diary, "A few Japs parachuted when they were hit, but some sailors and Marines on the 20mm opened up on the ones in the 'chutes and when they hit the water they were nothing but a piece of meat cut to ribbons."

*   *   *

Marvin Granville 'Pinky' Kennedy, captain of the new submarine USS *Wahoo*, had not had a very successful patrol off Truk, a Japanese staging base in the Carolines. And as a perfectionist, even a slave driver according to some, he was disappointed in himself. He had fired three torpedoes at his first target, a lone Japanese freighter. All had missed. A week later, *Wahoo* had met another freighter and this time Kennedy had let fly with four torpedoes. The first three missed, but the last one connected and Kennedy claimed a score of 6,400 tons (although post-war analysis of Japanese records showed no sinking at that time and place). Then he had missed two aircraft-carriers, *Chiyoda* and *Ryujo*. And they had been 'sitting ducks' too. The painfully honest and self-critical Kennedy made no bones about it on return to Pearl Harbor. He wrote in his report, "Made approach which, on final analysis, lacked aggressiveness and skill . . . watched the best target we could ever hope for disappear over the hill." Admiral Robert English, Commander of the Pearl Harbor based submarines, had been required to organize the Truk patrol by the personal order of Chester Nimitz. He was furious with Kennedy and wrote less than flattering comments by way of endorsement to the submariner's report. Nevertheless, although English had adopted the British practice of relieving unproductive submarine skippers, Kennedy held on to his command and eventually *Wahoo*, accompanied by *Gato*, *Tuna*, *Albacore* and *Grouper*, was ordered to resume patrols off Truk and the Solomons and to make their base at Brisbane.

They sailed from Pearl Harbor in mid-November 1942 and were all safely in Australia by the end of the month. This time Kennedy had two new faces in his wardroom. One was John Bradford Griggs III, who happened to be the son of English's Chief of Staff, a fact which can hardly have inspired Kennedy with self-confidence. The other was Dudley W. 'Mush' Morton, a thirty-five-year-old Kentuckian, who was sailing as a Prospective Commanding Officer observer. This was rather a misnomer. The PCO system was set up to enable officers already qualified as commanders to gain combat experience while waiting for a boat of their own. The bluntly outspoken Morton had commanded the elderly USS *Dolphin* a few months before, but was convinced that she was a death trap, smitten as she was by problems with fuel leaks, and had let all and sundry know that in his opinion she was overdue for scrapping. Morton had been on the verge of being returned to 'surface duty' by his division commander, John Haines, who was far from impressed by his rebellious attitude. However, Haines' boss, John H. 'Babe' Brown, liked Morton. He "liked the way Morton shook hands", and, in the American way of things, the fact that the junior man had been a star football player and in the wrestling squad at the Naval Academy counted a lot with him. It had been thanks to Brown's intervention that Morton had been rescued from the ignominy of transfer to surface work and sent to the PCO pool.

On her next patrol *Wahoo* encountered a convoy of three freighters, with a lone destroyer escort, south of Truk. Kennedy reasoned that, if he could knock out the destroyer first, he could then sink the merchantmen more or less at leisure. But he was unable to get a good angle of fire on the warship, so he torpedoed and sank the largest freighter, the *Kamoi Maru*. Instantly this brought an angry destroyer racing towards the submarine and dropping a cluster of about forty depth-charges. Kennedy dived deep and stayed there until dark. Then he crept up to periscope depth to look around. One freighter was well on her way to the horizon, the other had stopped to pick up survivors from the sunken ship and the destroyer was still on station.

Morton and Kennedy's executive officer, Richard O'Kane, (who was later to become America's top Second World War Submarine Ace in command of USS *Tang*) urged a second attack. With *Wahoo*'s new ultra-modern SJ radar, they argued, it would have been a simple job to take out the freighter in the darkness, and with a slice of luck they might even have been able to sink the destroyer as well. But Kennedy had had enough and they turned away without firing another shot.

By the time they tied up in Brisbane an air of disappointment and low morale pervaded the whole ship's company. "*Wahoo* was not making much of a record, " wrote Third Officer George Grider, "and we knew it. We had waited in the wrong places at the wrong time, like unlucky fishermen. We all felt thoroughly discouraged." The upshot was that, because of his continued lack of aggression, Pinky Kennedy did lose command this time. He was replaced by Mush Morton. Characteristically, Kennedy was even-minded about it. He wrote later, "In retrospect, I can see that it was right, but I was not so philosophical about it at the time."

The new captain was from a different mould. Big and bull-like, but easy-going with his subordinates nonetheless, Morton was consumed by a hatred of the Japanese that reached the very marrow of his bones. His appointment triggered an instant uplift of the crew's morale. Just before sailing from Brisbane on his first patrol in command, Morton assembled his men on deck. "*Wahoo* is expendable," he told them. "We will take every reasonable precaution, but our mission is to sink Japanese shipping. Now, if anybody doesn't wish to sail under those conditions, just see the yeoman. He has my full authority to transfer anyone who doesn't wish to volunteer. Nothing will ever be said about your remaining in Brisbane."

It was just the sort of speech that fighting men, on the very brink of the fight and simply itching to get on with it, wanted to hear. There were no refusals. Everybody sailed. It was 1700 hours on 16 January 1943 when they dropped their pilot in Moreton Bay, picked up their escort USS *Patterson*, and set course for New Guinea.

The yeoman, Forest Sterling, remembered the change of mood that Morton's pep-talk had brought about. "It was a different *Wahoo*. I could feel the stirring of a strong spirit growing in her. There was more of a feeling that we were trusted to get the job done. A high degree of confidence in the capabilities of our ship grew on us and we became a bit cocky. It was a feeling that not only was *Wahoo* the best damn submarine in the fleet but that she was capable of performing miracles."

The crew just loved Morton. He would laugh and joke with them as he wandered around the engine and torpedo rooms casually clad in off-duty garb, swapping tall tales and planning daring exploits against the despised enemy. But for all this, Morton was not at all well, although he concealed his discomfort admirably. When in harbour he would be hospitalized for treatment for a prostate problem and while on patrol this required frequent massage. None of this, however, was allowed to distract him from his main aim in life – sinking Japs.

Morton's orders were to reconnoitre a place called Wewak, on the northern coast of New Guinea, north of the Vitiaz Straits, which the Japanese were using as a supply base. Air reconnaissance had reported a considerable amount of enemy shipping there. But there was an immediate problem. He had no proper charts of that coastline, only an unmarked one. He was not even sure exactly where Wewak itself was, let alone possess any navigational details of its harbour. As it happened, one of the crew, Mechanic First Class Keeter, had bought an elementary school atlas in Australia. By making a blow-up of the appropriate page and superimposing it onto the unmarked chart of that coastline, Grider, who was a keen amateur photographer, produced a crude substitute. It was crude, but it worked. And soon *Wahoo* was poking her bows into Wewak Harbour. In time of peace Wewak is a beautiful and restful place, with beaches of dazzling sand backed by coconut palms. But in 1943 it swarmed with thousands of Japanese troops, was surrounded by artillery emplacements and its harbour was packed with the floating machines of war.

The Oxford Dictionary defines the verb 'reconnoitre' as "to carry out a reconnaissance", which in turn is defined as "a military examination to locate an enemy or to ascertain strategic features" or "a preliminary surveyor inspection". But to Morton it meant something much more. Having done all that was required of him by the Oxford

Dictionary, he found that his preliminary inspection of the strategic features of the harbour revealed the mastheads of Japanese ships, just as he had hoped. That was enough for Morton. In that case, 'reconnoitre' was to be taken as also meaning 'to sink'. He was going in! At 0330 on 24 January he dived, two and a half miles north of Kairiru Island, one of several islets which fronted the harbour. The approach run through the harbour was long and with dangerous sandbanks. But Morton was on the scent. He was in his element, perfectly relaxed, even enjoying the ride. He even cracked a joke when the boat scraped a sandbank. It was almost as if he were thriving on the adrenalin that the danger presented as the *Wahoo* slid silently through the murky water between enemy patrol craft. O'Kane, on the periscope, was utterly cool, making his observations to Morton in flat tones.

At 1318 O'Kane reported what looked like a bridge structure peeping from behind Nushu Island, about five miles further into the harbour. It was a Fubuki class destroyer at anchor, nursing several small RO class submarines against her flanks. What a target! Morton sent the crew to battle stations and was about to fire at the destroyer when O'Kane reported that the target had weighed anchor and was moving. It had been Morton's intention to fire high-speed shots from about 3,000 yards, which would have enabled him to stay deep as he retired. He set up *Wahoo* for a stern shot, but the destroyer swung left and spoiled the angle. At 1441 he fired a spread of three torpedoes from his bow tubes, range 1,800 yards. He watched their track. They were going to miss, aft, so he let her have another one. The destroyer's upper deck, rigging and superstructure were clustered with dozens of sailors, all acting as lookouts, and this time they spotted the tracks. It swung to avoid them and then turned to head straight for the *Wahoo*, at speed. And the Fubuki class could really motor. In their day they were among the fastest destroyers in the world. Morton kept his nerve and held the submarine's bows straight towards the advancing ship. He delayed firing his fifth shot until she was barely three-quarters of a mile away. It missed. The American sailors now froze. It was going to be curtains for them, of that they were sure. The destroyer kept coming and Morton let it get to 800 yards before he released the last 'fish' in his bow tubes. It only ran for twenty-five seconds before hitting its target amidships. There was a mighty explosion which broke her back and she started to settle rapidly, with swarms of men leaping from her decks into the water. On the nine-mile trip back to the open sea *Wahoo*'s crew listened to the furious noise of artillery fire from the shore and the solid thumps of a couple of aerial bombs behind them. Morton surfaced at 1930, well clear of the islands, and raced away on four engines for half an hour to put a few more miles between himself and Wewak. Then he cut to one engine, issued a rare tot of brandy to his relieved crew and set course through the gathering darkness to head for the Palau–Wewak convoy track, which passed between the islands of Wuvulu and Aua.

By dawn *Wahoo* was back on the hunt, criss-crossing the convoy route, hoping to find a likely target. A small fishing boat was the first vessel they saw, at 0830. You could not be sure of any stranger in this war and it may have been acting as a spotter for the enemy. A few tommy-gun shots across its bows brought it alongside the submarine for inspection. But all it contained was six Malay fishermen, including one who was blind. And two of the others were sick with scurvy. Mush gave them food and water, and *Wahoo* went on her way. It turned out to be a quiet day, but it was a lull before a storm.

Next morning at 0757, a smudge of smoke appeared on the horizon. Morton turned towards it and after three-quarters of an hour could plainly see that there were in fact two ships hull down in the distance. He dived to periscope depth and closed the range. They were two freighters, but their course was puzzling. It did not lead to, or come from, any known port. But never mind that, the important thing was that they were now large in his sights. He decided that his best firing position would be from about 1,300 yards on the beam of the nearest ship. At 1044 he fired two torpedoes at the leading ship and seventeen seconds later two at the other one. The first two found their target, with hits fore and aft, and one of the second pair scored too. Four minutes later, at 1045, O'Kane took a sweep around with the periscope to check whether the freighters looked like sinking. The first ship was listing badly and sinking by the stern, while the other was heading directly for the submarine, although painfully slowly.

But what the Americans had not seen was a third ship, a huge transport, which had been sailing out of their sight on the far side of her companions, and was now only a mile away. And, very conveniently, she was broadside on to the submarine. Morton needed no prompting. Three 'fish' hissed from *Wahoo*'s tubes, two of which

120

caught the big ship and slowed her to a crawl. Meanwhile the second freighter, although badly crippled, was still coming on determinedly, albeit slightly crab-wise. Morton loosed off two shots at her – 'down the throat'. One of them hit, but it did not stop her and *Wahoo* was forced to go deeper and swung to port at full speed to avoid being rammed amid such a rumpus of shell-fire and bullets from the transport that it was impossible to know exactly what was taking place. He crept cautiously back up to periscope depth eight minutes later to find that the first ship had sunk, the second was going down slowly but surely, and the transport had now stopped dead but was still afloat. He took up position three-quarters of a mile from her and fired what he intended to be the killer shot, but it ran beneath her and failed to explode. The men on the decks of the transport had spotted the torpedo's wake and now re-opened a hostile fire at *Wahoo*'s periscope with deck-guns and rifles. At 1135, seeing that the transport had swung a little, bringing her to an angle of 65 degrees on the submarine's bow, Morton sent another torpedo on its way. He wrote in his report:

"The torpedo wake headed straight for his stack. The explosion blew his midships section higher than a kite. Troops commenced jumping over the side like ants off a hot plate. Her stern went up and she headed for the bottom. Took several pictures."

At 1136 he swung and headed for the crippled second ship, which had appeared to be sinking, but was in fact now limping away. But *Wahoo*'s batteries were low and he was forced to break off, much to his disappointment.

His report went on:

"At 1155 sighted tops of a fourth ship to the right of the cripple. Her thick masts in line had the appearance of a light cruiser. *Kept heading for these ships hoping that the last one sighted would stop to pick up the survivors of the transport.* (author's italics) When the range was about 10,000 yards, however, she turned right and joined the cripple. Her masts and bridge-structure set right aft identified her not as a cruiser but a tanker. *Decided to let these two ships get over the horizon while we surfaced to charge batteries and destroy the estimated twenty troop boats now in the water. These boats were of many types, scows, motor-launches, cabin cruisers and nondescript varieties. At 1235 went to battle surfaces* (sic) *and manned all guns. Fired 4" gun at largest scow loaded with troops. Although all troops in this boat apparently jumped into the water our fire was returned with small caliber machineguns. We then opened fire with everything we had. Then set course 085 degrees at flank speed to overtake the cripple and the tanker.*" (author's italics)

In a few bland words, Morton had skated over what was, in reality, a nightmarish scene. His patrol report provided a far from vivid description of what had actually taken place. *Wahoo* had surfaced to find herself in a sea of Japanese. The water was so thick with bobbing heads sticking up from kapok life-jackets that it was impossible for the submarine to move forward without pushing them aside like driftwood. They were mostly huddled together within a wide circle, towards which those individuals who had become isolated were swimming or paddling desperately in search of solidarity. Dotted among them were the boats and rafts and general flotsam and jetsam. Mush Morton looked about him at the carnage. "There must be ten thousand of them," somebody remarked. "I figure about nine thousand five hundred of the sons-a-bitches," replied Morton. With that he ordered the deck guns to open fire. True, there were a few defiant pistol shots in return from the Japanese in the boats, but to Mush that meant that they were fair game to be mown down. The horrific massacre continued for about an hour, at the end of which they had destroyed all the boats and most of the men. The sea ran pink and the sharks were closing in. Then *Wahoo* turned away to chase the two fleeing ships.

They sighted the smoke from their quarry at 1530 and by dusk had caught up. Anxious to conserve his batteries, Morton stayed on the surface, hidden just below the horizon, but keeping their mastheads in sight by using his fully extended periscope – a trick known as a 'surface sweep', which gave him an enormous range of visibility. He dived at 1721 and started his approach, deciding to attack the tanker first, which so far was unscathed. At 1829 he fired a spread of three 'fish' at a range of 2,300 yards. A loud explosion was heard one minute and twenty-two seconds later. He surfaced to go after the freighter, but was surprised to find that the tanker was still floating.

It was now pitch dark and moonrise was not due for another three hours. There was plenty of time left to line up another surface shot whilst invisible in the enveloping blackness. But *Wahoo* was down to her last four torpedoes. And these were all in the stern tubes.

But the zig-zagging tanker was unobliging. *Wahoo* was now going full speed astern, with Morton trying to synchronize his aim with his weaving target. But he was unable to latch on to her satisfactorily. Then the solution occurred to him. He closed her from directly astern. When she zigged right he held his own course and speed. Then, when she zagged back he swung hard left under full power. This gave him a stern shot on a 90 degree track at 1,850 yards. At 2025 his chance came. He gave her two torpedoes, one of which blasted into her abaft of amidships, breaking her back. As the submarine passed her to chase after the freighter, only her bow section was still afloat, and that was listing badly.

The freighter's crew were now of course fully aware of *Wahoo*'s appearance. And it was quite clear that they were determined not to be sunk without a fight. They kept up continual random 'flashless' gunfire to keep the Americans at a distance. One shell splashed directly ahead of the submarine only to ricochet right over the conning-tower. They had got the range. Morton wisely dived, but the shellfire continued for a good quarter-hour. He had only been resurfaced for two minutes to resume the chase when a huge search-light began to sweep over the sea from their port bow. It was obviously from a warship. This could be a far more valuable prize and Morton swung towards it, noting that the freighter had followed suit. But barely ten minutes later he found himself at a perfect angle with the freighter, which was still shelling the submarine sporadically. He set his last two torpedoes at her, but he had fired in haste. Grider turned to a colleague in the conning-tower and said with impatience, "If either one of those torpedoes hits, I will kiss your royal ass." They both hit and moments later an escort destroyer appeared on the horizon, silhouetting the sinking freighter in its searchlight. And a most unusual little ceremony took place in *Wahoo*'s conning-tower as she melted away into the night.

At 2130, Morton set course for Fais Island. Next day, 27 January, *Wahoo* fell in with a large convoy of six ships – freighters and tankers. But he had no torpedoes left. All he could do was to tag the last one in the line, which did not seem to be armed, and shell it with the 4-inch gun. But *Wahoo* was still 6,000 yards away when she was spotted and the convoy ran to hide in a convenient rain squall. Then two of the larger freighters opened fire. By now the convoy's escort destroyer had been alerted and she raced onto the scene. Morton turned tail and fled, with the destroyer boiling after him like an angry watch-dog, sending salvoes of shells splashing uncomfortably close. He dived to 300 feet, with depth-charges rumbling all around. They did no damage but he stayed deep for a couple of hours before surfacing and running again for Fais.

Fais was rich in phosphorite, a valuable source of fertilizer. Morton reconnoitred the coast. There was no sign of any Japanese presence and he planned to expend his last few 4-inch shells on the refinery and warehouses that night. But in the afternoon a well-armed inter-island steamer appeared and moored to a buoy off the refinery. She looked like the Q-ship that *Gudgeon* had sketched on a previous patrol and she would have made a nice target for a single torpedo he noted regretfully. At 1600 he decided to leave well alone, took several more reconnaissance photographs and announced, "Let's head for the barn, boys".

Wahoo arrived back at Pearl Harbor on 7 February dressed with the trappings of triumph. Eight miniature Japanese flags fluttered from her signal halyard, one for each of the ships she had sunk and a straw broom was lashed to her periscope shear-legs to boast of a clean sweep. But the most prominent embellishment of all was the sheet painted with the words *"Kill the Sunza Bitches"*. Her fame spread like wildfire and the Honolulu papers were soon full of Morton's exploits. Admiral Charles Lockwood had taken over from English as Commander of Submarines Pacific, the latter having been killed when a Pan-Am Clipper on charter to the US Navy crashed into a mountain near San Francisco in a storm in mid-January. Lockwood dubbed Morton "The One-Boat WolfPack" as he presented him with a Navy Cross. And General Douglas MacArthur, who was in the habit of awarding medals without consulting another soul, sent him an Army Distinguished Service Cross from Port Moresby.

But the killing of the hundreds, maybe thousands, of helpless survivors from the transport was nothing but cold-blooded murder to many people, and there were many submariners among them, although no criticism of Morton's actions appeared in the notes appended to his patrol report by his Senior Officers. Indeed, their remarks were composed of nothing but the most glowing words of praise. Many interpreted this – together with all the honours and adulation showered upon Morton – as tacit approval from on high. But no official statement of policy was ever issued on the subject. It was just taken as one of those unspoken rules that submarine captains could follow Morton's tactics if they wished. Not many did.

Morton's second patrol in command of *Wahoo* took him into waters where, so far, no US submarine had intruded – the extreme northern reaches of the Yellow Sea where the Hwang-ho River empties into the sea after its long journey across China. It was a far from ideal vicinity for submarine operations because the water was very shallow, averaging a mere 120 feet. To a submariner it was little more than a puddle. But Morton relished the challenge. He found the area swarming with unsuspecting shipping – steamers, junks and sampans. *Wahoo* was like a cat in a coop full of day-old chicks and when the time came to sail for a refit at Midway she had sunk nine ships, including three freighters.

"Congratulations on a job well done," beamed Admiral Lockwood, "Japs think wolf-pack operating in Yellow Sea. All shipping tied up."

From the beginning of their involvement in the war, the Americans had been experiencing frustration with their torpedoes. In mid-January 1942, the submarine USS *Seadragon*, hunting in the South China Sea, had sighted several Japanese warships and no less than thirty big transports taking troops to beef up their presence in Malaya. She made eight separate attacks and fired thirteen torpedoes, only one of which hit. In March '42 Lucius Chappell in *Sculpin* fired nine Mark XIVs at three sitting targets off Kendari in the Celebes, all of which missed. The Mark XIV torpedoes clearly had major faults. They tended to run too deep and their magnetic exploders were unreliable. The designers managed to overcome the deep-running problem by the middle of the year, but criticism of the exploders fell on the deaf ear of their inventor, Ralph Christie. He inspected stocks and concluded that the problem was bad maintenance, poor skills and lack of training. Nevertheless, the problems continued. A furious Lawson 'Red' Ramage returned to Fremantle in *Trout* from a patrol off Indo-China. He had fired fourteen torpedoes, one of which prematured and five were duds. And on his next patrol the results were even worse – fifteen torpedoes and only one hit. Ashore, tempers began to fray. On one occasion a slanging match between Christie and Ramage came to the verge of fisticuffs.

By early 1943, more torpedo problems had arisen. First, there was a supply shortage. During 1942 the US Bureau of Ordnance had manufactured about 2,000 submarine torpedoes, but the Navy had fired 1,442. A new electric torpedo, the Westinghouse Mark XVIII, which had been promised six months before, had still failed to appear. And the magnetic exploder controversy still simmered.

Against all that, however, was Morton's experience with the Mark XIV. On his famous first patrol, he had fired twenty-four, all fitted with magnetic exploders. In general, they had performed reasonably well. Indeed, two of them had certainly saved *Wahoo* from destruction in Wewak Harbour. But his third patrol was a different story.

The codebreakers had learned that the Japanese intended to send a major fleet to sea to counter the April–May '43 US offensive in the Aleutians. Lockwood dispatched *Wahoo* to intercept. To her crew the coldness of the Pacific far north came as an unpleasant shock. This was a far cry from the balmy weather they had encountered for the past year and a half in Brisbane or around New Guinea or Midway or Honolulu. Lookouts, shivering despite being bundled in every stitch of clothing they possessed, tried in vain to peer through the dancing curtains of blizzard after blizzard. Sterling said his ears were so cold that he was scared to touch them in case they shattered. When it stopped snowing and sleeting and at last some cold sky emerged, he wrote, "There was no ocean to be seen, just a vast plain of thin ice. Jagged islands pierced this ice at irregular intervals. *Wahoo*'s nose was clearing a pathway through the ice so smoothly that it seemed to part at her approach. Morton lay in ambush for the Japanese fleet off the Kuriles, only to learn that the enemy had cancelled their sortie. Lockwood ordered him to proceed back on general patrol. On 4 May, the codebreakers steered *Wahoo* onto the track of a large seaplane tender, the *Kamikawa Maru*. From a range of only 1,300 yards, Morton fired three Mark XIVs. One hit, causing some damage, but another missed and the third one failed. He wrote in his report, "It is inconceivable that any normal dispersion could allow this last torpedo to miss a 510-foot target at this range."

On this patrol, ship after ship escaped because of torpedo failure of one sort or another. It was thoroughly disappointing and disheartening – and dangerous. Submariners were prepared to bear the normal additional risks that their special line of work entailed, but the possibility of losing their lives because of a now notorious 'rogue' Mark of torpedo was rather too much to ask. Morton broke off the patrol after only twenty-six days and sailed back to Pearl Harbor. In a filthy temper, he charged into Lockwood's office and in colourful sailor-talk listed his results. He had fired off all sixteen torpedoes and sunk only three ships. But at the same time there had been another three, all sitting ducks, which had got away owing to torpedo problems. Morton was one of Lockwood's stars. The Admiral always listened to Mush and finally gave in to his demands (and those of several other U.S. submarine officers) that the magnetic exploders should be de-activated and future reliance placed on old-fashioned contact exploders. But Morton's longstanding prostate problem needed attention. He looked tired and drawn. Lockwood sent *Wahoo* to Mare Island, California, for refit. And Morton went into hospital for treatment.

America had been at war now for a year and a half and the Mark XIV had been trouble from the beginning. By the time of Morton's verbal assault on Lockwood over 2,000 of them had been fired by the US Navy, with extremely poor results. It is arguable that Japan would have been brought to her knees much more quickly if the Mark XIV had been more efficient. Maybe, even, the nuclear horrors of Hiroshima and Nagasaki would never have occurred. It is surprising that nothing was done about it for so long, even on the grounds that great heaps of dollars were being thrown down the drain.

Lockwood had long itched to get his submarines into the Sea of Japan. As a giant natural harbour safely enclosed by the Chinese mainland and the islands of the Japanese archipelago, it was bound to be crammed with shipping. Moving the war closer to the Japanese homeland would sap enemy morale. There were only three entrances to the Sea of Japan – via the Tsushima Straits from the south, the Tsugaru Strait in the centre and the northern channel, La Pérouse Strait, which was ice-bound for much of the year. All these shallow passages were thought to be heavily mined, closely guarded and vigilantly patrolled. The Russian territory of Sakhalin makes the northern shore of La Pérouse Strait. Russian ships used it to and from Vladivostok during the summer months. A US submarine might gain entrance by slinking in behind one of them, or by following a course as if making for Vladivostok. And an entry via La Pérouse was likely to be the least expected by the Japanese because of the Russian presence. In practice the main problem would be not so much getting in, but getting out of the Sea of Japan. Any prolonged campaign against the shipping there could only result in the complete blocking of the three exits and the hunting of the raiders until they were either sunk or their fuel ran out.

Four days on the rampage in the Sea of Japan was thought to be the optimum time that a raider would have to retain a reasonable chance of getting home again. On the night of 4 July 1943 three U.S submarines, *Lapon*, *Permit* and *Plunger*, slid through La Pérouse on the surface amid a heavy traffic of brightly lit Russian ships. But it was a poorly handled escapade, netting only three small cargo ships whilst subjecting three of Uncle Sam's submarines to great danger. As a result, the captains of *Permit* and *Lapon* were stood down from their commands.

The Japanese were now aware that the Americans had been able to encroach upon the Sea of Japan but, nevertheless, Lockwood planned a second foray in the August. Mush Morton, now out of hospital, eagerly volunteered to have a chance to create mayhem in the hated enemy's backyard. He had privately devised a new system of attack, but he kept it strictly to himself. Proud of his prowess as a crackshot with a torpedo, he planned in future to fire only one 'fish' against each ship. He figured that if he could maintain his past record of being on target, this system ought to bring him an unprecedented bag of fifteen or more ships. *Wahoo* was to be accompanied by *Plunger*, whose captain, 1932 Olympic gymnastics gold medallist Benny Bass, had been the only one of the previous expedition's skippers to keep his boat. Morton raced through La Pérouse on the surface on the night of 14 August and Bass followed two days later, in full daylight, submerged all the way. Morton found a big convoy almost right away and put his new firing system into operation. The results were abysmal. From 15 to 18 August he fired ten torpedoes at eight freighters. Eight missed, one broached and the tenth was a dud. Bass's record was only slightly better. He fired thirteen to sink two ships. Putting all the blame for his poor results on his torpedoes, Morton radioed base for permission to return and reload. It was the first time that a Morton Patrol had drawn a complete blank. And no plaudits were to be seen in Lockwood's comments on Mush's report. Quite to the contrary, he was scathing about the 'one shot' theory and ordered that conventional spreads of two or preferably three torpedoes should be fired in future attacks. Following Morton's pleas to be allowed to return to the Sea of Japan to try to make amends, *Wahoo*, this time followed by Eugene Sands in *Sawfish* two days later, sailed from

Pearl Harbor on 9 September. She was scheduled to pass through La Pérouse, between Hokkaido and Sakhalin, on 20 September with orders to remain below 40° north after 26 September so as to keep clear of the advancing winter ice, and in any event to clear the area by 21 October. The two boats rendezvoused at Midway to top up with fuel on the way to Japan, and *Wahoo* left there on 13 September. That was the last that Eugene Sands or anybody else ever saw or heard of her or her crew of seventy-eight sailors and their Jap-hating skipper.

Commander Morton and his shipmates were posted missing, presumed lost, on 1 November 1943 and declared dead on 7 January 1946. Morton had won the Navy Cross with three gold stars (in lieu of three more Crosses), the Army Distinguished Service Cross, the American Defense Service Medal, the Asiatic-Pacific Campaign Medal, the World War II Victory Medal and the Purple Heart. In 1969 a new destroyer USS *Morton* (DD-948) was named in his honour.

It has often been said that two wrongs can never make one right, but an analysis of the heaps of praise on one hand and condemnation on the other for similar activities in the Second World War shows that old saw to be not necessarily true. It all depended on which side you had been.

*   *   *

The Japanese advance down the northern coast of Papua-New Guinea in mid-1942 was a serious threat to the Australian mainland. If they had been able to take possession of Port Moresby on the southern tip of the island as their jumping-off point, northern Australia, with thousands of miles of coastline to protect, would have been well-nigh impossible to defend. By September that year the invaders had taken Buna and advanced along the Kokoda Track – a gruelling journey over the 13,000-foot Owen Stanley Range, with its mist-shrouded, knife-edged ridges clad in thick, dripping jungle, and through slimy malaria ridden swamps, long kunai grass and sluggish, muddy streams – until they were at the Iorobaiwa Ridge, only forty miles from Port Moresby. In November Darwin itself had suffered an air raid. In some of the nastiest fighting of the war, the Australian defenders under Major-General Vasey had put up a staunch and heroic defence. They fought their way back along the Kokoda Track, over Templeton's Crossing, and had re-taken Buna by 14 December. By the end of January 1943 Brigadier Dougherty's Australian 21st Brigade, reinforced by American troops under MacArthur's command, had pushed the invaders back 200 miles, almost to Lae on the Huon Gulf. Here, there was a key Japanese airfield and garrison. Lae had to be taken if Japanese forces were to be swept from the area, but the Allied advance came to a standstill, caused mainly by the lack of advanced naval bases and the consequential supply problems, which were not helped by the difficult road accessibility to the remote Allied airstrip at a former gold-rush boom town, now a mere jungle village, Wau, which was subject to frequent attack by Japanese marauders. Already, the Papuan campaign had seen heavy Allied losses. The Australians had lost 2,037 killed in action and 3,533 wounded and the Americans 671 dead, with 2,172 wounded. Other deaths, presumably mainly by disease, had accounted for 244.

Wau was a thorn in the side from the Japanese point of view, simply because it was there. If their New Guinea campaign were not to lose momentum, or even to fizzle out altogether, Wau had to be taken out of the equation. As much as the Allies needed to eliminate Lae, the Japanese wanted to rub out Wau. They planned a major thrust on it from the north. But first, if this offensive were to stand any chance of success, heavy reinforcements needed to be poured in to Lae, which had to be held at all costs. At the same time, units of the 17th Australian Brigade were being moved up from Milne Bay to reinforce Wau.

The Japanese Chiefs of Staff decided to move 6,912 troops of the XVIII Army into Lae from Rabaul, on the northern tip of New Britain, to augment the existing garrison of 3,500. The only practical means of getting them into the place was by sea, so they began to assemble a sixteen-ship convoy at Rabaul. There were army troop transports, *Oigawa Maru*, *Shinai Maru*, *Aiyo Maru*, *Kyokusei Maru*, *Tamei Maru*, *Nojima Maru* and *Teiyo Maru*, plus the little 953-ton *Kembu Maru* which was laden with drums of aviation spirit, eight battle-hardened escort destroyers, *Shikanami*, *Uranami*, *Tokitsukaze*, *Yukikaze*, *Asagumo*, *Arashio* and *Asashio*, under the command of Rear-Admiral Masatomi Kimura, flying his flag in the destroyer *Shirayuki*, 'White Snow', and a battalion of 400 marines in the special service vessel *Nojima*. The loading of material and personnel was meticulously planned and divided between the ships, so that even if half of them were lost (which was recognized as a distinct possibility) it would still be possible to put a balanced well-equipped force ashore. Orders were issued that any air attack while the ships rode at anchor off Lae must not be allowed to interfere with the unloading operation; the work must continue regardless. With a blanket of high-level air cover and by slipping in behind the curtain of an anticipated weather front, they hoped to make the 500-mile voyage to Lae with minimal losses. Kimura set the sailing time at midnight on 28 February. But next day, at 1600 hours, the convoy was observed by an Australian reconnaissance plane to be proceeding at a steady plod of seven knots south-westwards towards the Dampier Strait under the low clouds of the awaited very welcome storm. The scout plane tracked the ships until 2130 that evening, but then lost contact with them in poor visibility. The Japanese weather forecasters had proved to be reliable. The protective weather front they had foreseen was, at least for the moment, keeping the convoy safe from attack. Kimura's best hope now was for the comforting veil of some prolonged filthy weather, although Vice Admiral Mikawa had promised a cover of 200 fighter planes if and when the skies cleared to expose the ships.

Laboriously hacked and bulldozed into the inhospitable terrain south of Buna were a number of Allied-held airstrips. These were the bases of the Fifth USAAF under Lieutenant-General George C. Kenney, augmented by the 9th Operational Group of the Royal Australian Air Force commanded by Air Commodore Joseph Hewitt. This combined force was composed of some 207 A-20, B-17, B-24, B-25, Hudson, Boston, Beaufort and Beaufighter bombers and fighter-bombers, plus 129 P-38, P-39 and P-40 fighter planes. Mikawa had gravely underestimated that strength. And, to add to his misfortune, the storm changed direction, swinging back over New Britain and the Solomon Sea. The promised Japanese air escort scrambled into the now clear sky from bases at Rabaul, where, incidentally, they had no fewer than five airfields, from Gasmata and from Lae itself. At Lae they were desperately low on fuel, fresh supplies of which were on board the painfully slow *Kembu Maru*.

For over a week the Allies had been aware of the build-up of ships at Rabaul and were fully prepared for action. Kenney had ordered the B-25s to be 'tweaked up' for strafing by removing the bombing equipment from their noses and replacing it with eight .50 calibre machine-guns, which gave them an enormous capability when it came to forward firing. And there was to be another painful surprise for the Japanese. Major Edward Larner's 90th Bomb Squadron of B-25s was equipped to operate a devastating new technique which came to be known as skip-bombing. It was not dissimilar in principle to Barnes-Wallis's bouncing bomb as used in the Dambusters raid, testing for which, coincidentally, was being carried out in Great Britain at that very time. The invention of skip-bombing as an anti-shipping tactic is credited to US Army Major William Benn. Hitherto, very low-level bombing carried the grave risk of a plane being destroyed by its own bomb-blast. With skip-bombing, the B-25s could run in at masthead level, drop their 500 lb bombs with five-second delay fuses *alongside* the target ship, so that they skipped on the water and crashed against the hull, and be away to a safe distance before the explosion. The effect was very much the same as if the ship had struck a mine. It had been tried successfully on a recent raid on Rabaul. Now, Kenney decided, it was time to give the enemy a full-scale demonstration.

At 0815 on the morning of 2 March a patrolling B-24 picked up the convoy again. It was thirty miles north of Cape Gloucester and about to turn south through the Dampier Strait. Twenty-nine bombers, including twelve Flying Fortress B-17s, immediately took to the air. Within two hours they were overhead, flying at 5,000 feet. And by midday they had sunk the *Kyokusei Maru* and inflicted damage on *Nojima* and *Teiyo Maru*. The destroyers *Yukikaze* and *Asagumo* rescued over 900 survivors from the *Kyokusei* before the slowly sinking transport disappeared. Mikawa, at base in Rabaul, could have ordered the convoy to scatter and make for safer water, even by turning back on Rabaul, but he did not do so. Such was the importance, as he saw it, of getting men into Lae that he commanded the two rescuing destroyers to peel off and steam there at full speed with their cargoes of survivors. They made it under cover of dark and landed the men safely. Early next morning these two destroyers re-joined the convoy, which was now only eighty miles from Lae, having been shadowed all night by an Australian Catalina. They were just in time for Kenney's big show.

The convoy was sailing in loose order, with forty Mitsubishi Zeros circling high above it. They were well positioned to give them the drop on any attackers – except skip-bombers. At about 1000 hours (0800 Japanese time), droning in from the south came a squadron of B-17s and A-20s, delivering a medium-altitude bombing attack.

They were sheltered by a pack of sixteen P-38s who climbed to engage the Zeros in a distractionary dog-fight while thirteen Australian Beaufighters swept in to strafe the decks of the ships. Then, right behind them, in roared the skip-bombing B-25s to deliver the sucker punch. They were flying so low that their slip-streams were disturbing the surface of the calm sea. Flying in twos, each plane with its eight forward machine guns spewing a deluge of fire onto the ships' decks, they swooped in to drop their bombs and soar away. The little *Kembu Maru*, sitting on a highly dangerous cargo of aviation fuel, was one of the first to die. Suddenly, with a mighty roar, she simply ignited to become a solid globe of flame. Never since Pearl Harbor, twenty-seven months before, had there been such an overwhelming aerial attack on ships. In fact, some historians consider the first fifteen minutes of the attack that day to be among the most destructive in the annals of sea-fighting. No fewer than twenty-eight of the thirty-seven 500 lb bombs released by the first wave of skip-bombers found their target.

One B-25 pilot, Lieutenant Roy Moore, landed at Port Moresby and wrote his battle report:

> "When within strafing range I opened fire with my forward guns. The decks were covered with troops, lined up facing the attacking planes with rifles in hand. However, my .50 calibres outranged them and I saw hundreds fall or go over the side ... then ceased fire and made a gradual pull-up to clear the masts. My bombs skipped into the sides of the ship and exploded, leaving a large hole at the waterline."

The convoy was in disarray. The big transports lost way and wallowed out of control, some on fire. They were sitting ducks for the next echelon of skip-bombers, and the next after that. By midday more than 200 bombs had fallen on the desperately twisting and turning ships. And desperate the twisting and turning was, because a badly holed ship is not always an easy thing to steer. Far above, the P-38s and P-40s, now joined by some Flying Fortresses, continued their scrap with the Zeros. Trails of vapour and smoke embroidered patterns on the sky. Flaming planes fell towards the sea. One B-17 lost a wing. Seven of its crew baled out, only to lose their lives in midair in the rain of cannon-fire. Three P-38s sent five Zeros spiralling downwards and then, in turn, were shot down themselves. Meanwhile, the Japanese were prevented from putting fresh planes into the air to relieve those in combat, who were now very low on fuel, by a halo of Allied fighters patrolling high over Lae.

The mayhem continued all afternoon. By early evening the surviving ships of the convoy were scattered all around the Huon Gulf, most of them badly holed. One by one they slowly filled with water, toppled over and sank, leaving only one, the 6,500-ton *Oigawa Maru*, still afloat but helpless. She had been hit in the first five minutes of the attack, long ago that morning, but by some miracle she had not so far received a *coup de grace*. The sea was spangled with the bobbing heads of swimmers, life-rafts, rubber dinghies, dead bodies and assorted debris strewn over an area of several square miles.

Japanese destroyers had for a decade been renowned for their speed, fire-power and manoeuvrability. Their 5.5" main armament was to be of little use that day, but most of the eight escorts were mounted with as many as thirty-two anti-aircraft guns, and had been known to push nearly forty knots. But none of this otherwise impressive display of armament proved to be sufficient defence against the unmerciful rain of machine-gun fire from Kenney's planes. Kimura's flagship, *Shirayuki*, had her stern bombed away in the first phases of the action. She sank quickly, leaving just enough time for *Shikinami* to come alongside and take off her crew and the wounded Kimura. The speeding *Arashio* was hit by a cluster of bombs, promptly lost all control of her rudder and collided disastrously with the *Nojima*, which was already no more than a crippled hulk. *Tokitsukaze* collected a bomb in the engine-room, which left her stopped, dead in the water. The remaining five destroyers fished some 2,700 survivors out of the sea and then four of them retired northwards through the Vitiaz Strait, leaving behind the *Asashio*, whose captain, Yasuo, had nobly elected to go to the assistance of the crumpled *Arashio*. It was a fatal thing to do. When another wave of Allied aircraft arrived, in the early afternoon, his ship was the only one seen to be moving in what appeared to be a maritime junkyard. Yasuo radioed base to say that he was under renewed attack, but no more was heard from him. Thus, only four of the sixteen ships that had sailed from Rabaul managed to escape to fight another day. They were the destroyers *Asagumo*, *Shikinami*, *Yukikaze* and *Uranami*.

Nightfall brought no relief for the Japanese derelicts. It became the turn of the fast motor torpedo boats of the US Navy to engage in some action. Ten of these, up from Tufi and Kona Kope, charged across Huon Gulf under the command of Lieutenant-Commander Barry Atkins. The weather had turned again and heavy seas battered these little fifty-ton plywood craft as they ploughed forward through the rain with their usual forty-plus knots reduced to little more than thirty. Atkins saw flickering flames in the distance through the murk. It was the *Oigawa Maru*. She had been burning now for nearly fourteen hours. Two torpedoes, one each from *PT-143* and *PT-150*, quickly dispatched her to the bottom. It was, in truth, little more than a target-practice exercise. There was no chance of them meeting with any answering fire. It seems that there was more danger to their fragile wooden hulls from collision with submerged wreckage, of which there was plenty. Indeed, two of them were forced to turn back owing to this. And Atkins' crews were fortunate not to run into any Japanese destroyers. Any one of these, even a battle-weary one, would probably have been more than they could have handled. In fact, Admiral Kimura did return with *Shikinami*, *Yukikaze* and *Asagumo* that night to rescue more men from the hulks of *Arashio* and *Tokitsukaze*, and hastily retire to Rabaul, but the two forces did not encounter each other.

Next day, 4 March, the bombers returned. A 500 lb bomb from a B-17 plummeted straight down the for'ard funnel of the *Arashio* and blew her bottom out, while the *Tokitsukaze* was sunk late in the afternoon. No Japanese ship was now to be seen on the surface of the Huon Gulf. But there were still hundreds, even thousands, of survivors clinging to wreckage and in boats. If the opening fifteen minutes of the action had seen some of the most intense destruction of ships in the history of sea-warfare, what happened next must count as being among the coldest butchery of human life at sea. There was no place for magnanimity in a war such as this. It was done out of military necessity, so it was claimed. The justification was that Japanese soldiers do not surrender and many of them were in swimming distance of the shore. They could not be allowed to make the beach and head for Lae to reinforce the garrison. Torpedo boats cruised among the flotsam machine-gunning every survivor they could find. Sometimes whole boatloads were spotted by planes, found by the boats and systematically destroyed. One boat, laden with survivors, managed to escape the carnage and sail 700 miles to Guadalcanal, only to be sunk there by a US patrol. Two torpedo boats came across a couple of Japanese submarines taking on a group of about 100 survivors. They opened fire with their machine guns and fired two torpedoes, but both missed and the subs crash-dived. They were destroyed by clusters of depth-charges. American A-20 Havocs, accompanied by Australian twin-engined Beaufighters, each armed with six machine guns and four cannon, zoomed back and forth across the Gulf, strafing without mercy any sign of life among the floating wreckage. The water was whipped into froth as the bullets rained down, churning the blood and dollops of flesh together with the oil from the sunken ships into a sickening soup. They only stopped when nothing more was seen to move. For all that, several hundred Japanese did manage to elude the sharks and swim ashore, only to be tracked down in the jungle by native hunters. "For a month," Samuel E. Morison wrote in his *History of US Naval Operations in World War II*, "there was open season on Nips, the natives had the time of their lives in tracking them down as in the old head-hunting days."

Major Edward F. Hoover, assistant operations officer of the Fifth Bomber Command, wrote after the war. "This was the dirty part of the job. We sent out A-20s and Beaufighters to strafe lifeboats. It was rather a sloppy job and some of the boys got sick. But that is something you've got to learn. The enemy is out to kill you and you are out to kill the enemy. You can't be sporting in a war."

It had been an overwhelming Allied victory and it was lauded as such by the Allied press, although almost nothing appeared about the massacre of survivors. Very little was written about the after-math of the battle. One of the rare articles that did appear, in the issue of *Time* magazine dated 15 March 1943, told how American fighter planes, flying low, had "turned lifeboats towed by motor barges and packed with Jap survivors into bloody sieves". It was the Japanese turn, it said, to receive some of the same ferocity which they had often displayed. Two weeks later it published a letter to the editor from a reader who had queried the morality of such cold-blooded slaughter. Instantly this triggered a flood of enraged correspondence from people who held the view that "morals" could play no part in a war of this nature. One said, "Another good old American custom I would like to see is nailing a Jap hide on every 'backhouse' door in America. "

Even when more of the truth came out later, little was revealed about the massacre and therefore only a sparse amount of material has survived to be available to researchers. All eight Japanese transports had been sunk, and four of the eight destroyers, plus a couple of dozen planes lost and over 3,000 men killed. The cost to the victors had been negligible. The 137 planes engaged had flown a total of 402 sorties between them. And they had all landed safely at base except for two bombers and three fighters. The Japanese plan to take Wau and its airfield was aborted and seven months later Australian ground forces took control of Lae. The Battle of the Bismarck Sea was a major milestone in the chronology of the Second World War in the Pacific. Coming almost immediately after all Japanese resistance ceased on Guadalcanal, it instantly removed any direct threat to northern Australia. In longer perspective, it served to underline the start of the Allies' island-hopping march to victory, although that victory still lay two and a half years ahead.

8

THE *TJISALAK* MASSACRE

The 5,787-ton Dutch-owned *Tjisalak* of the Java-China-Japan Lijn, built 1917, was on her way from Melbourne to Colombo with 6,400 tons of bagged flour and Dutch Navy mail on 26 March 1944 when she was torpedoed by the Penang-based Japanese submarine *I-8*, commanded by Captain Tatsunoke Ariizumi, in 02°30'S–78°40'E. The explosion killed six of the mostly Dutch 103 people on board, which consisted of her crew of seventy-six, including ten British Royal Navy gunners to man her four-inch gun and four Oerlikons, plus twenty-seven passengers. What happened next can only be described as a massacre.

The *Tjisalak* left Melbourne at 1000 on 7 March 1944. She encountered atrocious weather in the Australian Bight and her captain tried to find calmer water by steering a course closer to the coast to avoid damage to her. This put her twenty-fours hours behind schedule and of course used extra fuel-oil. Off Perth she received a radio message giving two new positions to pass through for safety. One was codenamed 'Fox' which was shown in the Captain's instructions as 27°S.70°E, but the other was given as 'O.N.', which he could not find in the book, and so he decided to steer a mean course for Colombo after passing through 'Fox'. Perth had asked for confirmation of these diversions and, although the freighter's radio office tried for two days to get through to them, they were unable to make contact. In the end, Durban picked up their calls and agreed to relay them to Perth.

Anxious about his fuel, the Captain decided to proceed at the economical speed of 10 knots until reaching the 500 mile zone and then increase to full speed and start zig-zagging. At 0530 on 26 March the Fourth Officer was sent down from the bridge to prepare the zig-zag diagram. Another half an hour's steaming and the Captain would be ringing down for Full Speed. At 0545, completely out of the blue, there was a tremendous explosion. The whole ship seemed to be lifted clean out of the water. A torpedo had struck her in No. 3 hold just abaft the bridge on the port side. She staggered and took on a heavy list to port and then slowly swayed back to lean about 15 degrees out of upright.

Dekker, the Second Mate, had just stood the middle watch, from midnight to 0400. Neither he nor the gunners on watch on the after-deck had seen anything unusual for the whole four hours, and it had been a beautifully clear night with excellent visibility. He had been pleased to climb into his bunk, as have most middle-watchmen through the ages, and by 0545 was deep in sleep. Wakened by the explosion, he hurried out on deck. The starboard alleyway was covered with oil, presumably blown up through the sounding pipes. The engines were already slowing down and great billows of steam were spouting from the stokehold. The lights were flickering and failing and the whole deck wore a sheen of fine white flour. Both wireless aerials had collapsed and the No. 3 hatch covers had been blown off. For some reason her rudder had become jammed to port. Several of the Chinese crew had already gone to their lifeboats.

Dekker was the ship's Gunnery Officer and went aft to the gun platform. The gun's crew were standing by, with the four-inch loaded and ready to fire. One of them said he had seen the track of a torpedo on the port side but there had been no time to warn the bridge. The order had been given to abandon ship, but neither Dekker nor any of the gunners had heard it. While the *Tjisalak*'s boats were being launched, they remained 'closed up' at their gun in accordance with instructions. They watched while one of the port lifeboats, containing the Second Radio Officer, Mr Blears, and three Chinese seamen prepared to pull away. Dekker noticed that Mr Blears had forgotten to take the boat's radio set with him and called him back to get it. Then he ordered him to pull away only a short distance as several of the gunners were non-swimmers and would need to be picked up later.

Suddenly a stream of machine-gun fire chattered from the ship's bridge. It was from the apprentice, who then jumped over the side and swam towards the waiting lifeboat. He had spotted a periscope at about the same second as one of the gunners shouted and pointed at it, about 1,000 yards away. Dekker gave the order to open fire. He said later, "The time was then about 0548. Everything went smoothly. It was beautiful to watch the way the gunners fired. Several times I had to call, 'Check, check, check!' owing to the lifeboats crossing the line of fire. The first shot was dead in line with the periscope and the second shot fell very close. The submarine had nearly surfaced. But then she suddenly dived again. We kept the gun trained on her and as she came up we fired again. I adjusted the range, but the gun would not bear more than Red 70° and she was at about Red 85°. The ship's list to port was rapidly increasing and by now the water was lapping round the gun mountings. I hoped that the ship would swing sufficiently to enable me to get another shot but we were unlucky. By 0600 hours she was listing at about 50° and we were unable to keep our feet, which were already in the water. We finally jumped over the side and within thirty seconds the *Tjisalak* had turned on her beam ends and sunk. The apprentice pulled his boat over and picked us up."

A sorrowful scene, the same which follows the sinking of any ship, spread across what on another day would have been a pleasant Indian Ocean morning. The rafts and lifeboats, each bearing a cluster of wretched men, sat among a scattered assortment of floating debris: planks, spars, bits of furniture and clothing, metal drums, crates and boxes of all sizes nodding tipsily on the swell. The men slowly rowed their boats around among the flotsam, looking for anything likely to contain food or fresh water. Four lifeboats had got away from the ship, but two of these were in a sorry condition, having been damaged by the torpedo explosion. Then the conning-tower and nose of the submarine poked out of the water and she came to the surface among them. A Japanese voice shouted in almost unintelligible English, "I want to see your Captain." The order was repeated twice more before the *Tjisalak*'s master stood up and was commanded to bring his boat alongside. One by one, the other boats were ordered to follow. Dekker had slowly pulled his boat to one side in the vain hope of being over-looked, but then came another shout, "Come alongside, and make it snappy, make it snappy!" As he made fast the boat's painter and climbed aboard, he found himself admiring the appearance of the sub. She was freshly painted and her bell and brasswork gleamed. Her officers and crew were all in uniform and were smart and neat, but the lack of discipline among the crew was surprising. They had become very nervous and several of them were scampering around the upper casing of the sub anxiously scanning the sky with binoculars.

As Dekker walked towards the fore-deck as ordered, to join a number of the freighter's Chinese crew who were already sitting there with their heads down, several of the European crew members, who had been taken below with the Master, now emerged and were ushered aft. With that the engines started and, after a Japanese rating had cut all the boats' painters, the submarine throbbed away. Meantime, more ratings had appeared on deck, armed with rifles, tommy-guns and Samurai swords. One held a coil of rope which he was carefully measuring off in lengths, staring coldly at the prisoners the whole time.

Raised voices could be heard from within the conning-tower. One was the Master's, shouting, "No, no, I don't know!" over and over again. The other was that of the submarine's young English-speaking commander. "Don't look back. Don't look back. If you look back, you'll be shot. Don't move!" he was bellowing at the prisoners squatting on the fore-deck. Then one of the Chinese fell or slipped or was pushed overboard and the Japs started firing at him in the water. They started picking out the Europeans, calling them out by name, starting with two of the gunners and ordering them to walk aft. Rifle shots cracked and all the time the commander was shouting, "Don't look back!" The names of the Fifth Engineer and the First Mate, F.E. Jong, were called out. Jong saw them shoot the Engineer through the head as he was walking astern. They shot at him, too, but he was a very tall man and that saved his life. Fired by a short Japanese, the bullet was travelling at an upward angle. It only grazed the back of Jong's head, knocking him into the sea, unconscious. He was fortunate to have been wearing his life-jacket which kept him afloat. When he recovered consciousness, he managed to swim undetected to a raft.

Everybody was ordered to take off his life-jacket just before it came to Dekker's turn. He turned to go to the after-deck. As he passed the conning-tower he caught a terrific blow to the left side of his head. He said, "This knocked me over to the right and as I was falling I saw another man on my right with a big sledge-hammer preparing to hit me. I managed to duck, but the hammer caught my right temple a glancing blow. As I fell to the deck I saw a man with a rifle pointed at me, so I rolled over the side into the water and dived under. I stayed under as long as possible and heard the sound of bullets ripping into the water overhead and the sound of propellers passing. I had to come up for air, but quickly dived again, because

141

there was the man with the rifle examining his magazine. When I came up for air again, the submarine was some distance away. I turned away from her and started to swim. I kept going for a long time. I was almost exhausted when I reached a piece of floating timber. In the distance I could see an upturned lifeboat, so I swam to it and dived underneath to hide in the 'air cushion'."

Meantime, three-quarters of a mile away, a murderous slaughter was taking place on the submarine. Wielding their swords, hammers and monkey-wrenches, the Japs were clubbing and slashing their prisoners to death and pushing the bodies from the blood-stained deck into the sea. Dekker had certainly been fortunate in smuggling himself away from this carnage. It was quite comfortable under the lifeboat, and it made sense to stay there until he was sure the Japs had departed. But after a few minutes he became acutely aware of a family of sharks swimming lazily round his hideaway. This was a far from comfortable situation. With a great effort, he hauled himself out and up onto the upturned keel of the boat. There was no submarine in sight, just two of the other lifeboats, which seemed to be empty. Suddenly there was the head of a swimmer approaching the boat. It was one of the Chinese, a man named Dancy. He was hardly able to haul himself out of the water, being totally exhausted and with two gaping wounds in the side of his neck from the blows of a Samurai sword.

Dekker decided that they should try to reach the other boats. He was sure he could see some small figures in one of them, but they were now some three or four miles distant and only visible when they were lifted on the swell. He tried swimming towards them, pushing his boat in front of him; he tried pushing a plank through the grab-lines and using it as an oar, and then he dived back underneath to retrieve one of the boat's oars and tried sculling with it. But all these methods were laborious and they made no headway. There was nothing for it but to swim. And there was only another hour or so of daylight left. They set off swimming through the mêlée of wreckage, making as much splashing as possible in order to scare off the sharks. Gradually, the boats became larger and clearer until one of them spotted the shouting swimmers. It was Jong's boat. He was sitting in the stem-sheets at the helm, utterly washed out and clearly still suffering from his head wound. With him were the Third Engineer, P.C. Spuybroek, and the Second Radio Officer, J. Blears. It was just about dusk.

Spuybroek had slipped unnoticed over the side of the submarine as soon as he had set foot on her deck. Diving right underneath her to resurface on the other side and quietly swim away, still unobserved, he was the only man to be entirely unwounded. The Japs had started to tie the remaining prisoners together in groups of two, four and six. One of the British naval ratings, boiling with anger, snatched a megaphone from the hand of one of the Jap officers and smashed it into the man's face. He was rewarded with a terrible slashing from a Samurai sword. Blears had found himself tied together with the Apprentice. When their turn came to be summoned towards their deaths on the after-deck, as they were passing the conning-tower, he whispered to the youngster, "Jump!"

A fusillade of bullets peppered the water around them as they started to swim and the Apprentice was hit in the neck. Blears was a strong swimmer. He managed to free himself from his bonds and took the wounded cadet on his back. For over an hour he swam as fast as he could away from the submarine, but at last he was so exhausted that he left the lad treading water while he went off to search among the wreckage for something that would serve as a raft to support them both. He found a piece of timber, but then collapsed with exhaustion. He never saw the boy again, but later drifted near a raft on which sat Jong and Spuybroek. They were paddling it towards one of the lifeboats and, having climbed aboard it, came back to pick him up. A few hours later they spied Dekker and Dancy.

As Chief Officer, Jong was in command, but he was drifting in and out of consciousness. He gave orders to raise the mast and set the sail, but Dekker did not do so. He did not want to make too much of a target for any Jap submarines still lurking in the area. For the same reason he had not used the boat's wireless set as he did not want his signals intercepted. And indeed these fears seemed to have been justified when, on the second day adrift, Spuybroek was on watch, standing in the stern. Suddenly he started and stared towards the horizon. He had seen a submarine and reported it to Dekker. And then they saw a flash from the vessel and a shell rasped through the air overhead. Then another, which fell short. And another. She was straddling the boat uncomfortably closely. And now she was close enough for them to see that she was no submarine. She was the US Liberty ship *James O. Wilder*.

She had been captured by the Japs, guessed Dekker, and they were now using her as a raider. Hence the unfriendliness. The five men in

143

the boat stripped off their clothes, resigning themselves to another swim. But Dekker's guesswork was wrong. They were about to jump over the side when the firing ceased and they looked up to see a crowd of European faces, including several women, peering at them from the rails. They pulled alongside and climbed aboard her. It was 1730 on 28 March. As Dekker stepped onto her deck a gun was thrust into his back and he was told to report to Captain Lunt on the bridge.

When Lunt heard the survivors' story he apologized for firing and explained that he had done so because the lifeboat had failed to fire the usual rocket. He was extra-anxious, he said, as he was carrying forty passengers, mainly forces personnel, including several ladies. After that he doubled the watches at the guns and the *Tjisalak* survivors were followed everywhere by an armed guard until they landed at Colombo at 2000 on 30 March. There followed a frustrating and distressing six hours. There were interrogation procedures to undergo and bundles of red tape to overcome. The Royal Naval Hospital could not take them in because they were Merchant Navy, and the General Hospital, to which they rode in a filthy ambulance, was full except in the paying ward. Jong and Dancy said they would stay there, such was their exhaustion, but for the others nothing could be done except to have their various wounds dressed by a most reluctant nun. They met a Royal Navy Chief Petty Officer outside, who said he was ashamed of the Service. He kindly contacted the Commanding Officer of the Royal Naval Hospital himself to make an appeal for help on their behalf, but this produced nothing but a bland apology about Regulations and that the regrettable situation would be reported.

The Dutch Naval authorities were only a little better. They responded to Dekker's telephone call by sending a car to take them to the Galle Face Hotel, which turned out to be full. They finished up by sleeping on a sofa in the ballroom after promising the night porter they would leave by 0700 in the morning. He brought them tea and toast, which he paid for himself and they had a shave and a bath. Later they were questioned again by British and Dutch Naval Intelligence, but refused to say anything further until they were fixed up with decent accommodation. In the end, they found themselves private billets in civilian houses.

Dekker wrote later, "I cannot speak too highly of the behaviour of all our gunners. They carried out their duty to the very last without question or wavering for a single moment. Their coolness under the very difficult circumstances resulted in accurate shooting. They met their deaths like the magnificent men they were. Acting Petty Officer Arnold was a born leader who inspired his subordinates to a grand performance in fulfilment of their duty. He was a man of whom the Royal Navy should be proud."

The men who remained and fought the gun to the last were:

Alfred John Arnold	Acting Petty Officer	C/J 100688
Frederick Mather	Able Seaman	P/JX 236841
Patrick O'Brien	Able Seaman	C/JX 277936
Frederick Drewery	Able Seaman	D/JX 313081
Albert Fieldhouse	Able Seaman	D/JX 349907
Frederick Parry	Able Seaman	D/JX 550844
John Joseph Burns	Bombardier Royal Artillery	3391333

As far as is known, Dekker, Jong, Spuybroek, Blears and Dancy were the only five survivors from the 103 people aboard the doomed *Tjisalak*. It was almost a total massacre.

9

THE TRAWLER *NOREEN MARY*

At a quarter past midnight on the night of 5–6 July 1944 a B-17 aircraft of Air Transport Command, USAAF, roared down the runway at Stornoway, in the Outer Hebrides and soared up into the patchy cloud over The Minches. Just one hour before, Captain H. Faber, Senior Flight Operations Officer at the airfield, had received information from the Royal Naval base at Lews Castle that a fishing trawler had been sunk by a U-boat to the north-east of the Isle of Lewis. The B-17's mission was to search for survivors.

The pilot's orders were to patrol an area between Tiumpan Head on the northern tip of Lewis's Eye Peninsula and the Point of Stoer on the Scottish mainland. He set a course of 070° magnetic and came down through the scattered layers of summer mist to an altitude of 1000 feet to get better visibility. Only minutes before, a flare had been sighted on the surface and reported by two Navy Hellcats. Taking a fresh course from Flying Control, the B-17 came within sight of the flare three minutes later.

The plane circled the spot, then made a run over it, dropping another flare to ensure the continued marking of the position. There appeared to be several pale-coloured objects in the water close to the first flare, but such was the poor visibility on that cloudy night that it was impossible to determine exactly what they were, even at that low altitude. Hundreds of ships had been sunk in the Western Approaches during the war and the objects could easily have been some kind of flotsam. There was plenty of it about. On the other hand, they could have been men in life-jackets. The airmen also spotted a small ship proceeding towards the flare. It looked like a Royal Navy corvette. The B-17 continued circling, making sure that its navigation lights were switched on to avoid a collision with the

Hellcats, which had also remained in the vicinity. The pilot refrained from illuminating the scene with his landing lights for fear of exposing the silhouette of the 'corvette' to a torpedo from any U-boats which may still have been lurking. At ten minutes past two he was ordered to return to base. Before heading for home, another marker flare was dropped. If indeed the shapes had been men, at least they would have been reassured by the knowledge that they had been found. Indeed, the 'corvette', which was probably the Admiralty tug *Lady Madeleine*, was bound to pick them up before long.

The Anti-U-boat Division's war diary report to the Chief of Naval Staff read –

SECRET – Report No. 1745.
9497 – at about 2145/5 *ss Starbank* reported U-boat shelling small vessels 10 miles west of Cape Wrath. One vessel appears to have been sunk. Details still incomplete. A/S surface and air forces are searching area.
9499 – ref 9497 HMT *Lady Madeleine* picked up two survivors from *s.t. Noreen Mary* sunk by gunfire from U-boat at 2200/5.
9505 – ref 9499. Aircraft of 15 Group has obtained sonar buoy contact in 58°15'N–9°.00W at 1453/6 and is hunting.

Eight of the *Noreen Mary*'s mainly middle-aged crew of ten were dead. Although she was a Granton, Edinburgh, boat, she had followed the common practice of fishing off the west coast at times when the herring were likely to be more plentiful. She had sailed independently from Ayr on 1 July, rounded the Mull of Kintyre and chugged north through the Minches towards the fishing grounds between the Butt of Lewis and Cape Wrath, where she fell in with a group of fellow trawlers. Her skipper, fifty-four-year-old John Flockhart, BEM, had not been to sea for eighteen months. In fact, he had retired and was not in the best of health. Mr Carnie, a member of the trawler's owners, the Newhaven firm Carnie & Gibb, later told the *Scottish Sunday Express*, "John had done his bit in the last war, but he apparently felt that he could do something more to help and he had a great love of the sea. He just took on the *Noreen Mary* to help out for a couple of months. The *Noreen Mary* was fishing with three other trawlers. She was broadside on to the U-boat when it surfaced and was shelled for three-quarters of an hour before she sank. The other trawlers were able to escape when they saw the U-boat."

On going ashore in Oban, the skipper of one of the other trawlers, Bob Smith, told the *Express*, "We had just finished dragging when a U-boat surfaced about a mile from us. It opened fire on the *Noreen Mary*, which was closest to it. There was no time to launch the boats. We cut away our trawl gear and scattered, but the *Noreen Mary* and her crew had no chance at all. There was nothing we could do to retaliate. For fully forty-five minutes the U-boat kept firing at the *Noreen Mary*. She was very badly battered and eventually sank."

The trawlermen on the other boats could only watch helplessly while the submarine carried out its savage and cowardly attack. One of them said later that they thought the U-boat crew must have been either doped or drunk. Visibility was perfectly good, so there could be no question that they had mistaken the identity of their target.

The dead fishermen were Skipper Flockhart himself, of Portobello, Edinburgh; his mate Alex Barnet, BEM, fifty-eight years old, from Leith; second fisherman Alex MacKenzie, forty-four, of Cockenzie; the first Engineer, William Jackson, fifty-three, of Eyemouth; the fireman George Gordon, thirty-nine, of Wallyford; the cook, Charles Lindsay, fifty-two, of Edinburgh; an eighteen-year-old apprentice from Glasgow, James Coates, and the only Englishman in the crew, forty-one-year-old Yorkshireman Wilfred Allan, a father of eight who had gone north from Scarborough about a year before to find work on some bigger boats.

The only two survivors were the Second Engineer, William Pryde, forty-one, of Edinburgh, and the fish-gutter, thirty-three-year-old James MacAlister from Portobello. MacAlister was interviewed by the Shipping Casualties Section on 18 August and gave his account of the incident. Sixteen months later, for some reason, he swore a deposition before a Notary Public in Edinburgh. It was largely an elaborated repetition of what he had first said.

> Deposition of James MacAlister, Member of the crew of the *Noreen Mary*.
> At Edinburgh the Twenty-first day of December Nineteen hundred and forty-five in presence of William Brunton Robertson, Solicitor and Notary Public, Edinburgh.
> Compeared James MacAlister, 21 Adelphi Place, Portobello, who being solemnly sworn and interrogated depones:
> "I am thirty-five years of age. I am presently employed as a Ship's Rigger with John Dinwoodie, Granton, near Edinburgh.

I have been a fisherman and a whaler practically all my days. In the month of July 1944, I was deckhand in the trawler *Noreen Mary* – a boat engaged in fishing on the west coast of Scotland, and it follows from what I have said that I was engaged in a peacetime occupation just as I had been engaged in that occupation for many years before. I was not engaged in combating the enemy, although it is the case that the *Noreen Mary* carried, like all other fishing trawlers, a gun, in this case a 'Savage Lewis'. In addition there was one rifle on board for the purpose of exploding enemy mines which might happen to be in the fairway; the vessel was not 'wiped'.

"On the last fishing trip of the *Noreen Mary* (from Ayr to the fishing grounds off the Butt of Lewis) there were ten of a crew – the skipper (John Flockhart), the mate (Alexander Barnett), second fisherman (Alexander Mackenzie), gutter (an Englishman whose name I forget), chief engineer (William Jackson), second engineer (William Pryde), fireman (George Gordon), trimmer (whose name I forget), cook (Charles Lindsay) and myself as deckhand. We had on board a catch of 325 boxes of fish.

"We left Ayr at 14 hours on 1 July 1944, proceeding independently for the fishing grounds off the Butt of Lewis. We started to trawl early on Monday morning, 3 July, at which time there were two other trawlers present. We continued to fish in the same area, with other trawlers joining up, until by the 5 July there were five other trawlers in our vicinity.

"Nothing of incident occurred until 2010 hours on 5 July when, whilst I was on watch, I saw two torpedoes pass down on our port side. They were together some six or eight feet apart, the nearest being about ten feet from the ship's side. Then I saw a conning-tower dead astern only 120-130 yards away, so I ran onto the bridge and called all hands. The ship's head was swinging to the S.E. (i.e. to starboard) at this time.

"By the time the crew had arrived on deck the conning-tower had submerged, and they would not believe that I had seen either the submarine or the torpedoes. In fact, the Mate asked, 'What pub have you been in?' We carried on fishing until 2030 hours when we hauled in our trawl, and shot it again at 2055 hours. The Mate then asked another trawler, *Starbank*, if she had seen anything, but she had not.

"At 2110 hours, while we were still trawling, the submarine

surfaced on our starboard beam, about fifty yards to the N.E. of us, and without any warning immediately opened fire on the ship with a machine-gun. We were eighteen miles west from Cape Wrath, on a north-westerly course (approx.) making three knots. The weather was clear and fine, sunny, with good visibility; the sea was smooth with light airs.

"When the submarine surfaced I saw men climbing out of the conning-tower. The skipper thought at first the submarine was British, but when she opened fire he immediately slackened the brake to take the weight off gear, and increased to full speed which was about ten knots. The submarine chased us, firing her machine-gun, and with the first rounds killed two or three men, including the skipper, who were on deck and had not had time to take cover. The submarine then started using a heavier gun, from her conning-tower, the first shot from which burst the boiler, enveloping everything in steam and stopping the ship.

"By now the crew had taken cover, but in spite of this all but four were killed. The submarine then commenced to circle round ahead of the vessel and passed down her port side with both guns firing continuously. We were listing slowly to port all the time but did not catch fire. The mate and I attempted to release the lifeboat which was aft, but the mate was killed whilst doing so, so I abandoned the attempt. I then went below into the pantry, which was below the waterline, for shelter. The ship was listing more and more to port, until finally at 2210 she rolled right over and sank, the only four men left alive on board were thrown into the sea. I do not know where the other three men had taken cover during this time, so I did not see or hear them until they were in the water.

"I swam around until I came across the broken bow of our lifeboat, which was upside down, and managed to scramble on top of it. Even now the submarine did not submerge, but deliberately steamed in my direction and when only 60–70 yards away fired directly at me with a short burst from the machine-gun. As their intention was quite obvious I fell into the water and remained there until the submarine ceased firing and submerged, after which I climbed onto the bottom of the boat. The submarine had been firing at us for a full hour.

"Shortly afterwards, I saw the second engineer hanging onto a big pond board, and seeing the ship's ladder nearby, I pushed one end of it over to him. He grabbed it and I was able to pull him over to the damaged lifeboat and lay him over the top. He was very badly injured and became hysterical; he shook hands with me and said he was going to jump overboard, the only thing I could do to prevent him doing so was to hit him on the jaw to make him unconscious. Since his wife has heard of this she refuses to speak to me. After ten minutes he recovered and was much quieter.

"The chief engineer and an apprentice trimmer were the other two men thrown clear of the ship, but I did not actually see them in the water. I heard them shouting for a time, but they were not seen again.

"The second engineer and I remained on the upturned lifeboat, and at daybreak I saw a trawler about half a mile away and after asking the second engineer if he could shout, to which he answered, 'Yes', I said, 'Well, if you have ever shouted in your life, shout now.' We made as much noise as we could and were heard by the crew of this trawler which was HMT *Lady Madeleine* who closed and lowered a boat and had us on board about 0500–0600. We searched the area which was littered with wreckage for other survivors for about an hour, but did not see any sign of life.

"Whilst on board the *Lady Madeleine* the second engineer and I had our wounds dressed; I learned later that the second engineer had forty-eight shrapnel wounds, also a piece of steel wire two and a half inches long embedded in his body. I think the shells must have been filled with this wire, as it definitely was not from any part of the ship's equipment. I had fourteen shrapnel wounds. The submarine was the largest I have seen, and she had a large conning-tower. She had two big guns, one on the after-deck and the other on the fore-part of the conning-tower. There was what looked like an Oerlikon (it was bigger than a machine-gun) on a stand on the fore-deck, but I was not able to see how many men fired it. The paintwork looked fresh, and there was no camouflage on deck. The hull was a lightish grey, and I saw a black swastika, picked out in white on the fore part of the conning-tower. Underneath the swastika there was a 'U' and underneath that '11', this number which was also seen by the trawlers *Starbreak* [sic] *Colleague*, and *W.H. Podd*, was painted in white. I did not see a crest. There was a peculiar erection on the bows of the submarine, which looked to me something like a catapult. It was a heavy structure, only two or three feet high. I do not think it was part of a net cutter.

"I saw two or three of the crew on the conning-tower, and a man at the heavy gun, but did not notice their uniform. I would not be able to identify any of them as I was constantly taking cover. Nobody on board the submarine spoke at any time.

"I understand that the *Starbreak*, which was in our immediate vicinity when the submarine surfaced, immediately began transmitting an SOS message. The submarine evidently heard her doing so and fired two shots in her direction, but they missed and she was able to get away. The other trawlers also cut their gear and steamed full speed for Stornoway.

"This is my fourth war-time experience having served in the whalers *Sylvester* (mined) and *New Seville* (torpedoed) and the trawler *Ocean Tide* which ran ashore.

"As a result of this attack by the U-boat, the casualties were six killed (the skipper, mate, one deckhand, second fisherman, cook and fireman), two missing (chief engineer and trimmer) and two injured (second engineer and myself).

"All of which is TRUTH as the Deponent shall answer to God. (Signed) James MacAlister and W.B. Robertson, Notary Public, Edinburgh."

The attacker of the *Noreen Mary* was the Type VIIC *U-247* of the *9th Unterseeboote Flotille* based at Brest. She had only been in commission since the previous October, after being built at Germania Werft at Kiel. Her short career, commanded by a twenty-four-year-old Berliner, Oberleutnant Gerhard Matschulat, had been somewhat less than glittering. On her first patrol she fired a torpedo at a British battleship and missed. It was on her second patrol that she sank what was to be her only prize, a 207-ton fishing smack. Matschulat's log reads –

1600	AM3659	Piston engine noises bearing 125° sound strength 2–3
	[German grid map ref]	Range 6000 yards. Steer right. 1613
		Steer right. Position . . .
		Moving into attack. 1613
		Position . . . Bearing 130°

1618	AM3659 Calm Sea. Visibility 6–8 sea miles.	Single torpedo from Tube 2. Missed. "Trier" torpedo passed by her bows.
1926		Engine noise bearing 230° sound strength 0–1 Fishing trawler. 9000 yards.
1943	AM3682 Calm sea. Visibility 10–12 sea miles. Light fading	Fishing trawler. Steer left. 9000 yards. Two-fan shot from tubes 1 and 4. Target turned away to starboard. Probably saw tracks in very calm sea.
2055	AM3683	Surfaced. Three fishing trawlers. Engaged the nearest one. She stops after three minutes. Fire sinking shot from tube 3 at "Noreen Mary" as she lay stopped.
2151	west of Cape Wrath	A miss. Misfired and did not clear. Sunk by flak shots into her side. Sunk by the stern.

The case of the *Noreen Mary* was presented by the Prosecution as part of the evidence against Karl Dönitz at the trial of major war criminals at Nuremberg in 1946. Submission of the following document as an exhibit can hardly have helped his case:

Comment of the German Submarine Command on the War Diary of *U-247* (Matschulat) for the period 18.5–28.7.44.
The sinking by flak of the fishing vessel in this area testifies to *great* offensive spirit and verve. As regards the sinking shot on the fishing vessel as she lay stopped, I should say that relatively more misses are scored when firing sinking than attacking shots, as the enemy, when lying stopped is usually still slightly moving –
Operations well carried out in difficult conditions.
Recognized success: fishing vessel *Noreen Mary* sunk by flak.
For the B.D.U –
Chief of Operational Division. (initials)

In the aftermath of D-day, 6 June 1944, the English Channel swarmed with Allied vessels of all descriptions as they poured men and supplies across to beef up the invasion forces. That the Germans should mount a concentrated submarine assault on these lines of communication was an obvious tactic. Their initial efforts had met with little success owing to the intensity of the Allied air and surface patrols. But even three months after the invasion of Normandy, some persistent U-boats still lurked in wait for an unwary prey. Alert British and Allied vigilance was still vital, but their anti-submarine patrols were hampered in their searches by unusually poor conditions. Strong tides, relatively shallow water and the innumerable wrecks which littered the sea-floor interfered with A/S transmissions and made accurate classification of contacts very difficult. And the Germans had learned how to take advantage of the presence of these wrecks. It was a simple matter for them to sit motionless on the bottom, in simulation of the carcass of a sunken ship, at the first sign that they had been detected by an inquisitive frigate.

The Ninth Escort Group was one of four Canadian Support Groups which had operated in the Channel and Western Approaches ever since D-day. On the morning of 31 August they were patrolling south of the Scilly Isles when orders were received from the C. in C. Plymouth to carry out an anti-submarine search along the convoy route to Hartland Point on the north Devon coast. An RAF patrol had made a suspicious radar contact at 0330 that morning about seventeen miles north-west of Trevose Head.

At 1845 the frigate HMCS *St. John* obtained a contact when she was about five miles due east of Wolf Rock, off Land's End. Although it faded and was lost, it was considered to have been promising enough to warrant continued investigation. Accordingly, *St. John*, with Lieutenant-Commander W.R. Stacey in command, HCMSs *Swansea* (Commander C.A. King) and *Port Colbourne* were detached to attempt to regain contact, while HCMSs *Stormont*, *Meon* and *Monnow* continued with their sweep along the convoy route. Two hours passed by before *Swansea* made a contact, although her radar operators were not confident that it was a submarine. It could have been a shoal of fish. *Swansea* dropped a single depth-charge, the result of which was seen by *St. John*, following astern, to be the appearance of a small oil slick. In turn, she fired a hedgehog pattern which produced still more oil and yet again at 2300, but by now it was too dark to observe results, and in any case

154

contact had been lost. However, there was no longer the possibility that fish could have offered a false target. The oil slicks had betrayed the definite presence of a submarine.

On the hunch that the submarine's course would be to the southwest, the three frigates began a down-tide parallel sweep at midnight. They had guessed correctly. At 0155 *St. John* plotted a contact 2050 yards away from her. She was about three miles from Wolf Rock Light, on a bearing of 200°. Stacey ran over the spot, with his echo sounder pinging a first-class trace. It looked as if he had found a bottomed U-boat. The target was absolutely stationary in forty-two fathoms of water. Not a sound came from it over the hydrophone, but a sharp peak, like a conning-tower, in the centre of the image was distinctly visible on the radar screen. A pattern of five depth-charges produced a rolling rumble of explosions, making the sea boil and glow with phosphorescence in the darkness. He repeated the exercise at 0320, by which time the early light enabled a considerable amount of oil to be seen on the surface. By now, the oil had spread to cover an area some two and a half miles long, which ought to have assisted the attackers' radar by smoothing the sea, but, frustratingly, contact was lost again at 0410.

The search continued throughout the forenoon and into the afternoon of 1 September until 1350 when Stacey signalled that he had obtained a solid echo sounder trace. He ran out and turned to pick up speed over the target and at 1414 another five depth-charges looped over *St. John*'s rails. Commander King, watching from *Swansea*, described the results as "startling". This time not only did more oil float to the surface but a large amount of assorted debris. Sea-boats were quickly lowered to collect this evidence, which was being rapidly scattered by the rising wind and sea. There were letters, shirts, photographs, a sock, a radio set diagram, a rubber raft, a cushion, a leather coat, a light list of the Bay of Biscay showing German swept minefield channels, and an engine maintenance book. There was a certificate commemorating the ten millionth engine revolution and part of the engine-room log of none other than *U-247*.

The carcass of *U-247* lies in 49°54'N, 05°49'W. There were no survivors from her crew of fifty-two. The Canadians had avenged the murders of the fishermen of the little *Noreen Mary*.

10

THE HELL-SHIPS (1) – *RAKUYO* AND *KACHIDOKI*

On US Independence Day 1944 a train rattled over the causeway into a sweltering Singapore and ground to a halt at the Keppel Docks station. It was carrying a party of Australian POWs on their way to Japan. The train had wound its way down the Malay peninsula with thirty of them crammed into each of its eighteen-foot steel trucks, the sides of which had been rendered scorching hot by the blazing equatorial sun. They had come from Tamarkan 'rest' camp, a grim place in the scrubby Siam jungle near Kanchanaburi, where they had been sent after toiling as slaves on the infamous Death Railway. But their journey to Singapore had been far from direct. It had taken them on what would have been, in peacetime, a grand and expensive tour, only within the scope of millionaires. They had left Tamarkan, it seemed, long ago, on 27 March. And now it was 4 July.

"All fit men go Nippon," the Tamarkan camp guards had suddenly announced. With a serious wartime shortage of domestic manpower, Tokyo had decreed that 10,000 of the fittest of these sick and starving specimens of humankind should be withdrawn from the various camps in South-East Asia and sent to Japan to work in the mines and munition factories. By any stretch of the imagination, no more than a handful of these men could realistically have been classified as 'fit'. Some of them welcomed the chance to get away from the steaming jungle, and the brutal and sadistic treatment they had suffered there. Japan could be no worse. It could even be better. Others took the opposite view. They knew, from reports received over hidden home-made radios that the Allies were at last on a winning footing in the Pacific. It would be a perilous trip. Packs of American submarines were wreaking terrible vengeance on Japanese merchant ships. The South China Sea was so packed with periscopes, it was joked, that you could almost walk on them to Yokohama. Their chances of being sunk were high. And even if they made it safely to Japan, their chances of early liberation from there would be slight.

The train pulled out of Kanchanaburi and away from the ghastly place which had been their home for nearly two years. Their journey took them through endless tracts of flat paddy-fields, stopping at trackside kitchens for them to clamber stiffly from their cattle trucks and be given meagre helpings of rice or a gulp or two of watery tea, ending at Phnom Penh, in Cambodia. At dawn next day they were marched down to the dockside on the wide and sluggish Mekong River. This was French Indo-China. Here was civilization. The streets seemed to be full of smiling white women, French and Eurasian, dressed in elegant clothes. Wide-eyed, the emaciated POWs gazed at them, receiving sympathetic and friendly glances in return. One or two women made surreptitious V-for-Victory signs. Some burst into tears at the sight of these men. The Japs had been careful to issue them with new clothes, simple green tunics and shorts, before allowing them into public view, but such things could not hide their skeletal condition.

At the quayside was a 300-ton river steamer, the *Long Ho*. They filed aboard. It was a roomy modern vessel, and Lieutenant Yamada, the Japanese officer in charge of the party, allowed those who could not find elbow-room in the for'ard hold to remain on the upper deck. This was comfort indeed. In fact, after the war, some of the prisoners actually recalled their trip in the *Long Ho* as being very pleasant. She steamed away from Phnom Penh, and next day she tied up 150 miles downriver at Saigon among the swarms of Japanese shipping which crowded the waterfront. It was 4 April 1944.

The POWs were marched to a former French Foreign Legion barracks near the Saigon docks to await sea transportation to Japan. Their new quarters were well-equipped with all the usual amenities of civilized life; plenty of fresh water, proper toilets, an electricity supply and a small shop which sold soap, cigarettes, toothbrushes and all manner of sundries. There was even a little golf-course! In residence there were about 250 British POWs, being the residue of some 2,000 who had been sent up from Singapore to work on the Saigon docks, but had later been drafted to work on the Death Railway to Burma. The Australians listened incredulously to the 'Pommie's' accounts of POW life in decadent Saigon. The work was not hard, the food was plentiful, the guards were decent and the accommodation was comfortable. And it was easy to slip into town at night. So easy, in fact, that venereal disease had become a problem among the British prisoners.

The following week, on Easter Sunday, 9 April, they packed up their few pathetic possessions and boarded motorized barges to take them down river to where a convoy was assembling off the Mekong Delta, at Cap St Jacques. There was a new-looking freighter at anchor in the roads with scrambling nets slung over her lofty sides. It was only with some difficulty that some of them, still weak from malnutrition and disease, managed to climb aboard. On this ship the holds were already full with cargo. So they were going to make the 2,000 mile trip to Japan entirely in the open, on the upper deck. Perhaps it was better that way. No sickening stink of excreta. No sticky bodies in suffocating heat. And a better chance of survival if they were torpedoed. It was a good trade in return for an occasional soaking in the rain. They ate a supper of rice and beans, and settled down for the night wherever they could among the deck machinery.

But they did not sail from Cap St Jacques. The ship's captain, having heard reports of the severe losses which Japanese merchant shipping was now suffering at the hands of the Allied submarine blockade in the South and East China Seas, refused to take them. He wanted no part in such a suicidal adventure. So that was why Saigon itself had been so crowded with shipping! Nobody was prepared to sail into Hell. "All men back to Saigon," the guards announced. And before the next day was out, they found themselves back in the French Foreign Legion barracks they had just left, while Yamada set about trying to find some other means of transporting his human cargo to Japan.

The good life picked up where it had left off in the wooden-built barracks. The men were sent out each day to work in the docks, or the hospital or the airfield. There were ample opportunities for stealing and for 'rackets', particularly for those who worked in the docks. Tinned foodstuffs were especially easy to filch, and whole cases of condensed milk, fruit and meat found their way into the barracks, either for consumption by the internees themselves or for onward sale on the black market in the town. A POW named Wheeler stripped the brass bushes from the door-knobs in the barracks and cleverly made 'gold' rings from them, even stamping them with a convincing 'hall-mark'. There was considerable demand for these gee-jaws among the local population and it was a profitable sideline after he had spent a busy day at 'work' on the airfield, furtively contaminating drums of fuel with handfuls of sugar.

The days rolled by. Then the weeks. They whiled away their leisure time with impromptu concerts. One of them had a clarinet, another a home-made banjo. Sporting contests, with running, jumping, throwing and boxing matches drew good crowds of excited prisoners. But all good things must come to an end. The day arrived when Yamada announced that he had arranged passage for them on a ship leaving Singapore. "All men go Singapore catch ship." It was 24 June 1944. They had been in Saigon for two and a half months and had just learned that the Allies were in Normandy.

It was back up the muddy Mekong to Phnom Penh, this time on the river steamer *Tian Guan*. And this time, in the stifling June heat, 300 of them were battened in the hold alongside a stinking cargo of dried fish. But they were still cheerful. At last the war seemed to be on the turn and their recent captivity had not been too unpleasant. They waited three days in Phnom Penh for the train to take them south to Singapore. When they saw it, a ribbon of small steel box-cars already half-laden with bags of rice, their high spirits sank instantly. The burning sun had made the box-cars like ovens. There was less than three square feet of space per man in each. And it was painful to touch the sizzling-hot sides.

With a snort and a jerk, the train rumbled off on its 1,100-mile journey. Bangkok looked wretchedly deserted. It had suffered badly at the hands of Allied bombers. At Bampong Junction the train swung south into Malaya. The Malayans, too, looked in poor shape after two and a half years of brutal Japanese occupation. They were not even getting enough of the normally plentiful rice. At stops in the cities, Penang and Kuala Lumpur, they saw hordes of people dressed in rags, clearly on the verge of starvation. Their desperate state was little better than that which the prisoners themselves had been in back in Tamarkan.

Eventually, a week after leaving Phnom Penh, a week in that baking-tin of a train, sitting with knees drawn up under chins, they left it at Singapore's Keppel Docks station to give a welcome stretch to their aching limbs. The poverty they had seen elsewhere in Malaya was not any different in Singapore. What had once been a city of brightness and vivacity now seemed subdued and gloomy. They marched through the seedy streets to some rows of vermin-ridden tumbledown bamboo shacks in the wooden-fenced POW transit compound at River Valley Road. This time nobody struck up 'Waltzing Matilda' to keep time with their tramping feet They had arrived at yet another temporary home.

∗ ∗ ∗

In Siam, a few miles through the jungle from Tamarkan, there was another euphemistic 'rest' camp: Tamuan. This one held British POWs. Mostly, they were the scarecrow remnants of the slave-labour gangs who had worked on the Death Railway, including the building of the famous 'Bridge over the River Kwai'. Many of them had been no more than conscripts when they had landed in Singapore, just in time for the surrender to the Japanese invaders in early 1942. Since then almost half of them had died, mainly from cholera, and been buried by their mates.

"All fit men go Nippon" came the order. New clothes were issued to the selected Japan Party, a motley collection of garb that looked like it had originated in a giant jumble sale; captured Dutch and British tropical green tunics mingled with white vests, floral patterned baggy shorts, brightly coloured straw hats and strange Japanese rubber shoes. At the leaving parade ceremony, Japanese officers in full dress uniform stood to attention on a platform outside their offices beside a six-piece British band, facing the lines of prisoners about to depart. The Japan Party swung past them out of Tamuan to the jangling clatter of the pots and pans tied to their haversacks and the music of the band. It was 'The Colonel Bogey March'. "Eyes left!" yelled the British officer in charge. The heads all snapped round in unison and a choir of raucous throaty voices sang out the well-known twin-syllabled chorus of defiant insult to their conquerors. "BOLLOCKS!" It had been their day, for once.

At Kanchanaburi there was the long train with its stinking steel box-cars. The British POWs knew the discomforts of such dreadful conveyances well, having come up from Singapore in them eighteen months before. They crammed themselves in. The Burma campaign was intensifying at this juncture of the war, and the southbound POW train was frequently shunted into sidings to make way for the many trains streaming north, crowded with Japanese troops. On their way to Burma, these trains would soon be passing over the rickety wooden trestle bridges that the prisoners had built in the

160

Siamese jungle, including the one over the River Kwai. If only one would collapse.

It took five days to travel the 1,000 miles to Singapore from Kanchanaburi. Singapore Harbour was almost deserted of ships. At the height of war you would have expected it to be bustling with activity. The absence of shipping may have been because of the massacre of Jap merchant ships by Allied submarines, which the POWs had heard about over the makeshift radios that some of the technicians had built in Tamuan.

With their new issue clothes now sweat-stained, torn and grimy, and the colourful straw hats battered and bent, they marched to an outlandish transit camp which consisted of unkempt three-decked open-sided bamboo huts crawling with rats. It had a stinking stream trickling through the middle and was surrounded by a high wooden fence. It was sandwiched between Havelock Road and River Valley Road. Now it is part of a city which has become a showpiece of cleanliness and the stream is a healthy free-flowing canal. In 1944 it was a rag-tag place of filth, misery and disease, and it was there that the British were joined by their Australian allies from Tamarkan on 4 July.

In common with all the other Far East POW camps, food was a constant problem for the starving inmates. Half a cup of boiled rice with a thumb-sized piece of fish was a typical River Valley Road supper, and it was not unusual for the diet to be supplemented by some grass or frogs caught in the filthy stream. The prisoners had long since grown to be skilful in the art of thieving, but at River Valley Road the guards were particularly strict about the pilfering and smuggling of extra rations. They carried out frequent searches of the ramshackle huts and the pitiful belongings of the prisoners, and any finding of 'illegal' material, even in trifling quantities, resulted in a savage beating for the 'culprits', on whose prostrate forms the blows and kicks would continue to rain long after they had lost consciousness. The condition of the three-tiered bamboo huts quickly deteriorated to the extent that they became dangerous. One night in the middle of July one of them collapsed. POW number 169, *"hyako, roku juzyu"*, Douglas Spon-Smith, Gunner 907144, Royal Artillery, and his pal Tom Pounder were lucky to have been sleeping on the top row. They crashed to the ground, but their fall was cushioned by those underneath, who were buried under a mass of bodies and the wreckage of the upper platforms. It was a miracle that nobody was killed, but a couple of dozen or so were seriously injured and taken off to Changi Hospital.

Not long after daybreak on 4 September a buzz of anticipation ran round the hellish colony. Something was afoot. And sure enough the cry was soon heard from the guards. "All men go Nippon. All men go Nippon." They were going to sail that day. At seven o'clock that morning the combined Japan Party mustered for final inspection before departure. There were 1,500 British and 718 Australians – total 2,218 apprehensive, ragged, sick and starving men. This time there was no leaving ceremony, no Japanese brass to see them off, no bowing formalities and no 'Colonel Bogey'. They just formed up into one long file and marched quietly out of that wretched place on the three-mile journey to the docks. Many of the sick, ravaged by malaria, beri-beri, dengue fever and dysentery, fell to the back of the column despite being helped along by their mates. One of the hated Korean guards took exception to this and ran up and down the line, snarling and jabbing at them, whilst friendly Chinese onlookers took the risk of passing them cool drinks.

Alongside the quay sat two sea-weary passenger-freighters, which some of the POWs themselves had been helping to load with rubber, copra and scrap iron; the *Rakuyo Maru* and the *Kachidoki Maru*. The red-balled ensign of the Jap merchant fleet hung limply from each of them, but neither of them bore any indication by way of markings on her rust streaked grey sides that she would be carrying prisoners of war, nor even a red cross for the protection of the hundreds of sick. The ships were of the same age and broadly similar in appearance, but they had started life on opposite sides of the world in 1921. The 9,500-ton *Rakuyo Maru* was born in the Mitsubishi yards in Nagasaki, but the *Kachidoki Maru*, slightly larger at 10,500 tons, had been originally launched as the *Wolverine State*, built for the United States Lines by the New York Shipbuilding Company in Camden, New Jersey. Later she was sold to Dollar Lines and re-named as the *President Harrison*. With the coming of war, she was chartered to the US Navy and had been cornered by a Japanese cruiser off the coast of China whilst carrying American sailors and marines to the Philippines. Her crew ran her onto a reef to render her useless to the Japs, but their captors managed to salvage and repair her and put her back into service as the *Kachidoki Maru*.

The ships were in the process of loading a cargo of rubber, and the long file of prisoners was directed through a large dockside ware-

162

house full of the stuff. Each man was given a block of rubber about the size of a suit-case, supposedly to be used as a life-raft if necessary. The blocks were of dense heavy raw rubber. Would they even float? One cynic said it was probably just a clever way of increasing the amount of cargo for Japan. They fell out of line on the quay, tossed down their few pathetic belongings and settled down to wait to go on board. As the morning wore on, so did the day get hotter. The sun was scorching down and they were already hungry and thirsty. At last the guards began to strut up and down, shrieking at them to get up and form into lines. They numbered off in Japanese. They had long since learned how to do this, not without the cost of more than a little pain for those who got it wrong. "*Ichi. Ni. San. Shi* . . ." ran the ripple of clipped calls down the ranks. Some Japanese officers stood on the bridge of the *Rakuyo Maru*, looking down at these proceedings. Lieutenant Yamada was among them, nodding his head approvingly.

They trudged up the gangways, prodded on their way by the pointed bamboo canes of the Korean guards; 900 British onto the *Kachidoki*, the Australians and 600 British onto the *Rakuyo*. On each ship one of the holds had been left open, the obvious intention being that the prisoners should occupy them. These dark, airless oven spaces had had wooden mezzanine decks installed in them, effectively doubling their capacity by dividing them in two horizontally. But this meant that the available air for each man would be halved, and the headroom reduced to about three feet. On the *Rakuyo Maru* nobody made a move to enter the hold, they just settled down wherever they could, on the hatch covers of the other holds, in deck lockers or under winches. But the Japs, excitable and dangerous, wanted them in the hold. Sullen and recklessly stubborn, they refused to go. It was a stand-off. The atmosphere became almost palpable. The Korean guards advanced, this time with fixed bayonets, jabbing and prodding. The POWs swore and ranted, but they were forced to back away until they were at the top of the hold companionway and eventually to yield under the weight of their own numbers. Conditions in the holds were unspeakable, as was the norm for all the Japanese prison-ships. A plate screwed to the bulkhead in *Rakuyo Maru* read, in English, "This space is designed for 187 third-class passengers." With the double deck, that gave an equivalent of 374, even if we are generous enough to ignore the airspace and headroom differences. Into that space the Japanese proceeded to pack 1,318 men, forcing them in on top of each other like inanimate cargo. If there was room to sit at all, it meant sitting with knees drawn up tightly under their chins. The sickly-sweet stink and the airless heat were overpowering. Sweat and excreta from the helpless dysentery cases, who were quite unable to make the difficult trip over the crammed limbs and bodies of their comrades to the *benjos* (toilet boxes which hung over the side of the ship), dripped from the upper wooden deck onto those below. Pounder and Spon-Smith were among the last group to cram themselves into the hellish hold of *Kachidoki Maru*. It was impossible to get down the steps without treading on a man, and once down there was a very real danger of becoming suffocated under the mass of bodies. The only light for the 900 men was from a single glimmering electric bulb. It was not powerful enough to illuminate the farthest corners of the compartment, which remained in darkness.

The senior British and Australian officers managed to arrange a conference with their captors, which included the *Rakuyo*'s captain and Lieutenant Yamada. The result was a rare victory for humanity. It was agreed that all the seriously sick cases and one-third of the 'fit' ones could remain on the open deck. The latter would be rotated in accordance with schedules drawn up by their own officers. All men topside would quietly go below in the event of stormy weather or if the ship came under attack. Any breaking of this rule and they would all be battened down for the remainder of the voyage. On the *Kachidoki* an even better deal was negotiated. All POWs were to be allowed topside during the hours of daylight once the ship had left harbour, provided they kept well for'ard, and away from No. 3 hold, which held some Japanese wounded. At night they would all be confined to the hold, with hatch open. Access to the *benjos* would be granted on request, but no queues must be allowed to form. Again, any transgression would mean an immediate end to the deal.

It was well into afternoon before the ships left their moorings and moved out into the roads where the convoy was to assemble. The Keppel Harbour was chock-a-block with ships this time. Had these been bottled up by the onslaught of American submarines? If so, it was clear that danger lay ahead.

Another day and a half passed before the convoy was ready to sail, heading north-east past the Anamba Islands and through the South China Sea towards the Formosa Strait. They had been joined by two other passenger-freighters and two tankers. The prisoners were reassured by the strength of the escort. What looked like a light cruiser was ahead of them, three frigates were on the flanks and astern and two sea-planes droned around overhead. The 'cruiser' was, in fact, the *Shikinami*, a 2,000-ton Fubuki class two-funnelled destroyer. Perhaps the POWs would have been even more reassured if they had known more about her. The Fubukis, although not structurally strong, had been easily the most powerful destroyers in the world when they were introduced around 1930. *Shikinami*, meaning 'Rolling Waves' (carried six 5-inch guns, thirty-two anti-aircraft guns of various calibres, nine 24-inch torpedo tubes and thirty-six depth charges. And when new she could steam at a blistering thirty-nine knots.

*   *   *

The FRUPAC unit at Pearl Harbor, Hawaii, housed what was the US Navy's most closely guarded operation. Armed marines patrolled outside the fence that surrounded the ordinary looking concrete Administration Building known as Station Hypo (H) in the Navy Yard, although none of them had the faintest idea of what was going on in its musty basement. The acronym stood for Fleet Radio Unit – Pacific. For the best part of twenty years a team of brilliant minds had worked there, wrestling with Japanese codes. And they had succeeded in breaking them. By 1944 over a thousand people worked at FRUPAC, intercepting, code-breaking, translating and processing a stream of secret information which guided Admiral Nimitz and General MacArthur in their tactical and strategic approach to the Pacific war. In early September a coded Japanese signal was intercepted. It revealed that an "important convoy" of six ships, plus escorts, would sail from Singapore on 6 September for Japan. They would be joined, en route, on 11 September by three more ships from Manila, plus their escorts. The signal went on to give exact details of the course the convoy would be steering, including midday positions for the ten-day voyage. No mention was made of the fact that any of the ships would be carrying POWs. Nor had there been any request for safe passage from the Japanese, which they had sometimes done on previous occasions for Red Cross or hospital ships, and which had always been honoured by Vice Admiral Charles Lockwood, commander of the US submarine fleet in the Pacific, even though it was strongly suspected that the ships in question would be carrying troops and/or war *matériel*.

In the top secret Submarine Operations Room, located in the Navy Yard over the torpedo shop, Captain W.J. 'Jasper' Holmes and Commander Richard G. Voge stood in front of the large wall-chart which consisted of a map of the Pacific theatre dotted with black magnetic shapes representing the current positions of the US submarines on patrol. Holmes, a veteran submariner, had been specially delegated by Lockwood to receive such signals. Voge had already made several patrols in command of USS *Sailfish*, early in the war, before being appointed as Lockwood's Operations Officer. Both of these men possessed an encyclopaedic knowledge of the Japanese navy. They plotted the course of the convoy on the map from the information revealed by the unscrambled signal. It would be sailing north-east through the South China Sea towards the Formosa Strait. On the way, it would be passing through an area code-named by the Americans as 'Convoy College', off the north-west coast of Luzon, the main island of the Philippines. And there were three US submarine wolf-packs already lurking there. Each pack had been given a code name based on the name of its commander. They were 'Ben's Busters', 'Dunc's Devils' and 'Ed's Eradicators'.

Voge immediately set to work on formulating a plan of attack. All three packs had one boat absent from the scene, reducing their strength from three boats each to two. The Busters and the Devils had sent *Sealion II* and *Spadefish* away to Saipan, in the Marianas, to re-load with torpedoes, and *Tunny* of the Eradicators, which had been damaged by Japanese bombers, was limping back to Pearl Harbor for repairs. He decided to send two of the packs, the Busters and the Eradicators, to string their four boats out along the course of the convoy. The Busters, with *Growler* and *Pampanito*, would have first strike, whilst the Eradicators, with *Barb* and *Queenfish*, would lie in wait farther along the course, about seventy miles to the north-east, to sweep up any escapees from the main attack. Before going into the attack the boats would rendezvous at 2200 hours on 11 September, plumb in the middle of the South China Sea, at 115° East, 18°40' North, at which point they would be as far as possible away from any shore-based Japanese aircraft at Hong Kong, Luzon or Hainan Island. Meantime *Sealion II*, now with a full load of torpedoes, would make all possible speed back from the Marianas, hopefully to rejoin the Busters in time for the action.

166

Voge's encoded orders were received by the submarines on the night of 9/10 September. *Growler* was carrying out a surface patrol of the north-west coast of Luzon and was the nearest boat to the rendezvous point. It was a dangerous place to be, with the Japanese in the process of reinforcing the island's defences as the threat of invasion steadily increased with each US victory in the Pacific. But the submarine's low silhouette and grey camouflage blended perfectly with the sea. She was well-nigh invisible. Her skipper, Commander T.B. 'Ben' Oakley, was a thirty-two-year-old New Yorker. He had been on four fruitless patrols as a junior officer before being given his own command, *Tarpon*, which was one of the US Navy's older boats. He had taken over *Growler* in April 1944 after her previous commander, Howard Gilmore, had sacrificed his life for the sake of his crew and his boat by crying "Take her down!" as he lay fatally wounded on the bridge. Oakley now had command of a famous boat and was only too aware that Gilmore would be a hard act to follow. His first patrol in *Growler* had produced just one minor scalp – a 2,000-tonner named *Katori Maru*. In the course of the war so far he had sailed thousands of miles and could show just that one 2,000-ton bucket and a frigate as trophies. He received the orders from Pearl Harbor with relish. There was no doubt that Ben Oakley was ready.

Pampanito was 300 miles away to the east. Her captain, Commander P.E. 'Paul' Summers, the thirty-one-year-old son of a Tennessee dentist, was the most junior skipper in the pack. For all his junior status, he was well experienced, having made no less than seven patrols in *Stingray*, albeit unproductive ones. This, his first patrol in command, had fallen to him when he was promoted in *Pampanito* to take over from a skipper who, in Pearl Harbor's eyes, was unsuited for the task ahead. Now, after two patrols in *Pampanito*, Summers himself was acquiring a reputation as an aloof, unaggressive captain who did not communicate well with his juniors. On the first patrol the boat had nearly been lost under a deluge of depth-charges after making an ill-conducted attack on a minor convoy in the Marianas. On the second sortie a Jap submarine had sent two torpedoes so close that they almost shaved *Pampanito*'s flanks. To make matters worse, on 30 August in going in to attack a convoy in the Bashi Channel, between Luzon and Formosa, Summers had taken the boat on an entirely wrong course and had consequently missed the main action. He was in serious danger of losing the confidence of his crew. In fact, some had already left. Now, on his third patrol in command, he steered west towards the rendezvous at a surface speed of seventeen knots.

Meantime, *Sealion II* spent the entire day of 10 September hurrying westwards from the Marianas, making seventeen knots on the surface. Her skipper, Commander Eli Reich (pronounced 'rich'), the thirty-one-year-old son of a New York policeman, had fired nineteen of his twenty-four torpedoes in the action of 30 August, hence his hasty 1,300-mile trip back to Saipan to re-load and re-fuel. A quiet mild-mannered devout Catholic, he was possessed of a calm but ruthless 'academic' type of aggression. Reich was not without connections. His wife, Jacqueline, was an aide to none other than the Navy Secretary himself, James V. Forrestal. *Sealion II* made the Philippines that same evening and, under cover of darkness, Reich worked his way through the strongly patrolled Babuyan Islands off the northern tip of Luzon, a highly dangerous manoeuvre, to slip into the South China Sea and head for the rendezvous.

By 2130 on the 11th both Summers and Reich had made contact with *Growler*, which had lain in wait submerged. By 2230 Oakley had given them their orders by megaphone and they had formed themselves into line abreast for the attack; *Growler* taking the central position, with *Sealion II* eight miles to port and *Pampanito* eight miles to starboard. Oakley ordered a course of 213 which would bring them into direct contact with the oncoming convoy, which the decoded signal had revealed would be on a course of 033. It was a dark cloudy night, but visibility was fair, with a sliver of moon due in about four hours' time. The wind was light, about Force 3. It was a good night for submariners to go hunting.

It was an hour past midnight when *Growler* made the first radar contact with the convoy. It was dead ahead, fifteen miles away. Oakley's course 213 had proved to be spot on. Twenty minutes later *Sealion II* picked it up too, and five minutes after that so did *Pampanito*. Reich recorded that there appeared to be "at least nine large vessels and an uncertain number of smaller escort vessels". At a closing speed of well over twenty knots, there was no time for delay. *Growler*'s crew went to battle stations. Oakley lined up on a big tanker in the middle column of the convoy. The forward torpedomen waited, with their six tubes primed for action. Oakley was on the point of firing when suddenly he noticed that one of the escort destroyers was hurtling towards them. They had been spotted, without doubt. "Check fire! Check fire! New target!" he shouted. The destroyer was now less than a mile away. The muzzles of its two twin-barrelled forward guns jutted menacingly. At 0154 precisely, at the almost point-blank range of 1,150 yards, Oakley fired three of his forward tubes and swung the boat hard to port, bringing his stern tubes to bear if they were needed. In this he had made another contribution to naval history. It was the first and only time that a bow to bow 'down the throat' surface attack would be made by a US submarine. It was a very dangerous thing to attempt. Afterwards, some critics labelled it foolhardy. Presented with only the narrowest of targets, the chances of a direct hit were slim. If this failed, there was the near certainty of being rammed. On the other hand, if the destroyer saw the torpedoes streaking towards it, and tried to avoid them by turning, the chances were that one of them would hit it. It needed a mere forty-nine seconds' wait for Oakley to know which way the game had gone. The destroyer blew up with a mighty flash of an explosion and heeled over. Oakley and his crew breathed more easily, but they were not yet out of danger, because the blazing wreck of the Jap ship was still under way, floating almost broadside, and heading straight towards them. It was now so close that Oakley could feel the heat of the flames. He saw a "horde of Japs" swarming onto its superstructure to try to jump clear. It was just 200 yards away when it plunged to the bottom of the South China Sea. And that was the end of 'Rolling Waves', IJNS *Shikinami*.

To her credit, she had seldom been idle throughout the war and had seen much action. From December 1941 until February 1942 she had been on constant troop convoy and carrier escort duties in the Java Sea. It was *Shikinami* which fired the final torpedo which sank the USS *Houston* (CA-30) at the Battle of Sunda Strait on 1 March 1942. She was at the Battle of Midway, 4/5 June 1942, the Battle of the Eastern Solomons on 24 August and on 12 October the Battle of Cape Esperance. She was on stand-by for the Battle of Santa Cruz on 26 October and spent 12–15 November in the naval battles for Guadalcanal, which had become almost a second home to her, having made countless runs to the place on transport escort duty. 1–4 March 1943 saw her at the Battle of the Bismarck Sea, where she not only managed to escape damage from intense bombing attacks by Allied aircraft but was able to rescue Rear-Admiral Masatomi and others from her sinking sister, the *Shirayuki*. Since then she had had little respite, busily hopping around the islands of the East Indies on escort work. On 19 July 1944 on the way to Singapore where she would to pick up the POW convoy, she had rescued survivors from the torpedoed light cruiser *Oi*. Now 'Rolling Waves' herself had gone, taking her captain, Takahashi, with her. The only evidence that she had ever existed were a few flames still flickering on the surface and the bobbing heads of her 128 survivors waiting to be rescued by the frigate *Mikura*.

Now that the presence of American subs was known to the convoy, they needed to work fast if the attack was to be fruitful. Oakley saw that there were two freighters, both now in sight of his stern tubes. He let them have four torpedoes and quietly noted three hits, although neither ship was sunk. But one of the escort frigates now came surging towards *Growler*, firing 4-inch shells as it came. Then another joined the attack. Oakley turned away, zig-zagging furiously, at nineteen knots. Gradually, he was able to pull away from the slower frigates. By 0225 he had lost them, and secured from battle stations. It had been a busy hour's work.

On the bridge of *Sealion II* Eli Reich saw and heard the results of *Growler*'s torpedo attacks. By 0230 the moon had started to rise and the convoy had closed to about three and a half miles. He decided it was time to go into the attack and sidled in to within 3,000 yards, picking out a large tanker at the head of the port column for his first target. He fired two from his bow tubes, but the second one ran crazily off target. There was a serious fault with the gyro setter. There was nothing to do but turn away, repair the problem and then resume the attack. But even as he gave the order to do so, two escort frigates came charging towards the submarine, spitting shells from their forward guns. Reich turned hard to port and the chase began, just as it had with *Growler* only minutes before. Likewise, *Sealion II* had longer legs than the Japanese frigates and was able to gain safety to secure and re-load her tubes.

Summers, in *Pampanito*, was about to have another embarrassing time. He had completely wrong guessed which way the convoy would swing after Oakley's initial attack. At 0300, he realized that for the past half-hour he had been chasing shadows. Worse still, he was now between the Japanese ships and the moon. The silhouette of *Pampanito* would be clearly visible to any sharp lookout. He turned south-west to bring the boat round to the port quarter of the convoy. If he could not get into a reasonable position to attack soon, the first streaks of dawn would be breaking through and, now that the Japs had been alerted, daylight could well bring an air attack with it. All in all, the first act of the drama had produced unimpressive results for the Americans. By 0500 Eli Reich had worked *Sealion II* to a position five miles off the starboard bow of the convoy, which was now heading north-westerly towards Hainan Island. There was only about half an hour to go before broad daylight. To be safe, he dived to periscope depth and selected a tanker and a large freighter as his targets. *Pampanito*'s crew, too, were at battle stations, now dead ahead of the convoy, also at periscope depth.

At a range of 2,500 yards and closing, Reich fired three of his six forward tubes at the tanker, then swung to port to target the freighter and let it have the other three Mark XIV steam torpedoes, each loaded with nearly 700 lbs of hyped-up TNT. The tanker exploded in one single roar, throwing an enormous mountain of flame high into the tropical dawn. Burning oil spewed from her to spread all around in great lakes of fire. (There was some dispute about the identity of this ship. Japanese records showed it to have been an 8,400-ton passenger-freighter, *Nankai Maru*, but that does not agree with several eye-witnesses, who insisted that it was a tanker. Indeed, there is some evidence which suggests that Reich hit two ships with his first salvo, which then collided with each other.) Reich's second salvo scored two hits out of three. One torpedo crashed into the bows of the freighter, the other caught her in the engine-room. But she did not sink, thanks to the cargo of raw rubber which had been crammed into her holds in Singapore. She was the *Rakuyo Maru*.

The convoy scattered and escort frigates began scurrying back and forth, furiously throwing depth-charges into the sea and firing their guns. Reich dived, to take his boat deep to safety. And once again Summers was frustrated. He had been in a perfect position to attack the leading ships and had been on the point of firing when the sky lit up with flames and pandemonium broke loose. He had not even known that Reich was there. Ever cautious, he chose not to pursue the fleeing freighters. There would be another day.

*   *   *

Hundreds of scantily clad sunburnt POWs lay on the exposed for'ard deck of the *Rakuyo Maru*. Most of them were asleep, or trying to sleep, with their thin undernourished bodies stretched out wherever a space could be found. Suddenly there was a tremendous bang and a huge sheet of flame shot up into the sky, no more than half a mile away to starboard. The noise woke the sleeping men. Those who could clambered to their feet to peer at the pyre of the *Shikinami*. Somebody shouted down the hatch to the hundreds more men in the hold, "They've hit one of the destroyers . . . It's on fire and listing . . . It's sunk!" Alarm bells began to ring all over the prison-ship. The Japanese guards and crew panicked wildly, rushing back and forth, excitedly shouting to each other. Within moments, some of them were actually sitting in the lifeboats. Reaction among the prisoners was mixed. Some of them lined the starboard rail and began cheering, elated at the thought that rescue could at last be close at hand. Others were terrified, realizing that their presence on board was not known to the attacking submarines. They were convinced that the hell-ship would be sunk by their Allies. Then the Japanese guards remembered the deal they had struck in Singapore. In the event of enemy action, all men were to go below. The guards, now calmer, advanced with rifles and bayonets to drive their reluctant captives down into the hold and out of sight.

On *Kachidoki Maru* there was a near disaster. In the confusion following the explosion of the *Shikinami*, with the convoy hurrying to scatter, a large tanker came swarming towards the prison ship. *Kachidoki*'s siren blew a sequence of short warning blasts and she turned hard to port. But it was too late. The tanker caught her on the starboard bow and, with a thunderous grating rumble, ran along her complete length, throwing up a mountainous cascade of sparks and slivers of burnt paint which showered all over the crowd of POWs on deck. *Kachidoki* heeled over at an alarming angle, some said 45°, and continued rocking until she had righted herself, while the POWs hung on to anything they could grab.

When Reich's second salvo hit the *Rakuyo Maru* in the forward hold, it caused her to duck her bows under her own impetus. This sent an avalanche of sea-water rushing over the fo'c's'le. The POWs, now back on deck and mostly awake, were caught by surprise. Many were knocked off their feet. For a moment several thought they would drown, being unsure as to whether the ship was still even underneath them. One Australian was washed all the way from the point of the bows back to the bridge structure. It was a miracle that many were not swept clean over the side. In the hold, there was a moment of panic when the water came pouring through the open hatch. There was a chaotic scramble for the ladder, with men screaming, "Let me get out!" as they pushed and fought with each other. But as soon as it was realized that they were not going down order was restored. They had been lucky. The torpedo had hit on the for'ard side of the bulkhead between 1 Hold and their 2 Hold and the cargo of rubber had absorbed much of the shock.

The *Rakuyo Maru* settled down about twelve feet at the bow, with a distinct list to starboard, and drifted out of control. Nevertheless, the Japs decided to abandon ship. They lowered away the ten lifeboats on the boat-deck. Some of the POWs rushed towards the boats, but guards with tommy-guns prevented them from getting too near. But that did not stop some of them. One jumped into a small blue rowing-boat, which held the ship's captain. The POW, a furious Sydneysider called Tommy Moxham, saw that the boat was still tied to the ship, so he snatched the captain's samurai sword and severed the rope with one swipe. Then he turned round and heaved the captain straight over the side, and reached down to hold him under until he drowned. Then he swarmed up a Jacob's ladder to go back on board the *Rakuyo*. Two more Australians found themselves in another rowing-boat with two Jap officers in full dress uniform with long swords. The officers ordered them to row, which they started to do, but at a given word they capsized the boat and drowned the Japs. On board there were many acts of revenge against their captors. They had waited a long time for this. One big Digger picked up a sword and hacked about six Japs into pieces, another strangled a Japanese officer and then chopped a few more up with a sword. A gang of POWs went for'ard and killed the bow deck gun crew. Big Frank McGrath, of the Australian 2nd Pioneer Corps, picked up a baulk of timber and laid into some Japs as they came up a ladder. He decked about four of them. Then two of his mates threw them into the sea. After only a few minutes most of the Japanese had either fled in the boats or been killed. McGrath, now in the water, himself strangled two of them. He was in the process of throttling a third, but the man pulled him under. Neither of them re-surfaced. Only a small number of Japs now remained on board *Rayuko Maru*. These men assumed an amazing change of attitude. As if by magic, they were suddenly friendly towards the POWs.

With the twin dangers of another torpedo striking the helpless *Rayuko*, plus the possibility of her drifting into collision with one of the still fiercely burning ships close by, the safest place seemed to be in the sea itself. Life-jackets were in very short supply and the lumps of raw rubber which the Japs had issued in Singapore had proved, as suspected, totally useless. There were about sixty small wooden rafts, each about the size of a billiards table. Anything else that would float followed; furniture from the dining-hall, oil-drums, a staircase, packing boxes and a hen coop. Even the wooden *benjos* were unlashed from the ship's sides and let fall into the sea. Seeing that there was no immediate likelihood of the ship sinking, some of the POWs took the view that it would be prudent to stock up on supplies before departing. Raiding the galley and cabins, they found sake and cigarettes, cakes and cigars, beans, bread, sugar, various types of tinned food, and even great fistfuls of Japanese money. But most important of all, there were some kegs of fresh water. This was the first time in years that they had had access to such bounty. They gorged themselves on cakes, guzzled water and had a quiet smoke before setting off.

Soon there was a line of bobbing heads and assorted 'rafts' stretching away from the *Rakuyo*. There was a firm current running, which fortunately was carrying them away from it as well as from the burning wrecks of the others and the patches of fire on the sea. In the water the deadly business of 'account settling' continued. There was a Japanese officer trying to swim with a couple of samurai swords and a clutch of water canteens round his neck. He asked some POWs, very politely, if he could board their raft. They pushed his head under the water and held it there until he ceased struggling. Rafts, each paddled Indian style by upwards of a dozen bloodthirsty POWs with bits of wood or bamboo, or even bare hands, raced to head off those full of terrified Japanese. But some of the POWs, having given some thought to their chances of survival, took a Jap or two on board their rafts as 'hostages'. This meant that they were less likely to be machine-gunned when the Jap rescue ships arrived. By 0600 there were over 1,200 men in the water and the straggly line of bobbing objects met the horizon.

Ben Oakley, in *Growler*, had been making his way back to the scene of action as fast as he could after eluding the chasing Japanese frigate. It was nearly 0630 when he first saw the two burning ships. He dived, to avoid being seen, and went to battle stations. Almost immediately he saw one of the escort frigates through his periscope. Lining up his target, he let it have six Mark XVIII electric torpedoes from his bow tubes and dived deep. The Growlers, lying doggo, listened to a whole range of bangs and crackles, some very loud, others more distant. But they were not explosions of depth-charges intended to destroy the submarine. They were the sinking frigate *Hirado*'s own depth-charges exploding within her.

This all took place within the sight of the POWs on the rafts. Oakley, of course, had no idea that they were there at all. Another frigate stormed over to attack *Growler* with several depth-charges, but she had obviously made no sonar contact because she was very far off the mark. Coupled with *Hirado*'s explosions, this wild attack created huge shock waves in the surrounding water, the effect of which on the POWs in the sea was terrifying. One said that it felt like his stomach was being squeezed into his throat. The tremendous concussions caused many of them to vomit blood and evacuate their bowels at the same time, which probably caused, or at least hastened. the deaths of several. Still unaware of the POWs' plight, Oakley sat quietly at 350 feet for the rest of the morning, then cleared off to the east, still submerged towards the rendezvous point.

With full daylight came a pale yellow sun. It shone on a ghastly scene. The two burning ships still sat on the smooth, oil-covered sea, smoking sullenly. *Rakuyo Maru* had sunk still lower in the water and was drifting helplessly with the current amid oil-drums, wooden planks and all the other floating litter from the drama. And in the water itself were many hundreds of men, each clutching desperately at something which floated, some with horrifying burns and injuries, and all struggling to steer clear of the oil, patches of which were still aflame. The shock of the depth-charges had weakened them severely, and exposure, thirst, the salt and the oil had also taken their toll. They kept clustered together as far as possible, and were in two main masses; one with perhaps 900 men and the other with about 300. But the two groups had drifted far apart and, being low in the Water, were now out of sight of each other. Many of those with still enough strength to paddle a raft or swim, seeing that the *Rakuyo* was still afloat, decided to go back on board to search for food and water. They were surprised to find that many men had not left the ship at all. These were making rafts and trying to launch one of the lifeboats which the Japanese had left behind. They managed to get it into the water with difficulty, and with about sixty in it and another seventy-five hanging onto it, they headed for some of the Japanese lifeboats. The hope was that when the rescue ships came for the Japs, they too would be picked up. By noon the flaming sun was like a furnace. Many of the POWs were bare-headed, having lost their hats or bandannas. And all were being mercilessly scorched by the rays and the salt. The two burning ships had finally sunk, but the rubber-stuffed *Rakuyo Maru* still obstinately refused to die. Wallowing in the water, lopsided and awkward, she was the only ship in sight.

*   *   *

Sealion II and *Pampanito* had been pre-occupied with playing mouse to the escort frigates' cat whilst at the same time trying to keep track of their own target, the convoy, and await their chance to make another attack. The tracks of both the hunters and the hunted now criss-crossed over many square miles of the South China Sea. Towards noon Summers, in *Pampanito*, suddenly lost the convoy from his radar screen. Was he about to miss yet another opportunity to redeem the reputation of his luckless boat and bring more humiliation to his exasperated crew? By fully extending his periscope whilst on the surface, he was able to broaden his range of sight by eye to the fullest. After half an hour's sweeping the horizon a smudge of smoke was spotted. It was the convoy, or rather the survivors of it. Summers relaxed and broke radio silence to inform the other Busters of the Japanese ships' position and its westerly course. He was going to shadow them, out of sight on their starboard side, and await nightfall.

Reich, in *Sealion II*, was surprised to receive this information, but he was sure that it was unreliable. He had been heading on a north-easterly course, which he was convinced would put him in an ideal position for attack as the convoy neared the Formosa Strait, and that fresh contact with it was imminent. And so he carried on north-eastwards at speed on the surface, vainly hoping to head off ships which, in fact, were sailing in almost the opposite direction far behind him. He was now drawing near to the position where the Eradicators, *Barb* and *Queenfish*, neither of whom were aware that there had been any action at all, were waiting to act as long-stops. They saw *Sealion II* as she tore past them, but neither she nor they made any radio contact. Reich did not see them and they assumed that he had received orders to operate independently.

Eighty miles to the west, Summers continued to dog the four remaining ships of the convoy. By mid-afternoon it looked as if they were heading for the safety of Hong Kong. Once they made it there,

Summers would have missed yet another shot. He dived and made ready to attack, but as he did so the Japanese altered course back towards Hainan Island. He stood his crew down from battle stations and resumed tracking. It would have to be a night surface attack after all. By now he must have been seething with frustration.

*　　*　　*

All day, as the creaking carcass of the *Rakuyo Maru* slowly settled itself down, inch by inch, into the South China Sea, gangs of POWs scrambled aboard to scavenge for anything which might improve their chances of survival. They made more rafts from hatch-boards, bundles of bamboo, oil-drums and cork mats. They found clothing, whisky, cigarettes, food and water. By late afternoon, though, it was clear that she was going. The last raft-load had paddled only about a hundred yards from her when she gave a long tired hiss as the remaining air was forced out of her and then went quietly on her way to the bottom, 6,000 feet below. The *Rakuyo Maru*, or 'Falling Leaves', had finally fallen.

Almost immediately some Japanese ships appeared on the scene – two frigates and a merchantman. Never would the POWs have admitted, only hours before, that they would ever be pleased to see a Japanese again for the rest of their lives. But having clung to the fine threads of life all day, covered in oil, caked in salt, blackened by the sun, ravenously thirsty and hungry, and many suffering from wounds, burns, sickness and sheer exhaustion, the hate in their hearts was forgotten for the moment. Rescue was at hand. That was the main thing now. The frigates quietly sniffed their way through the oil and debris on the water, like hounds in a rubbish dump, and came to a stop by the cluster of lifeboats. These were, of course, manned mainly by the Japanese survivors, but there was also the boat which had been launched by the group of Australians who had gone back on board and who had hoped that by joining the Jap group they would increase their chances of rescue. Dozens of others now approached the frigates, paddling rafts or swimming. But the Jap sailors would only allow their own countrymen to come aboard. Any POW who tried to climb up was pushed or cudgelled away. The Japanese captains were in a hurry to vacate the area. They did not want to expose their ships to a torpedo attack from any submarines still lurking around. They did not even bother to recover any of the boats, just their own people in them. One of the frigate captains came to the rail with a megaphone and called to the furious cursing men in the water, "Goodbye!" With that, the ships steamed away towards the main mass of men, about a mile away. Some of these rafts, it will be remembered, held a few Japanese as 'bait' for rescue. But that was a vain hope. Jap sailors manned the rails of the frigates and pointed guns at the POWs to hold them off, while their own people were picked up. On one raft they held their Jap hostage down out of sight with his mouth gagged. After the ships had left they beat him to death, leaving him soaked in blood. British ex-coal miner Wilf 'Barney' Barnett said, "Some of our lot were dying of thirst. I watched them drink his blood. It was horrible." As the frigates turned away, they performed one last despicable act of inhumanity. They swung round hard and tore deliberately through the middle of the bunched island of rafts and wreckage. Men were washed up high on the bow-waves to fall helplessly back into the water. Without doubt, several more met their end at that point.

There was a rush to claim places back on a raft or one of the now empty lifeboats. Night was beginning to fall and the sea was getting up. Those in the boats rowed around picking up as many men as they could find. Desperate shouts of "Over here! Over here!" rent the darkness. But many were missed. In all, the lifeboats picked up about 350 men, but that still left over 1,000 bodies stranded in the middle of the South China Sea. One Australian recalled, "The last thing I saw that night was a bloke on the horizon, standing on a raft, all by himself."

After the ramming by the frigates many men lost their will to live. Some of them had been through the hell of Dunkirk, then survived the horrors of the Death Railway and River Valley Road, only now to encounter more inexpressible barbarism. For some it was the last straw. They simply put their heads down and died. Then something happened which made an unforgettable impression on those who witnessed it. Wafting across the dark water came a deep singing voice. Soon it was joined by hundreds of others, loud, throaty and defiant: *"Rule Britannia, Britannia rule the waves. Britons never, never, never shall be slaves . . ."*

*   *   *

Pampanito had been dragged uncomfortably close to the south China coast by the convoy. By early evening, she was only a few minutes flying time from Hainan Island and Summers had had to dive several times to avoid being seen by patrolling aircraft. This did not make it any easier for the Americans to shadow their prey and at 1955 hours the worst happened. They lost radar contact with it. The submarine's officers were now growing angry at the repeatedly missed chances to attack the enemy. Summers thought hard. The convoy's intended destination was Japan, in the opposite direction to Hainan. What would he do in the place of the Japanese commodore? He decided that he would not go to Hainan at all, but head for Hong Kong 300 miles nearer to home, re-group, and then make a run for it, clinging to the coast of China all the way under a land-based air shield. He altered course to the north-east, towards Hong Kong, and just over an hour later radar contact was regained. The Japanese ships were dead ahead, fifteen miles distant. Summers had been wrong, but for once he had been lucky! The convoy was indeed still headed for Hainan, not Hong Kong, but he had picked up the tail of one of its zig-zags. He closed with them at speed on the surface.

There they were, the *Kachidoki Maru* with three good-sized freighters and, as far as he could see, four escorts. They were making about eleven knots and zig-zagging on a mean course of 280. It was a perfect night; no moon, a very calm sea and just a few low flat clouds, making for good visibility. Summers planned his attack straight out of the book – all ten torpedo tubes, six for'ard then four stern, in two salvoes. *Pampanito* ran in fast for the kill. But then, more almost unbelievable catastrophe! The for'ard torpedomen had just flooded the tubes, prior to opening the outer doors, when the torpedo jammed in number four tube. Its propellers were whirring hysterically. If it had armed itself and exploded, it would have sent them all to Kingdom Come in an instant. The Torpedo Officer, Lieutenant Ted Swain, who had not been hesitant in voicing his criticisms of Summers' tactics, and Torpedoman Jim Behney, raced to deal with the crisis. It was only Behney's colossal strength which saved the day. He broke the linkage to the No. 4 Tube rudder setter, which freed the gyro controls to the other five tubes. Only a minute later Summers fired them – five Mark XVIII electrics, range two miles – then swung hard to starboard to bring his stern tubes into play.

It was good shooting. Six of the nine torpedoes found their mark – two in *Kachidoki Maru*, two in one of the freighters and one each in the other two. Summers pulled away to observe and record the results. *Kachidoki Maru* and one of the freighters had already sunk. Another was incandescent with crimson fire and the fourth could not been seen through the curtain of smoke, although it had certainly been hit. At last they had thrown off the ignominious nickname of the 'Peaceful Pamp'.

It being after sunset when the torpedo struck, most of the 900 British POWs on *Kachidoki* were below, confined to Number 2 hold, as per the deal which had been made before sailing from Singapore. Tom Pounder and Doug Spon-Smith and a few dozen others were still hiding on the upper deck, strictly against orders. It was a fine calm evening and they had been enjoying the cool air after the day's hot sun. Suddenly the guards started screaming and shouting at each other. Then there was a muffled thud. It seemed to come from the far after-end of the ship, but it was strong enough to make the deck shudder beneath their feet. Seconds later came another thud, this time from somewhere amidships. They knew instantly that the *Kachidoki Maru* had been torpedoed. One or two of them crept down the ladders into the darkness of the hold to warn their mates, quietly, so as not to spark off a panic stampede to escape. Amazingly, they found that many of them were annoyed at being disturbed, saying that they simply did not believe it, and the noise was only depth-charges exploding somewhere near. But then the engines stopped and an officer shouted, superfluously, for calm. The ship had, in fact, been torpedoed, but was not sinking, he assured them. How wrong he was. And thanks to this wrongful information, valuable minutes were to be lost which cost men their lives.

In the traditional British fashion, orderly queues were formed at the foot of the ladders and men started to climb quietly out onto the deck. But the *Kachidoki was* sinking fast, and as soon as this was realized the scramble started. Many of the helplessly sick were trapped in the hold. Others found it impossible to escape because the ship had settled so quickly and so far by the stern that the ladders were lying aback. The men on deck rushed to cut loose the life-rafts and throw them over the side along with anything else that would float. A frantic search for life-jackets and water-bottles started. The orderly queues quickly melted away and those who could were now fighting to get out of the hold. It was every man for himself. Those who made it to the upper deck were jumping into the water forty odd feet below, plummeting down in their dozens, whether they could swim or not. Doug Spon-Smith was one of those who could not. His mate Pounder was a strong swimmer and leapt in without hesitation, but Doug 'froze' for a few seconds on the rail before making the plunge. He rose to the surface, spluttering. He had lost his shorts and his eyes were stinging with oil. There was no sign of his friend. Somehow he thrashed his way towards a raft. There were about two dozen men on it already, including six unarmed Japanese soldiers. The Japs knew they were heavily outnumbered and were wisely keeping their mouths shut. Indeed, scarcely a word was spoken as he dragged himself aboard. He had been lucky.

The sea was like a frothing cauldron, churned into a boiling phosphorescent lake by hundreds of struggling bodies. The *Kachidoki*'s forward deck gun rolled back with a loud rumble and crashed down the hatch on those trying to get out of the hold, together with several other pieces of deck equipment which had become unshipped. It will never be known how many were killed by this, or how many failed to escape from the hell of Number 2 hold. The Japanese were still shrieking and rushing about. One of their officers was shooting his own badly wounded men next door in Number 3 hold with his revolver rather than leave them to drown. And on the bridge the anguished captain shot himself.

Some were killed in the water by rafts and other objects being thrown overboard from above. One man said that he knew he had killed another by falling straight onto his head when he jumped. "I looked for him, but he never came back up," he said. Another rose towards the surface with bursting lungs after being sucked down by the ship to find that he was jammed under a raft. He said afterwards that he had ceased to struggle, was feeling pleasantly drowsy and was almost done for, when some semi-conscious instinct made him roll over to freedom and fresh air, where he trod water, gasping and spluttering and vomiting a mixture of sea-water, oil and his supper of rice.

Somebody shouted, "She's going!" And she was. She now sat bolt upright in the water, pointing her bows directly at the sky. Then she slid slowly backwards, to disappear with a final shuddering rumble, amid a vortex of giant bubbles. Only sixteen minutes before she had been steaming along at eleven knots, bound for Hainan Island.

Probably around 300 British POWs and 400 Japanese crew, wounded soldiers and passengers have the *Kachidoki Maru* as their tomb, 360 feet down on the bottom of the South China Sea, in 19°18' north, 111°53' east.

The oil that spewed from *Kachidoki*'s fractured tanks caused extreme discomfort for the many hundreds of men, both POWs and Japanese, in the sea. It floated like a thick, black duvet on top of the water and many of them were unlucky enough to drift into it. Immediately, it turned hair into a solid cake, clogged ears and noses, stung and blinded eyes, and, if swallowed, caused violent vomiting. Soon most of their bodies were coated with the stuff. Some died and their otherwise near-naked bodies were floating in the sea wearing a black oily shroud. However, the oil did make for some blessings. It helped to calm the water, (the wind was getting up), it helped to keep them warm, and it made them all more buoyant. Most important of all, it was probably the oil which deterred any major attacks by sharks, which usually proliferate in that area. Indeed, there was no official reporting of any injuries by sharks among either the *Rakuyo* or *Kachidoki* survivors, although Eric Halfhide did recall seeing instances where sharks were snatching at men's legs.

Places on rafts and in lifeboats were at a premium. So rapid had been the sinking that only a few lifeboats had got away and these were occupied mainly by armed Japanese who defied the POWs to try to board them. One Britisher did manage to clamber aboard a lifeboat full of Japanese, but as soon as he did there was the flash of a knife and the POW fell dead with a blade embedded in his back. Otherwise, the oil-covered POWs clung to rafts or whatever floating object was available. Six were on an upturned table, three were on a big section of broken wooden deckhead, one of whom was a Japanese soldier keeping the other two at a safe distance with his rifle, two were on a *benjo*, one of whom had a shattered leg, six were taking turns to lean on a hatch-board which would only support two at a time, twelve more were doing the same with a makeshift raft, seven others were crowded on a small raft, one of whom was a Japanese officer. They pushed him off and held him under. Two were riding on top of a crazily rocking galvanised tank of some sort. It was a scene of extreme desperation.

One POW, George Huitson, was fortunate to find a raft with room to spare. Luckily for him, it held some Japanese soldiers, and one sailor, who did not object to him joining them. They seemed subdued. Their officer sat looking miserable all night, but the sailor was surprisingly cheerful. He turned to an amazed Huitson and quoted Nelson's signal in perfect English, *"England expects every man to do his duty."*

*　　*　　*

The *Rakuyo Maru* POWs in lifeboats drifted some way from those on rafts and bits of flotsam during the night. Three of the boats grouped themselves together under the natural leadership of Vic Duncan, one of the *Perth* sailors. They had only a limited supply of over-cooked rice scrapings and some water, but with the aid of makeshift sails fashioned out of blankets, Duncan reckoned that they could make the China coastline, about 200 miles away, in about a week.

Another little flotilla of six boats was commanded by a senior Australian officer, fifty-year-old Brigadier Arthur Varley. Varley had been incarcerated in Tamarkan along with his son, John, but the Japs had not selected the younger man for the Japan party. This group had drifted farther still away from the main body, until it was almost out of sight, apparently heading eastwards for the Philippines. They were never seen again. None of them regained Allied-held territory. None of them were ever reported by the Japanese as recaptured POWs.

As for those in the water, their terrible ordeal continued, bringing with it more horrors than they would ever have imagined. Coated in oil, caked with burning salt and roasted by the glaring tropical sun, their thirst tormented them to the limit of endurance. "Whatever you do, don't drink salt water!" some of the sailors among them had warned, time and again. But by the second day dozens of them had given way to the temptation and gulped it down.

The results were predictable. Madness overcame them. Some suffered from hallucinations. "I'm just going to that island over there to get some grub," said one, pointing at the empty sea. With that he swam a couple of strokes and sank out of sight. Another announced that he was going to milk his cows, dived off and disappeared in the same way. Others raved crazily, completely out of their minds. Vicious fights broke out as different groups tried to push each other off rafts. One lunatic grabbed another and bit his neck to drink his blood. Two men fought over a small fish that one had caught. They struggled violently in the water until their strength expired and both went under. Future author, POW Ernest Fieldhouse, swam to a raft and asked for water. A strong pair of hands grabbed him and pushed him under the water. He managed to free himself after a tussle, but was horrified to look up and see a man with mad staring bloodshot eyes and foam dribbling from his mouth and snot-filled nostrils. Some drank their own urine, which had the same unhingeing effect on their brains. Eric Halfhide collected a few drops in his cupped hands to moisten his cracked lips. He said that he had never tasted anything so repugnant in all his life.

Dawn on the 13th found the oil-coated *Kachidoki* survivors cold and miserable, clinging to bits of wreckage and rafts. At bayonet and knife-point from the Japs, a team of POWs had just heaved with all their strength on ropes attached to the capsized lifeboat to bring it back upright. The Japs had then piled in and were about to make off in it when two rescue frigates appeared. Astonishingly, it picked up about 200 POWs as well as Japanese. Then a trawler came along and about another 150 were hauled out of the water. Among them was Tom Pounder. But this still left 200-odd behind. Among them was Spon-Smith. Neither friend knew at that stage what had happened to the other. The blessing was that there were now two empty lifeboats and much more room on the rafts.

The frigates and the trawler headed for Hainan, with the POWs huddled together on the fo'c's'les to keep warm, like "a load of monkeys". Even more astonishingly, they were treated kindly, and given rice and water. It was insipid fare, but it was better than nothing. They had survived. They were alive. But what was to happen next? The following morning, the lookouts in Vic Duncan's *Rakuyo* lifeboats spotted smoke on the horizon. Then they heard several long bursts of what sounded like the rattle of distant machine-gun fire. Soon three Japanese escort sloops hove into view. What was the purpose of the gun-fire? Had the Japs murdered Brigadier Varley and company? One of ships swung out of line and made for the lifeboats. It circled them slowly, with all its guns trained on the POWs. Was this going to be the end for them? "If you believe in Christ," Duncan advised his men, "say your prayers now." But they were as surprised as the *Kachidoki* men had been the previous day when they saw scrambling nets being lowered over the sides of the sloops and Japanese sailors beckoning them to climb aboard. Was this some kind of trick? Were they to be interrogated and then thrown to the sharks? No. They were given hot, sweet drinks and brandy trifle! And, no, the captain knew nothing about Varley. He just pointed at the other two sloops, which suggested that the Brigadier was on board one of them. But, of course, this was untrue. It can never be proved, but in all likelihood it would seem that the gun-fire was, indeed, the massacre of the 200-strong Varley group.

These ships also set course for Hainan, about 200 miles to the west. The following evening, as they passed the tanker set on fire by *Pampanito*, the *Zuiho Maru*, she was still burning brightly, as she had been now for forty-eight hours. It was 1100 on the morning of 15 September when they tied up alongside a tanker in a small harbour on Hainan Island, probably Sangai. It was here that they saw their comrades from the *Kachidoki* for the first time since they had sailed from Singapore. They were appalled by what they saw. Men with broken unset limbs; men with their flesh horribly burned by both oil and sun; men blinded by the oil in their eyes, being led around by the hand by their mates; men lying helpless in their own filth, starved and covered in oil. Rowland Richards, an Australian medical officer, had tended many cases of every kind of hideous tropical disease imaginable, and injuries too, on the Death Railway and at River Valley Road. He was a more hardened medical man than most, without doubt. But the sights that he saw that day were too much, even for him. He threw up.

Next day, 16 September, all the POWs were transferred to a big 20,000-ton whale factory-ship, the *Kibibi Maru*, in which they were to sail to Japan. Unbeknown to them, the *Kibibi* had been converted to carry fuel oil. With just one hit in her side from an American torpedo, she would erupt like a volcano.

*   *   *

The Eradicators, *Barb* and *Queenfish*, had not heard a sound about the whole operation, neither from the other submarines nor from Pearl Harbor. They had waited patiently off the coast of north-west Luzon, keyed up for action, but all this had brought them by way of reward had been a skirmish with some Jap sub-hunter frigates and a bone-shaking from their depth-charges. To make matters worse, Fluckey and Loughlin had wasted no less than ten expensive torpedoes for no hits. There had been no sign of any units of the awaited convoy. Had Oakley, Reich and Summers made a clean sweep and sunk the lot? Ed Swinburne decided it was time to call it a day. The Eradicators headed east for the Bashi Channel.

Eventually, the news came through that Oakley was to hand over command of the pack to Eli Reich, and take *Growler* to Fremantle in Western Australia for refit. Summers was still patrolling off Hainan Island. Reich informed him that he too would be making for that area. Duncan's *Rakuyo* survivors were fortunate that neither *Pampanito* nor *Sealion II* sighted their rescue sloops on the way to Hainan. They cannot have been very far away and of course neither of the American skippers yet knew that they had attacked ships carrying POWs, and that 2,218 of their own allies had been thrown into the South China Sea. *Pampanito* came within a whisker of that awful news when she sighted several lifeboats in the distance. One of them seemed to have men in it. But it was five miles away and Summers was already on course to investigate two smudges of smoke on the horizon. He made the reasonable assumption that the lifeboat contained Japanese survivors from the ships he had attacked and doubtless they would be picked up soon by their own side. And so he did not close the boat, but continued his pursuit of the smoke. In all probability, however, the men were British survivors from the *Kachidoki*, in one of the boats left behind by the Japanese. As for the smoke, that evening two blips showed on *Pampanito*'s radar. They were two small trawlers. Summers decided that they were not sizeable enough to justify expending torpedoes and left them in peace. He entered in his log, "Very disheartened". He would have been even more so if he had sunk them. Almost certainly, they were among several small ships involved in the rescue and would have been packed with British POWs.

Reich reckoned that most of the prey off Hainan must have scampered for safe haven following the attack on the *Kachidoki* convoy (luckily for the occupants of the *Kibibi Maru*) and that richer pickings were more likely in the Luzon Straits. He rendezvoused with Summers and the pair set off east at daybreak on 15 September.

Their course took them about forty miles to the north of the position where *Sealion II* had sunk the *Rakuyo Maru*. They were dangerous waters, with the needled Japs still on the hunt for the submarine pack. By mid-afternoon *Pampanito* had had three 'aircraft approaching' scares, although none of these came close enough to make an attack. Nonetheless, the lookouts were very decidedly keeping alert. The afternoon watch had just been relieved, a few minutes before 1600 hours, when twenty-one-year-old signalman Herman Bixler was carefully sweeping his section of the horizon with his binoculars. The sea was dead calm and visibility was good. Bixler blinked, looked away and then peered again through his glasses. Yes, he could see a large amount of flotsam and a lifeboat in the distance. But Summers was wary. This could be a Jap decoy trick. A little later they saw two rafts full of wildly waving men. Some of them were semi-naked and from a distance they seemed to have dark skins.

Again Summers assumed these men to be Japs. And, given his unawareness of the true state of affairs, again it was a reasonable assumption. He gave the order to break out the small arms. Anybody who wanted to shoot a Jap should grab a tommy-gun. Several sailors gathered on the foredeck, fully prepared to kill. The gunner's mate, Hauptmann, toted a double-barrelled 12-bore shotgun. *Pampanito* drew nearer to the rafts. The sailors held their weapons at the ready. Then they heard angry, jumbled shouting coming from the dark men. At first it was unintelligible, but then one voice rang clear, above the others, "First you bloody Yanks sink us. Now you're going to bloody well shoot us!"

The Americans stared in astonishment. But they were still suspicious. "One man only to come aboard," ordered Hauptmann as he tossed a rope across. It was grabbed by a former Australian school teacher, thirty-one-year-old Frank Farmer, who thus became the first Allied soldier to return to friendly forces from the Death Railway. For the record, it was 1634 hours on 15 September 1944, in 18°42' north, 114°00' east. Farmer always insisted that it was not the angry shout that stopped the American sailors from opening fire, but the sight of Harold 'Curly' Martin's hair, still showing defiantly blond despite the oil which covered the rest of his body.

The Americans' astonishment instantly turned to acute anguish when they learned that over 2,000 British and Australians had been on board the ships they had attacked. Learning that there were more rafts, with more stranded men in the area, Summers carried on the search until 2015. By then it was fully dark, but he had rescued seventy-three men. Dozens of crew members poured out onto the upper casing to help the castaways climb aboard. Gently, they lowered them into the boat, stripped them of their oil-soaked rags and tried to remove the worst of the oil from their bodies by washing them in diesel. Summers headed for Saipan at full speed, while *Pampanito*'s pharmacist's mate, Maurice Demers, did his best to clean up their unexpected guests and make them as comfortable as he could with his limited available medical supplies. The submariners willingly gave up their bunks to accommodate the patients, some of whom were so thin that two of them fitted easily into a single bunk. Demers, helped by every member of the off-watch crew in one way or another, worked all through the night, tending these half-dead humans, administering shots of morphine, doses of quinine and vitamin tablets, bathing oil and dirt from bloodshot eyes, and raking great lumps of it from ears and mouths. They were drifting in and out of consciousness. Some could not even speak. The *Pampanito* had become an emergency ward as she tore flat out through the South China Sea, towards the Balintang Channel, Saipan and safety. Maurice Demers did not sleep or eat for four days and three nights.

Meantime, at 1715, Summers had radioed *Sealion II* and Pearl Harbor to inform them of his awful discovery. Reich, of course, had immediately made full speed to cover the twenty-eight miles to the spot. Unlike Summers, he had time to plan his operation, but there would be almost no time in which to carry it out, because the light was already beginning to fade. He divided his rescue crew into three teams. One would swim out to the rafts and attach ropes to them for pulling in. The second would help the survivors to climb on deck. The third would strip them of their oil-soaked rags and get them below as quickly as possible.

The first sign that they were nearing the area was when *Sealion II* passed several dead bodies in life-jackets, floating in the oil. Then, with the boat flooded down, to bring her upper casing nearer to the surface of the sea, the forward hydroplanes were swung out like wings and the swimmers got down onto them with their lines ready for the rescue. It was 1840 hours when they started hauling them aboard. *Sealion II*'s crew experienced the same sense of shock as *Pampanito*'s had done at finding fellow-humans in such a state. But there was another, over-riding factor which affected them, and them only. These were survivors from the *Rakuyo Maru*, and it had been the unwitting *Sealion II* herself which had fired the torpedoes which consigned these men to their fate. If it was possible, their rage rose to new heights towards the Japanese for such mindless slaughter.

Reich had barely an hour and a half in which to work. By 2000 hours he had picked up twenty-three Australians and thirty-one British. Then he had to make one of the most difficult decisions of his life. Accommodation space was very limited, more so than in

Pampanito mainly because *Sealion II* had fired fewer torpedoes. Medical supplies, too, were inadequate to deal with any greater numbers. "That's all," he ordered. It was time to go. It meant leaving hundreds of men in the water, but there was no alternative. Each boat already held over twice the number of bodies she was designed to accommodate. And they had taken enormous risks in lingering, stopped, for several hours 600 miles inside enemy-held waters. Reich entered in his log, "It was heart-breaking to leave so many dying men behind." One submariner said that sometimes in the night, years afterwards, he could hear the desperate voices calling from the darkness, "Over here! Over here!"

As the sound of the sub's engines faded into the night, the spirits of those who were about to spend their fourth night in the water reached their nadir. Some men threw their hands up in despair and disappeared beneath the surface. It was simple suicide. Some waved and shouted angrily after the Americans. Some just prayed.

The pharmacist's mate in *Sealion II* was a twenty-one-year-old Virginian, Roy Williams. Like Demers, he too started on a full-time first-aid marathon. All the rescued were exhausted, malnourished, weak and dangerously dehydrated. Eric Halfhide was so thin that when hands reached under his arms to lift him up on the deck of the sub, he yelped with pain. Half the men had skin problems of some kind caused by contact with the oil. In particular this seemed to have affected the area of the scrotum, which was cracked, sore and swollen. One man was thought to have tuberculosis. There were five cases of malaria. Williams took a five-gallon drum of hydraulic oil to clean away the caked oil from their bodies. Then those who were able to remain on their feet were given a warm soapy shower and their painful skin ulcers dusted with sulfa powder.

Pearl Harbor radioed Ed Swinburne, commander of the Eradicators, at 0400 on the morning of 16 September and called for him to assist with the rescues. *Barb* and *Queenfish* turned about and headed west at top speed. On the way they passed *Pampanito*, barging through the choppiness (the weather was deteriorating) in the opposite direction, with *Sealion II* storming along a couple of hours behind her. None of them broke radio silence.

At 2100 the Eradicators were still 135 miles short of the rescue spot when it became Swinburne's turn to make a difficult decision. A large convoy appeared on the radar, range 34,000 yards. No information about this had been heard from Pearl Harbor. Somehow or other FRUPAC must have missed it. What should Swinburne do? Delay the rescue mission or attack the Japs? He reasoned that his prime purpose was to fight the enemy.

Approaching stealthily on the surface in the moonless darkness to within about 3,500 yards, Loughlin in *Queenfish* could make out the shapes of the two largest ships in the convoy. He fired his last four torpedoes at one of them and two minutes later the China Sea was momentarily lit up by the flash of a huge explosion. He had sunk a 10,000-ton transport, but was now completely out of torpedoes. He took *Queenfish* away to the rear of the convoy so as to track any scattering ships, and *Barb* moved in to take up the attack. Fluckey primed his remaining nine torpedoes and set sights on two of the leading ships. They looked like tankers. But just as he was about to fire they turned on a zig-zag, to reveal a much larger ship which had been sailing on their far side. Fluckey could not believe his luck. It was an aircraft-carrier! The 22,000-ton flat-top *Unho*, 'the Cloud Falcon', a strange looking contraption, 591 feet long with no superstructure. He moved closer, now inside the circling escorts, to get a better shot at her. He fired six tubes, three at the carrier and three at one of the tankers, but one of the escort sloops was now charging towards *Barb*. It was less than half a mile away and suddenly there was an aircraft overhead as well. Fluckey crash-dived. *Barb*'s crew held their breaths and waited for the depth-charges, which never came. But they did hear five of the torpedoes explode. They had sunk the 11,000-ton tanker *Azusa* as well as the Cloud Falcon. The Eradicators now had only three torpedoes left, all in *Barb*'s tubes. At 0055 on 17 September they turned to resume their rescue mission. It was going to be a race against the weather. A typhoon was brewing.

It was almost dawn when they reached the farthest position to where it was calculated the rafts would have drifted, allowing for prevailing currents and wind. The wind now blew at twenty knots, the sea was becoming decidedly angry and the skies were black with rain. But there was no sign of any survivors. Five miles apart and keeping a constant and careful watch for Jap planes, they began to sweep. Four hours passed before the first pieces of wreckage and slicks of oil hove into view. The debris was strewn right across the seascape, as far as the eye could see. But there seemed to be no sign of life among it. The two submarines gently nosed their way through the dismal setting. It was nearly midday before the first dead bodies were seen, clad in life-jackets and floating in the oil. They were Japanese. Then some were seen which had European faces. Then more. The repulsive stench that arose from them was sickening and the Americans on the bridge tied handkerchieves over their noses as they scanned with their binoculars. Could anybody have survived here for five days? It was 1255 when two rafts with men on them were sighted through *Barb*'s raised periscope. They were only just alive when the submariners lifted them aboard ten minutes later.

Barb and *Queenfish* searched all that day, and the next, until the weather had reached such a pitch of violence that they could barely see past the nearest wave. With sadness in their hearts, they turned away. Their prime purpose now was to sail to safety with the thirty-two British and Australian human beings they had just pulled out of the South China Sea.

*　　*　　*

The 656 POWs who had been put aboard the whale factory ship *Kibibi Maru* had had a narrow escape. Their convoy left Hainan on 16 September – the same day on which the Eradicators were sinking the *Unyo* and the *Azusa* a few miles out. The prisoners were housed on what had been the factory deck of the big ship, more or less on the waterline. It was a voluminous space, with room for everybody to settle down on beds of straw, like animals in a cavernous steel stable, among the redundant whale-butchering paraphernalia of vats, winches, heavy chains and little trucks on rails. Many of the men were naked, their last few remnants of clothing having fallen to pieces long since, rotted by sun and salt. No daylight was allowed to enter the compartment. A chain of lamps studded along the bulk-head emitted a weak glow which reflected eerily on the men's sun-blackened skins to give them the appearance of weird spectres. And all the while the whale-butchering machinery clanked and rumbled with each movement of the ship. Dysentery was rife, as well as scabies and pellagra. It was understandable that the Jap guards kept well away from them. It was a long trip up to the *benjos* on the upper deck. Many could not control their bowels, and their excrement lay all around. On the voyage about eight of them died. Their mates wrapped the bodies in straw mats and consigned them to the sea with some words of prayer. Such things held no dread for them now. They had become inured to death.

191

The *Kibibi* ran the gauntlet through the Formosa Strait and docked at Moji, Japan, on 28 September 1944. The prisoners were eventually issued with some clothing before being sent on to various camps – Fukuoka, Sakata and Kawasaki. It was one of the coldest Japanese winters on record. Allied submarines and aircraft had, by now, got Japan firmly under lock and key. Almost no supplies were getting in. The people were starving and freezing. The POWs were reduced, on occasions, to killing dogs for food. More of them were to die before US forces arrived to liberate the 600-odd survivors in late August 1945. Not that that was the beginning of anything like a happy ending for many of the survivors, even the outwardly healthy ones. For them, to awake suddenly in the night bathed in the sweat of a hideous nightmare, shaking with panic, became common-place for many years afterwards.

*   *   *

The survivors rescued by the submarines were, by comparison, the lucky ones. Five of them died as *Pampanito* and *Sealion II* raced through the night to safety, despite the efforts of Demers and Williams to save them. They were John Campbell of the Gordon Highlanders in *Pampanito* and Britisher Douglass Rolph plus three others in *Sealion*, none of whom it was possible to identify. They cleared the Balintang Channel undetected by Jap patrols and by dawn were in the open sea with 1,300 miles to go. Rolph died at 2230 on 19 September, less than twelve hours before they were to tie up alongside the tender *Fulton* at Saipan.

The Eradicators caught the typhoon and found heavy going as they headed east from the rescue area, making barely eight knots in mountainous seas and winds reaching 75 miles per hour. Two Englishmen, Londoner Harry Winters and Yorkshireman Cyril Grice, died in *Queenfish*. Grice had remained unconscious the whole time and was probably never aware that he had been rescued.

The four submarines safely delivered ninety-two Australian and sixty British ex-POWs to Saipan, where on 15 June the garrison of 43,000 Jap troops had been all but wiped out when the island fell into American hands and 4,000 Jap civilians had committed suicide by blowing themselves up with grenades or jumping from cliffs, whole families together, rather than be captured. The hell-ship survivors were taken to the 148th Field Hospital, which was composed of a group of tents on a hillside. It was far from being a safe place, because there were still a few Japanese troops hiding out in caves and remote dugouts. These were being flushed out with flame-throwers by US marines and soldiers. But the hospital itself was almost devoid of patients, leaving the staff free to lavish all their attention on the emaciated forms of the new arrivals. Ernest Fieldhouse had never been a giant, but he was found to weigh under five stone. In his official report Colonel Wadsworth, the commanding officer of the hospital said that he had found that 95% of them had had malaria, 67% had recurrent dysentery, 61% had tropical ulcers, 20% had palpable livers, all had skin lesions of one type or another, and all showed various signs of vitamin deficiency. There were nine cases of acute bronchitis, five of corneal scarring and one of tuberculosis. Clearly, the first objective of the medicos was to nurse these skeletal figures back into condition and to build them up for the long journey home. So there was food, and plenty of it. But they found it far too rich, and, besides, many of them were now having difficulty in moving their bowels. For these the diet for several days was little more than vitamin pills and laxatives.

With six of their number still unfit to travel, eighty-six Australians, clad in US Army summer khaki, left Saipan in the Liberty ship *Alcoa Polaris* on 28 September bound for Guadalcanal, where they would join the minelayer USS *Monadnock* for the last leg of their homeward journey. Sea traffic was heavily congested in the Pacific at that time, owing to the build-up for the invasion of the Philippines, and it was not until 18 October that *Monadnock* sailed into Moreton Bay, Brisbane. Bar two, the sixty-strong British contingent at Saipan were all passed fit to travel and on 1 October they were taken out in landing craft to board the liberty ship *Cape Douglas* for Honolulu, then to San Francisco in the troopship *Orizaba*, a train journey right across the USA, via Chicago to New York, there to board the liner *Queen Mary*, which berthed at Greenock on 9 November. They had had many adventures between Saipan and Scotland, with anecdotes enough to fill another book. For some the rush of joyful adrenalin, and still thankfully youthful exuberance, induced by their freedom from years of hell, was too much. Surrounded by the bright lights of Chicago and New York, they went wild. Military discipline could take a back seat. That was their attitude. And it was understandable. Just seven weeks before, these young men had been half-dead, half-starved, caked in salt, smothered in thick stinging oil and scorched by an unmerciful tropical sun as they battled for their lives in the South China Sea. But now they were going home. For many there was a life ahead which would be beset with ill-health in one way or another. But at least they were alive and for them there had been a relatively happy ending. The stark and saddening statistic which puts the whole deplorable story into perspective, and is its grim epitaph, is that there were only 758 survivors of the 2,218 prisoner-slaves who sailed as a half-suffocated cargo from Singapore in the stinking holds of the Japanese hell-ships *Rakuyo Maru* and *Kachidoki Maru*.

11

THE HELL-SHIPS (2) - *LISBON MARU*

Their wide-flung Co-Prosperity Sphere was an unwieldy enterprise for the Japanese to manage logistically, and *Rakuyo* and *Kachidoki* were not the only hell-ships to sail, unmarked and crammed with POWs under monstrously inhuman conditions, to wherever extra labour was required throughout the war. Not by a long chalk. Many of them were attacked unwittingly by Allied warships and aircraft. At least, thirteen more of them are known to have sunk. There was the *Suez Maru*, torpedoed off Kangean Island on her way to Java on 29 September 1943 with 548 prisoners on board. All perished. *Montevideo Maru* was torpedoed by the US submarine *Sturgeon* off Bagador Lighthouse, Cape Bojiduru, Luzon at 2.25 a.m. on 1 July 1942 and 1,035 Allied prisoners, mainly soldiers of the Australian 8th Division, were lost. *Tyofuku Maru* was on her way from Singapore to Japan on 21 September 1944 with 1,287 prisoners on board. 907 men were lost when she was sunk by US aircraft north of the Philippines. *Nichimei Maru*, Singapore to Moulmein in Burma, lost 53 men from the 1,000 prisoners on board when she was sunk by a submarine on 15 January 1943. *Tamabuko Maru*, taking 772 POWs from Singapore to Japan, was torpedoed by USS *Tang* off Nagasaki in sight of the Japanese coast on 24 June 1944; 560 lives were lost, the survivors being picked up by a passing Japanese whaler. *Harahiku Maru* had barely left Belawan harbour in Sumatra on 26 June 1944 when she was torpedoed and 177 of the 720 of her cargo of prisoners were killed or drowned; *Shinyu Maru* was sunk by the submarine USS *Barb* off Mindanão on 17 September 1944. There were 81 survivors among the 750 prisoners on board, who were rescued from the sharks by USS *Narwhal*. The captured Dutch ship *Van Waerwijck* was torpedoed by the British submarine

HMS *Truculent*. Of the 800 prisoners on board, barely 200 escaped with their lives, including a dog named Judy who survived to the end of the war in a prison camp with her master. *Junya Maru*, built by Duncan & Co. on the Clyde, was sunk by the British submarine HMS *Tradewind* on the voyage from Sumatra to Japan on 18 September 1944 and 1,477 out of 2,200 mainly Dutch POWs on board were lost, along with 4,200 Japanese slave labourers. This was the greatest loss of life at sea in a single incident that the world had seen up to that time.

The 7,000-ton *Oryuko Maru* was carrying 1,619 POWs, 1,000 shipwreck survivors and 700 civilians from Manila to Japan when she came under attack from US carrier-borne aircraft. She went aground in Subic Bay in the Philippines, but the attacks continued for another two days. Many men died, battened down in their stinking oven of a hold, if not from the bombing, from suffocation, thirst or disease. In the foetid darkness, naked bodies crawled over each other like ants, crazy with thirst and searching for water. Some of the Americans killed each other in their madness. The survivors were told to swim ashore by their captors and to remove their shoes and clothing because it was a fairly long way. But the Japs had set up machine guns on the beach and as the prisoners neared the shore they were raked with fire. Those who were not killed were re-taken as prisoners. They were transported by truck and train to San Fernando. On the way fifteen of the more seriously wounded were either bayoneted or beheaded. The rest were put aboard two other ships, the *Enoura Maru* and *Brazil Maru*. They reached Takao Bay in Formosa (Taiwan) where the *Enoura* was damaged so badly by an aircraft torpedo attack that she was unable to continue the voyage. All the prisoners were transferred to the *Brazil Maru*, which sailed from Formosa for Japan on 14 January 1945. When she arrived at Moji, less than 500 were still alive of the 3,319 who had sailed in the *Oryuko Maru*, and of these another 150 were to die within a month of their arrival.

But it would be inappropriate to close without telling the story of one other hell-ship. It is true that the number of men who sailed in her to die was fewer than in some of the others and her story may also be surpassed, arguably, in terms of horror by that of some of the other hell-ships. But it is unequalled for the height of callous indifference to the value of human life which it reveals. Indeed, it contains instances where such cold disregard had evolved into a vicious pleasure. She was called the *Lisbon Maru*.

Petty Officer Telegraphist Alf Hunt, D/JX 143909, from Stratford-on-Avon, had been in the Far East since 1938, serving on board an ancient 645-ton river gun-boat HMS *Cicala*, mainly on anti-pirate patrols up the Pearl River to Canton. On the outbreak of war against the Japanese, Alf was drafted to the motor torpedo boat *MTB 12* of the 2nd Flotilla. It was a lucky move for him, because *Cicala* was bombed and sunk at her moorings by attacking Jap planes a few days later on 2 December 1941. But his luck did not hold. On 17 December, with the enemy closing in on Hong Kong, the MTBs were sent out to attack their landing craft. It was a fierce fight, taking place more or less in the harbour itself and *MTB 12* was sunk after crashing into the sea-wall. Alf was the only survivor. He struck out for the beach, which was only 200 yards or so away. Severely wounded and weak from loss of blood, he made it to the foreshore and collapsed in a monsoon drain. Later it was discovered that he had wounds to his left arm, shrapnel in his back, three bullets in his left leg and an ugly groove where a bullet had pierced his tin-hat and ploughed its way across his forehead. The Japs had got ashore by this time and Alf was discovered by two soldiers who were engaged on cutting down the barbed wire defences. They pulled him roughly out of the drain, still barely conscious, and, taking a length of barbed wire, bound his hands together with it. Then they bundled him to a large house which was being used as their headquarters. He was dragged before a middle-aged colonel whose chest was emblazoned with medal ribbons. Alf was sufficiently in possession of his senses to notice that some of them were British awards from the First World War. The colonel looked at the barbed wire around Alf s wrists and immediately flew into a rage. The painful binding was quickly removed and the soldiers who had captured Alf stood bowing and hissing whilst the colonel ranted at them. The furious harangue ended with the colonel roundly slapping their faces with a shoe. Alf had understood not a word of it, of course, but it was reassuring to see that the colonel, at least, seemed to be a decent sort. He was taken to a building in Argyle Street which was being used as a reception centre for prisoners.

When Hong Kong finally fell to the Japanese on Christmas Day 1941 many of the British garrison were taken prisoner, although five MTBs of the 2nd Flotilla managed to escape thanks to the loyal co-operation and resourceful guidance of a one-legged Chinese

Admiral, Chan Chak, who was 'on loan' to the British from Chiang Kai-shek They eventually made it to safety at Rangoon, in Burma, after a series of adventures. It is remarkable that within weeks some of them were home in Great Britain.

In Hong Kong most of the officer-captives were assigned to the prison in Argyle Street. The Other Ranks were transferred to the mainland and marched to Sham Shui Po Barracks, a disused army camp on the foreshore. This place was in a decrepit state, having been looted by the local population. No fittings of any use remained. Even the wooden doors had been removed and the sanitation was non-existent. Their first task was to dig latrines and establish a 'hospital' for those among them who, already, had succumbed to sickness brought on by the inhuman conditions. The prisoners were left in no doubt as to the attitude which their captors bore towards them. If there were any uncertainty in that regard it was to be fully dispelled over the next four years. At Sham Shui Po food was minimal and consisted almost entirely of watery rice. Within a short time there was not a cat or a dog to be seen around the place. Dysentery and pellagra were widespread. A diphtheria epidemic broke out and men began to die, but still no medical supplies were provided by the Japanese.

The guards were a brutal bunch of thugs. The slightest transgression of the 'rules' would result in a merciless beating which would be kept up until either the victim became unconscious (or worse) or the guards grew tired of the sport. Kicks, punches and beatings with rifle-butts became commonplace. No mail or Red Cross parcels got through. The prisoners' morale sagged. They felt they had been forgotten and cut off from the familiar values of life. Indeed, some of them felt (and still do feel) that Hong Kong, and therefore their freedom, had been sacrificed cheaply by their Government.

The days and weeks dragged into months. Some of the fitter men would have welcomed some light work, just for something to do, but as yet the Japanese had not put them to any kind of work. They were simply vegetating. Overall their health was still suffering owing to the poor diet. The sanitation for the patients in the 'hospital' consisted of emptying toilet buckets over the sea-wall. When a rumour spread around the camp in mid-September 1942 that they were to be shipped to Japan it was met with a certain amount of optimism by many of the inmates. There were some who thought that they would be bound to receive better treatment in the Japanese homeland, where the Japanese army would, perhaps, be anxious to appear more humane in its treatment of prisoners. Others thought that there would be a far better chance of rescue by the Allies if they stayed in Hong Kong. The rest simply felt that anywhere else would make a welcome change from the everyday dreariness of Sham Shui Po. And the rumour was eventually confirmed. A draft of selected prisoners would be sailing soon for Japan to relieve the shortage of factory labour.

Among the Royal Navy men chosen were Alf Hunt and Jack Hughieson, another telegraphist, also ex HMS *Cicala* and MTBs, and others from the destroyer HMS *Thracian* and the gun-boats HMS *Robin* and HMS *Moth*. With them were soldiers from the 1st Battalion Middlesex Regiment, the 2nd Battalion Royal Scots, the Royal Corps of Signals, the Royal Engineers and the Royal Artillery. Twenty-one-year-old Hughieson, from Edinburgh, had been captured on Christmas Day 1941 at Bennetts Hill, along with some Royal Marines and some Gurkhas. Before being marched away to Sham Shui Po he had been forced to witness the violent systematic rape of six nurses by Japanese soldiers. It was so sickening that he had stood behind a broad-shouldered Marine to block the view.

Altogether, 1,816 men were drawn up on the parade ground before a Lieutenant Hideo Wada and addressed through his interpreter Niimori Genichiro. "You are going to be taken away from Hong Kong," Wada announced, "to a beautiful country where you will be looked after and well-treated. I shall be in charge of the party. Take care of your health. Remember my face." They were then given a cursory medical examination, presumably to ensure their fitness to travel. With that, they were marched out of camp, clutching battered suitcases, kitbags and pathetic parcels of cherished personal possessions, to be bundled onto barges and lighters at Sham Shui Po pier and taken out to a large cargo ship at anchor in the middle of the harbour. It was the 7,000-ton *Lisbon Maru*. She was already getting up steam as the prisoners were hustled up the boarding ladder onto her deck. They could see that she had 4-inch guns mounted both fore and aft, but she bore no markings of any kind to indicate that she was carrying Prisoners of War. In the words of one of them, "It was the start of the most traumatic and tragic event of my life, a time when I finally decided that there was nothing to live for and that death would be a welcome release from all my suffering."

About 750 men were crammed into each of the two main for'ard holds, with the remainder in Number Three hold abaft the bridge. Space was so limited that there was no room for everybody to lie down at the same time on the packed earth which covered the floor of the hold. Presumably this was the residue of an earlier cargo or ballast. Eventually it was decided that the only way to ensure that men were able to rest properly was by arranging a sleeping rota. The officers were huddled on a small half-deck part way up the bulk-head. No blankets of any kind were issued. To add to the discomfort, nearly every man in the draft was suffering from some disease or the effects of long-term malnutrition. Dysentery and diarrhoea were rife and the stench was appalling even before the voyage began. The rest of the day was spent taking on board 778 wounded Japanese soldiers, who were packed onto a wooden mezzanine deck within the holds. Many of these men, too, were suffering from dysentery and diarrhoea, and their uncontrollable bowels caused frequent spatters of faecal matter to fall on the prisoners packed below them. A heavily armed guard of twenty-five was commanded by Lieutenant Wada. This meant, of course, that the Japanese author-ities did not only ignore the right to safe passage of their POWs but also that of their own sick and wounded troops. There was every reason to mark *Lisbon Maru* as a hospital ship as well as a carrier of POWs. But it was not done.

At high tide on 27 September Captain Kyoda Shigeru weighed anchor and the hell-ship slid from harbour and headed north-east towards the Formosa Strait. She was carrying four lifeboats and four life-rafts which Shigeru had decreed would be reserved for the Japanese, and two life-rafts for use by the 1,816 POWs if necessary. There were enough kapok life-jackets for about half of the prisoners. (At the War Crimes trials after the war, interpreter Niimori insisted that every man had one, which he checked personally at each roll call.)

A rare piece of good fortune for the prisoners was that their food was more wholesome, albeit only slightly, than what they had been accustomed to at Sham Shui Po. Sometimes their evening meal of the usual rice was supplemented by a small piece of tinned meat and a mouthful of vegetables. There was even an issue of cigarettes. But water was severely limited. There was barely enough to drink and certainly none for washing. As for toilet facilities, these consisted of wooden *benjos*, a sort of box-cradle which was slung over the side of the ship. But there were far too few of them for the numbers of men on board, especially as most of them were suffering from illnesses affecting their bowel movements. Very quickly the heat and the stench of sweat and excreta, coupled with the inevitable sea-sickness which affected many of them, created an intolerable atmosphere and the Japanese were persuaded to allow a few men on deck by rota.

The Gato class American submarine USS *Grouper* (SS 214) had been first commissioned only seven months before, but she was already a veteran of the titanic Battle of Midway, where she had survived the blasts of 170 depth-charges and bombs. The night of 30 September 1942 saw her on her second war patrol in the East China Sea, south of Shanghai. It was a fine night, with a very bright moon which made the calm sea shimmer like sequins. At around 0400 hours, she sighted a cluster of twinkling lights about 4,000 yards away. On investigation these proved to be nine Chinese sampans engaged in a night's fishing. But sliding quietly past them was the large shape of an unmarked 7000-ton freighter. It was far too bright to attempt a surface attack and, rather than risk hitting one of the sampans with a torpedo, *Grouper*'s captain, Lieutenant-Commander Clarence Duke, decided to pace the freighter to establish her course and speed, and wait for daylight.

Duke dived just before dawn and brought *Grouper* to within 3,250 yards of her target. At four minutes past seven he fired a spread of three torpedoes, which all missed. On board the hell-ship the unsuspecting prisoners were in the midst of roll-call, having been roused from an uncomfortable night's sleep at 6.30 to dress hurriedly and join the usual morning rush for the *benjos*. Duke fired a fourth torpedo. It ran true, and two minutes and ten seconds later there was a loud explosion. The *Lisbon Maru* swung violently to starboard and came to a stop. On board, chaos reigned. The guards, yelling loudly, rushed around in high agitation, pushing all the prisoners on deck back down into the hold, including some of the very sick who were permanently 'topside' in isolation. Then the four-inch guns opened up, firing at the submarine, which had come up to periscope depth. Shells were bursting all around *Grouper*. None of them found their target, but they were far too close for comfort. Duke noted that the *Lisbon Maru* had hoisted a red flag which resembled the letter B for Baker. This flag would normally be flown to indicate "am taking on or discharging dangerous cargo", for example explosives or ammunition. Its purpose here remains unclear. Possibly it was a ploy to deter the submarine or any other vessels from coming too close to her.

The freighter had stopped and had gone aground on a sandbank, but she was far from destroyed. Duke dived and lined *Grouper* up for another shot. At 0845 he fired a fifth torpedo, set at a depth of six feet. The range was a mere 1,000 yards, but his shooting was very poor and he missed. By now the *Lisbon Maru* had listed to starboard and Duke went round to her portside, where more of her underbelly was exposed. At 0938 he fired one of his stern tubes, set at zero depth. The range was so close that it needed a run of only forty seconds. *Grouper* dived instantly as the torpedo left its tube. She was down 100 feet before the explosion was heard. But as she was diving there was a droning sound from the sky. It was a Mitsubishi Davai 108 bomber. And it had spotted her. Two minutes later she was shaken by the uncomfortably close blasts of three depth-charges from the aircraft.

Grouper stayed close at hand all through the day, occasionally coming under depth-charge attacks, although they were never close enough to cause her any damage. At 1900 hours Duke surfaced and left the area, still unaware that the disabled ship he had been stalking was crammed with his own allies. His reasons for lurking in the vicinity for so long without making any more attacks are not clear. He had fired five torpedoes up until 0938, but does not appear to have expended any more during the rest of the day. *Grouper* had six bow tubes and four at the stern, and would have been loaded with twenty-four torpedoes at the start of her patrol. She had sunk the *Tone Maru* on 21 September, but it does not seem likely that she can have been low on torpedoes when she met up with the prison ship. On board the *Lisbon Maru* none of the prisoners were allowed on deck for any reason whatsoever throughout the rest of the day, not even to visit the *benjos*. With so many of them suffering from dysentery, the nauseous conditions can only be imagined. For seven hours no food was issued and water was refused. In the hold the air became thick and the suffocating heat was unbearable.

The senior British officer, Lieutenant-Colonel H.W.M. 'Monkey' Stewart, OBE, MC, of the Middlesex Regiment, bravely began to argue with Lieutenant Wada, insisting that the hatches should be opened slightly at least, in order to avoid men suffocating. Interpreter Niimori's reply was, "There is nothing for you to worry about. You are bred like rats, and so can stay like rats." Captain

Shigeru was sympathetic to Stewart's request, but Wada was reluctant to concede, saying that his guard of a mere twenty-five soldiers could not hope to contain the POWs if they decided to riot. It developed into a vehement argument between Shigeru and the menacing Wada, which was won by the guard commander, who told the browbeaten ship's captain that he bad no right to interfere in military matters. At 2100 the hatches were battened down and roped with tarpaulins. The prisoners were now without food, water or sanitation. The single electric light bulb which bad been their only means of illumination flickered, dimmed and finally died when the donkey engine failed. Nearly two thousand men were now incarcerated below the water-line in an unventilated steamy cess-tank of a ship. A struggling stack of sweating, defecating, nauseous, terrified humankind was trapped in utter darkness without any means of escape.

Wada's reported comments in the *Japanese Times Weekly* of 20 October 1942 made a mockery of the truth.

"That we must rescue the British POWs was the foremost thought which leaped to our minds when the ship met with disaster. It was just the hour for the roll-call of the prisoners. They were somewhat taken aback and were about to stampede. 'Don't worry, Japanese planes and warships will come to your rescue,' we told them. The commotion died down. It was encouraging to note that they had come to have such trust in the Imperial Forces during their brief POW camp life."

On the afternoon of 2 October the destroyer *Kure* and the merchant ship *Toyokuni Maru* appeared on the scene and took off the 778 wounded Japanese troops. The three captains conferred and arrangements were made to tow the crippled *Lisbon Maru* off the sandbank into shallow water. Her only occupants were now the twenty-five guards and her seventy-seven crew – plus 1,816 helpless POWs. In the holds the departure of the wounded Japanese troops had allowed the entrance of some fresh air and there was now more breathing space for the prisoners. Apart from this welcome relief, conditions had rapidly deteriorated. There had been no food or opportunity to visit the *benjos* for twenty-four hours. The air supply soon regained its thick foetid state. By tapping on the bulkheads in Morse or calling by voice through a small vent, the men were able to communicate with those in the next hold. Things were getting desperate in Number Three hold, they learned. It was flooding with water and the pumps had to be manned, but the suffocating conditions made it impossible for more than a few strokes to be made before the pumper fainted and had to be relieved. Number One hold reported that two diphtheria cases had died. In Number Two hold, Lieutenant-Colonel Stewart conserved precious oxygen by ordering the men to lie down flat and keep still, with no talking. He had made repeated requests for water and at 0400 hours Niimori appeared at the hatchway and lowered down a bucket on a rope. It was full of urine. By dawn on 2 October the problem of foul air had progressed to the point of being dangerous. And the *Lisbon Maru* was lurching around unsteadily as the water entered her different compartments. It was clear that she would not remain afloat for much longer.

The Japanese remained deaf to all entreaties by Stewart that they should open the hatches. But the British officer did not intend that 1,816 men should drown like rats without a struggle and gave permission for a small group of volunteers to break out of the hold to try to persuade the Japanese to give them a fair chance of saving their lives. Somebody produced a large butcher's knife which their captors had not detected and in the jet blackness Army Lieutenant Howell, who was the Hon. Sec. of the Hong Kong Kennel Club, climbed a steel ladder and tried to use it to cut open one of the hatch covers. But the shortage of oxygen defeated his efforts. At 0900 hours the prison-ship gave a tremulous stagger, which prompted Howell to try again. And this time he succeeded. Together with Lieutenant Potter, who could speak a little Japanese, and a few others, he climbed out onto the deck. They saw some Royal Artillerymen trying to emerge from Number Three hold through some portholes which looked out onto the well-deck. They managed to unscrew a door in the bulkhead and let them out. Then, taking care to walk slowly and calmly so as not to give the slightest impression of any rebellious intention, they all turned towards the bridge to ask to talk to the captain. Before they had taken but a few paces, some of the guards shoved the muzzles of their rifles through the hole in the hatch and fired indiscriminately into the blackness below, killing one man and wounding Lieutenant G. Hamilton of the Royal Scots. They fired again, this time at Howell's group on deck. One or two were wounded, including Potter, who died soon afterwards. Discretion being the better part of valour, the party quickly returned to the hold and reported to Stewart.

The prisoners had forced their exit from the hold in the nick of time, because almost immediately the *Lisbon Maru* gave another drunken lurch and at last the water began to flood in. She settled quickly by the stern, with her submerged afterpart lodged firmly on the sandbank and her bows pointing at the slowly brightening sky. Now the sea poured in through the hatchway of Number Three hold. Some of the men inside managed to get out, but many were beaten back by the force of the rushing water and were drowned. In the other holds too, farther forward, it was time to abandon ship. Using knives and any other implement which would cut, they severed the ropes and tarpaulin coverings and levered away the baulks of timber forming the hatch covers. Although there was a scramble to get out, there was little loss of discipline. Jack Hughieson was following the first man up, a sailor with a knife, when the men behind him tried to clamber in front of him. He felt himself about to be submerged under a mad rush of feet and instinctively kicked out. Turning, he saw two men fall back into the hold, their faces contorted with panic. It is unlikely that they managed to get out before she went down. Speaking nearly sixty years later, he said he had never forgotten the expressions on those faces, or quite forgiven himself for what he had done to them. Many men formed orderly queues and climbed out quietly, but when a number of them had gained the deck the guards opened fire on them. Several men fell before they had taken more than a few steps. Some of the guards were overpowered by sheer weight of numbers, given a quick vindictive beating and unceremoniously heaved over the side.

Then it was a case of every man for himself. Pausing only to help a few mates out of the holds, men started to jump over the side into the sea in their dozens. Alf Hunt, who was one of the last out, remembers burning his hands by sliding thirty feet down a rope. And all the time they were being fired on by Wada's guards, even after they were in the water. Many were killed as they tried to swim away.

Only about three miles away, looming out of the water like a dozing family of hump-backed sea monsters, were the steep cliffs and 800 foot peaks of the Chu San archipelago. For a thousand years these islands had been the destination of Buddhist and Taoist pilgrims and were covered with religious shrines, monasteries and cave temples. Appropriately, they were believed by many to be the home of Kuan Yin, the Goddess of Mercy. Alf knew none of this, but he was a strong swimmer and he struck out towards them. For the second time in the war he was set to swim for his life. But by this time some other vessels, including a destroyer, had come to stand by the stricken *Lisbon Maru*. And from these now came the crackle of small arms fire which poured down onto the hundreds of swimming men. It was a massacre. One or two of these craft even steamed up and down among the desperate swimmers, running them down. Many of them were cruelly mangled by the churning screws. Dozens of dead bodies were floating in the water. Bullets threw up spurts of water all around Alf Hunt as he swam as fast as his undernourished limbs would allow. Luckily, there was a strong current running towards the islands and he was quickly swept away from immediate danger.

Jack Hughieson had simply dived over the side and started to swim towards the islands. For as long as he could hold his breath, he kept underwater to avoid the machine-gun bullets which he could hear splattering into the water just above him. Surfacing, he found himself alongside Lieutenant-Commander Green, whom he knew well. Green was suffering badly from dysentery and was very weak with dehydration. Hughieson helped him along and promised him that if he did not make it he would let his family know that he was thinking of them at the last. Every few minutes the older man's reserves of strength would vanish altogether and he would start to sink. Jack dived to save him several times, which sapped his own scant energy. Luckily, the high salinity of the water in the China Sea makes for easy buoyancy and once they were clear of the destroyers' machine guns, swept along by the powerful current, they were able to rest by floating on their backs for a while. Even so, Jack Hughieson was almost dead-beat himself and the islands did not seem to have come much closer. In a state of complete exhaustion, he resigned himself to his fate. Just stop swimming and let yourself sink down. It would be easy. He started to think of his mother and family in faraway Scotland, fully accepting that these would be his final thoughts on this Earth. Then a tinkling voice said, "Hello. I save you." And he looked up into the face of a Chinese fisherman peering over the side of a boat. Jack never did see the going of Green, but made it his business after the war to keep his promise to the Lieutenant-Commander.

By the time Lieutenant Hamilton had dragged himself out of the hold there were no Japanese left on board the prison-ship. He dived into the sea intending, like Alf Hunt, to swim to the islands. There were four Jap ships standing by, he noticed, but none of them seemed prepared to rescue the swimming men. In fact, Hamilton saw several men kicked back into the water when they tried to climb up ropes to board these ships. He made good progress in the favourable current, but had not gone very far when he saw that the Japs had had an apparent change of heart and were now picking up prisoners. He turned and swam towards one of them. It looked like a small patrol vessel. Somebody threw him a rope and he was pulled up by some of the POWs who had already been rescued. Three days later they put into Shanghai and were paraded on the dockside. A few of them were clad in just a pair of shorts, but most of them were completely naked. They had lived for three days and nights, shivering as they huddled together under a rotten tarpaulin on the upper deck, with just four ship's biscuits per day and two small cups of watered-down milk.

When the roll was called only 970 answered their names out of the 1,816 who had sailed from Hong Kong. Two hundred or so of the missing men had made the Chu San islands, either by swimming or having been picked up by Chinese sampans and junks, but the remainder had all lost their lives. Sadly, some of the swimmers had reached the shore only to lose their lives by being dashed against the rocks by the speeding current.

It is beyond doubt that the intention of the Japanese was to say that the *Lisbon Maru* had been torpedoed without warning and had gone down so quickly that they had been given no chance to release the POWs from the holds. Indeed, that is exactly what the *Nippon Times*, an English language newspaper published in Japan, did say about the incident. If that were so, why were all the Japanese personnel transferred to the other ships during the night whilst the prisoners were left battened down? The truth was that there had been plenty of time for every single man on board the *Lisbon Maru*, both British and Japanese, to have been rescued. And the Japs had only changed their minds about taking POWs aboard the rescue ships when they saw some Chinese sampans performing the same humane act. But the sadistic Niimori made no mealy-mouthed excuses. He did not mince his words as he addressed the near-naked mass of dejected survivors as they trembled with cold on the Shanghai quayside. "You should have all gone down with the others."

En route to the islands, Alf Hunt fell in with another swimmer,

Royal Engineers Corporal Reg Westwood. They were destined to become lifelong friends and keep in regular touch even though Reg made his home in Canada after the war. Together, when they were little more than youths, they took a breather aboard a passing five-foot plank on that desperate day in the East China Sea. Eventually they beached in a sandy cove among some scattered rocky outcrops on an island called Tai Shan. A fresh spring was tinkling down the steep cliff nearby to make a rivulet across the sand. Their throats were parched with salt and they stuck their heads into the refreshing coolness to drink deeply. There were some steps cut into the cliff and after resting awhile to catch their breaths they set out for the top. They were greeted by half a dozen smiling Chinese fishermen from the village. These poor people gave them food and clothes and sheltered them, well-hidden, in a hay-rick.* Later, it came as a surprise to learn that the refreshing "spring" with which they had slaked their thirst on the beach was, in fact, the overflow from the village toilet! "No matter," recalled Alf nearly sixty years afterwards. "Whatever it was, it still tasted like nectar to us."

After two days a force of Japanese marines landed on the island and the game was up. Hunt, Hughieson, Westwood and others were taken to Shanghai and reunited with the other *Lisbon Maru* survivors. By now exposure to cold had begun it take its toll and hypothermia was added to the list of physical afflictions which beset the prisoners. Leaving behind thirty-five of the more serious dysentery cases, the remainder boarded another prison-ship, the *Shinsei Maru*, and sailed for Osaka in Japan. Large numbers of them were not to complete the journey. Five men died on board. Fifty very sick men were put off the ship at Moji and fifty more at Hiroshima. Five hundred went on as far as Kobe, which left a mere 290 who reached their destination. Of these, around 200 were to die during the first winter owing to disease, malnutrition and exposure. The Japanese kept no records and therefore it has never been possible for the families of those who died to know whether they lost their lives in the East China Sea, or whether they survived the sinking only to die later in Japan.

Stories of life in the prison camps on the Japanese mainland are manifold. Each man who was robbed of three or four years of his

---

* In 1949, the British Government expressed its gratitude to these people, who had risked their own lives to help the survivors from the *Lisbon Maru*, by presenting them with a motor fishing-boat, a supply of diesel and some cattle.

young life there, but was able to survive under conditions of unspeakable filth, torture, starvation and disease, could fill a volume with his own experiences. Jack Hughieson's experiences were typical of many. While working in the docks at Osaka, he dropped an unwieldy sack of rice. For this he was rewarded with a blow from a rifle-butt which smashed one of his knee-caps. Another time, when caught with a small piece of 'illegal' salt-fish in his possession, he was made to dig a grave and climb into it. Lying there, flat on his back, he was convinced that he was about to be buried alive, but they just put a wooden cover over the hole and left him terrified for a couple of hours in complete darkness. He was put to work in a new 'hospital' at Ichioka, between Osaka and Kobe, which was in reality the boxed-in terracing of a derelict sports stadium. It was strewn with piles of soggy, rotting rubbish and human excreta and the first job of the prisoners was to clear it with their bare hands. There, he came under the heel of a particularly nasty Japanese officer. One day somebody stole a few eggs belonging to the Jap, who flew into a screaming rage. He lined up twelve of the starving prisoners, selected at random, and drew his sword. "Who stole my eggs?" he demanded from the first man in line. No answer. He asked again. The man said he did not know. With that he was made to kneel and the big razor-sharp sword came flashing down on the back of his neck. The head was not completely severed, but remained suspended by a few pieces of skin and flesh as the blood gushed forth several feet. Next man was Ernie Irvine, a US Navy medic. Same question. Irvine did not know either. Jack was next in line. He remembers staring transfixed at the blood running down the sword blade as Ernie faced the Jap. Again the question. It looked as if the American had only a few seconds more to live, but a sudden inspiration saved his and all their lives. "You've just killed the man who stole your eggs!" he exclaimed, pointing at the corpse.

Later, Hughieson was put to work in the infamous Medical Unit 731. It was, in truth, no more than a vivisection laboratory. The prisoners' job was to carry in the emaciated bodies of men who were no longer fit for work and place them on the examination table. Medical students would gather round to be lectured as the bodies of the still-living creatures were opened up for observation and study. Many times Jack saw living torsos cut from throat to groin and entrails removed and placed to one side to reveal various working organs of interest. The only saving grace, if by some massive generosity of spirit it can be called such a thing, was that these long-suffering, once fit and strong young men were already beyond help and were about to die in any event And many times, for the rest of his life, Jack Hughieson would awake in the middle of the night bathed in the sweat of some horrific nightmare.

Interpreter Niimori Genichiro was brought before a British Military Court in Hong Kong in October 1946 on eight war crimes charges. All the charges involved brutality in one form or another. First, a Mr F.B. Miles, civilian manager of the American Club in Hong Kong, testified that the accused was responsible for several deeds of atrocity towards prisoners on land. When the Court came to deal with his activities on the hell-ships, Niimori tried to blame his superiors for battening down the prisoners on the sinking *Lisbon Maru*. Then he claimed that he had not known they were battened down and if he had been aware of their plight he would have done something to help them. But the Court heard that it had been Niimori who had been the main force behind the cruel treatment suffered by the prisoners on the *Lisbon Maru*. And that was not the sole voyage for which his activities were on trial. He had made a further trip on a prison transport, the *Toyama Maru*, taking Canadian POWs from Hong Kong to Japan. A soldier from the Royal Rifles of Canada, Rifleman Doucet, had been unable to produce a sweater for inspection. It had been a gift from the Red Cross, but Doucet had sold it to a Japanese guard in exchange for food. He was given such a severe beating by Niimori and one of the guard corporals that he died of his injuries in Marumi Camp, Japan, a few weeks later. There are many who would say that the sentence of fifteen years' imprisonment which Niimori received was extremely lenient.

Captain Kyoda Shigeru appeared before Lieutenant-Colonel R.J. Laming at No. 5 Court, held at Jardine Mathieson's premises at East Point Godown, Hong Kong on 23 October 1946. It was to be a twenty-four-day hearing, which would indicate the thoroughness with which the War Crimes Trials were conducted. He had taken his ship to sea through dangerous waters with a hopelessly inadequate number of lifeboats and rafts, and he had ordered that these should be reserved strictly for the Japanese. It was Shigeru's unsuccessful efforts to influence Niimori and Wada to open the hatches which persuaded the Court to impose a sentence of only seven years.

The story of every Far East POW consists of tales of unspeakable cruelty. But apart from the chilling effect that the saga of the hell-ships brings to the mind of a civilized reader, there is a question which must baffle the armchair strategist. Why did the Japanese allow thousands of enemy lives as well as their own to perish unnecessarily when ultimately it defeated their purpose? And it was all for the sake of some paint and a few diplomatic telegrams. The omission to mark these ships and to ask the Allies for safe passage was the sole reason that they were being torpedoed as early as mid-1942. And the physical condition of the prisoners who did arrive in Japan was such that often they were unable to carry out the work which was required of them. This fact, at least, was realized by the Japanese War Ministry. The following order preceded instructions that prisoners should arrive at their destination 'in a condition to perform work'.

Army Asia Secret Order No. 1504 – 10 December 1942.
Recently, during the transportation of prisoners of war to Japan, many of them have been taken ill or have died, and quite a few of them have been incapacitated for further work due to their treatment on the journey, which was inadequate.

Yet the lesson of the unmarked ships was still not learned by a myopic Japanese High Command. In the later stages of the war, when Japan became desperate for labour in her mines, docks and factories at home, she was driven to shipping POWs from the far-away jungles of Siam to fill the gap, but still the ships sailed without any distinctive markings or safe passage clearances to run the gauntlet of Allied submarines. In the month of September 1944 alone Japan denied itself the work of 9,000 pairs of hands because of this inexplicable intransigence.

In all the long history of maritime affairs, there cannot have been many stories of disasters at sea which sadden the heart more than those of the Japanese hell-ships.

12

THE OTHERS

In the course of the Second World War 5,150 Allied merchant ships were sunk, 2,828 of them by Axis submarines. In the year 1942 they were going down at the average rate of thirty-three each week. Thousands of Allied merchant seamen lost their lives in the conflict. The British Merchant Navy alone lost over 30,000. Many of the sinkings took place far away from land and men were left in lifeboats with little hope of reaching safety. Many were even fired on or rammed whilst in a lifeboat or on a raft, or while swimming for their lives towards one. Others were murdered in cold blood on the deck of the submarine which had sunk their ship. We have been able to look only at some of the more notable cases. It would need several more volumes to tell the sad story of each and every one of them. And the fact that such records as do survive are often little more than brief standardized notes presents further difficulty to the researcher. However, it would be unfitting to omit completely what, for want of a better phrase, might be called the 'others'. Perhaps the accounts of a handful of them may be used to pay some small tribute to the memory of each one of those brave men who lost his life so unjustly.

The Case of the trawler *Ebb*

It was four o'clock in the morning of 28 July 1942. The little 259-ton fishing trawler *Ebb*, owned by General Sea Foods Co. of Boston, Massachusetts, was chugging at a steady nine knots towards the Sable Island fishing grounds in the Atlantic, off the south-east coast of the Nova Scotia hammerhead. She had already decked thirty-eight tons of cod, which now lay on ice in her hold, but her skipper Philip Colbert had thought he would try for better luck off the Western

Bank. Forty-five miles from Cape Sable, the lookout shouted that there was a submarine off their starboard quarter, on a parallel course. It was the *U-754*, commanded by twenty-nine-year-old Kapitänleutnant Hans Oestermann, a native of the little Saxon town of Bremervörde. Without any warning, at the range of a mere fifty yards, the submarine opened fire with 88-mm and 20-mm guns. Colbert hove-to immediately, but the firing did not cease. The trawler's four officers and thirteen crew abandoned ship under a hail of shells and bullets. Colbert and four of his men, seamen Edward McDonald, Leo Ryan, Michael Shea and one other were killed, while seven of their shipmates were wounded. The U-boat circled around, firing about fifty more shots at the fishing-boat before she finally sank. It was astonishing that the 21,000 gallons of fuel oil that she was reported to have been carrying did not explode. She lies in 43°18'N–63°50'W. Although the *Ebb* had carried a radio-telephone, there had not been time to send out any distress calls, and it was by a very fortunate chance that the surviving three officers and nine men were picked up fourteen hours later by the British destroyer HMS *Witherington* and landed in Boston on 30 July.

The very next day *U-754* was bombed and sunk by a Hudson bomber from 113 Squadron of the Royal Canadian Air Force. There were no survivors from her crew of forty-three. Her own grave is in 43°02'N–64°52'W, only a few miles from that of her unarmed victim.

The Cases of the *Ascot*, the *British Chivalry*, the *Sutlej* and the *Centaur*

The *Ascot* atrocity took place in the Indian Ocean, just south of the equator. The 7,000-ton British ship had sailed from Colombo on 19 February 1944, bound for Madagascar. Ten days out, just after midday, a torpedo was spotted by the gunners on watch, streaking towards their starboard beam. There had been no warning given and there was no time for evasive action. The torpedo exploded in the *Ascot*'s engine-room, killing four of her engine and boiler-room men. Her starboard boats were completely destroyed and she seemed to be going down quickly. Orders were given to abandon ship and the rest of the crew, fifty-two men, took to the two portside lifeboats and a raft. The *Ascot* settled in the water, but she did not sink as rapidly as had at first appeared. Ten minutes later a submarine surfaced about a mile away. It was the Japanese *I-37*, under *Shosa* (lieutenant-commander) Hajime Nakagawa. Within the space of the previous seven days Nakagawa had sent the British ships *British Chivalry*, a 7,100-ton tanker, and *Sutlej*, a 5,200-ton freighter, to the bottom of the Indian Ocean. On 22 February twenty survivors on rafts and lifeboats from the *British Chivalry* were machine-gunned by the crew of *I-37*. Their thirty-eight shipmates spent the next thirty-seven days drifting aimlessly before their boats and rafts were spotted by a passing ship which landed them at Durban. Similarly, on 26 February, fifty men of the crew of the *Sutlej* were slaughtered, leaving twenty-three survivors. Of these, five were rescued after forty-two days and the other eighteen after an ordeal of forty-nine days on their rafts.

Nakagawa had started his career of criminal carnage on 14 May 1943 when, as captain of *I-177* he had torpedoed the Clyde-built Australian hospital ship *Centaur* off Cape Morton on the Queensland coast. *Centaur* had been clearly marked as a hospital ship, painted in brilliant white, with a green band and red crosses twenty feet high on her sides. At night floodlights illuminated her special markings, with red neon lights shining on her funnel and green ones following the green band around her waist. She could not have been mistaken for anything other than a hospital ship, except perhaps a floating fun-fair. Within three minutes she had gone to the bottom in ninety fathoms of water, taking 268 people with her, of which 252 were medical staff.

Now Nakagawa circled the wallowing *Ascot* and began to shell her. Soon she was ablaze from prow to stern. He turned his attention to the lifeboats. The British seamen noticed that, strangely, one man in the submarine's conning-tower seemed to be a European. And he was wearing a European-style naval officer's cap in contrast to the khaki-clad Jap sailors with their soft-peaked headgear. The Japanese captain demanded that the *Ascot*'s master, first engineer and radio officer identify themselves. When he received no instant reply, a burst of machine-gun fire spat forth from the submarine. At this the master stood up and was ordered on board. In anger at the slow response, a Japanese officer slashed at him with a bayonet. We are told that he suffered injuries to his palms. Presumably he tried to defend himself by grabbing at the weapon. He was thrown into the sea, but managed to gain one of the boats. At that, machine-gun fire was sprayed onto the lifeboats and raft. Such was its intensity and direction that all fifty-two occupants were forced to jump into the water to save their lives. Ten of them were shot dead whilst swimming. The submarine went away, but returned thirty minutes later to resume firing on the survivors, who by this time had got back into the boats.

Again those who were able to do so took to the water. One badly wounded sailor, barely conscious, was unable to move and was left in the boat. With remarkable courage, Gunner Walker of the Royal Marine Artillery stayed behind to shield him. From his position in the lifeboat Walker was able to act as a spotter for the men in the water, calling out to them the whereabouts of the submarine so that they knew on which side of the boat and raft to hide. Despite the artilleryman's brave efforts the wounded sailor was hit again and was killed. Walker himself collected two bullets in his leg from the sporadic bouts of machine-gunning which took place until darkness fell, when at last *I-37* made off and was not seen again.

By next morning, both boats and the raft had drifted far apart, although they could still see each other in the distance. However, by good fortune on the following day, 2 March, one of the boats came alongside the raft. It was waterlogged and very badly shot-up and contained only one man, a member of the crew named Hughson, who climbed onto the raft to join the other seven survivors. The second lifeboat, in which were the master and others, Hughson said, had been rammed and sunk by the submarine. His boat had also been attacked in a similar way, but most of its occupants had dived into the sea, only to be killed in the water by machine-gun fire. He alone had stayed in the boat and he was the sole survivor. The submarine took the boat in tow, with Hughson prostrate in the bottom, feigning death. After a while, the boat was cut adrift and rammed again, causing more damage. He had not dared to move a muscle all night, but at daybreak had risked peering over the side. There was no sign of any Japs and he hoisted the boat's sail. Although she was half full of water, which made for difficult progress, he had managed to find the raft.

After their three-day ordeal, the eight survivors of the fifty-six bodies who had sailed from Colombo in the *ss Ascot* were fortunate to be seen on their raft by the Dutch ship *mv Straat Soenda*, which picked them up at 1330 on 3 March and landed them in Aden.

At the end of the war, Nakagawa was arrested and tried as a war criminal. He spent just four years in Sugamo prison.

The Case of the SS *David H. Atwater*

The elderly freighter *David H. Atwater*, owned by Atwacoal Transportation Co. of Fall River, Massachusetts, was homeward bound with 3,911 tons of coal from Norfolk, Virginia, on 2 April 1942. About 10 miles east of Chincoteague Inlet, Virginia, she was shelled without warning by the German VIIC class submarine *U-552* commanded by Kapitänleutnant Erich Topp. This was a famous Second World War U-boat, nicknamed the Red Devil. And this was not the first time she and her aggressive captain had been involved in a controversial sinking.

At dawn on 31 October 1941, six weeks before the USA entered the war, Topp had attacked the eastbound convoy HX156. He fired a torpedo at one of the destroyer escorts. Her magazine exploded, blowing her apart. She sank within minutes, and 100 of her crew of 144 lost their lives. She was the USS *Reuben James*, the first US Navy ship to be lost by enemy action in the war. The bland German reaction was that the Americans, although not at war at that stage, had been escorting British convoys and had been attacking U-boats.

Now, five months later, in the course of a rampage of destruction off the Virginia-Carolina coast, Topp, completely unaware that he himself was being stalked by two patrolling US destroyers, *Emmons* and *Hambleton*, had dived to stalk the unsuspecting *David H. Atwater*, then surfaced at 2115 to attack her in the safety of darkness. The crew were given no chance. As they prepared to launch their boats and abandon ship, the U-boat opened up on them with her 88mm gun at a range of 600 yards, followed by sweeps of machine-gun fire. Ninety-three shots were fired by the Germans, fifty shells of which struck the ship, killing the master, Captain Bill Webster. Not waiting for the boats to be launched, most of the freighter's crew jumped into the sea. US Coastguard Cutter no. 218, *Legare*, heard the gunfire and saw the flashes. She raced onto the scene, arriving at 2130 to find only two feet of the *David H. Atwater*'s mast still showing above the water, a few dead bodies and just three survivors from the crew of twenty-seven. In one of the lifeboats was a dead body and the other boat was riddled with bullet holes. There was no sign of the Red Devil, which had quietly slunk away from the scene to resume hunting.

It seems that the Allies laid no charges against Topp at the end of the war for the machine-gunning of the *Atwater*'s survivors. He had been the third most successful submarine commander in any Navy in the Second World War. After the war he became an architect, but rejoined the Navy in 1958, later becoming a staff member of the Military Committee of NATO. He retired finally in 1969 with the rank of *Konteradmiral*.

The Case of the MV *Tulagi*

The 2281-ton British vessel *Tulagi*, owned by Burns Philp & Co., was registered as a Hong Kong ship. But on 27 March 1944, with her home port firmly under the heel of the Japanese invaders, she was trudging up through the Indian Ocean to Colombo from Australia, heavily laden with 1,850 tons of flour. She was just south of the equator, east of Diego Garcia, when she was sunk by the Type IXC *U-532*, commanded by Korvettenkapitän Ottoheinrich Junker. Junker tried to enhance his 'score' by reporting the sinking as that of the 4,734-ton Australian *Age*, but that ship was never recorded as lost!

The *Tulagi* carried a crew of forty-nine, plus five Royal Navy gunners. Only fifteen of these men got away from the scene of the sinking, on two rafts. For fifty-four days the two rafts kept together, drifting helplessly on the ocean currents. Then, for reasons which may never be known, they separated. It proved to be a disastrous event for one of them, which held eight European sailors. It was never found. The other, with the remaining seven survivors, landed on Alphonse, one of the Amirante Islands in the western part of the Seychelles Group north of Madagascar, just five days after they had separated, having drifted 1,500 miles in fifty-nine days. The details of their ordeal are not recorded and can only be imagined.

Junker, a then forty-nine-year-old torpedo specialist from Freiburg, headed back to Germany from Djakarta in January 1945. He had sunk eight ships for a total of 46,895 tons. *U-532* was surrendered at Liverpool on 10 May 1945 and Junker spent the next three years in captivity. He was reported as still alive in August 2000, thus being possibly the oldest surviving U-boat commander of the Second World War.

The Case of the SS *Jean Nicolet*

The 7,176-ton Liberty ship *Jean Nicolet* was on a voyage from Fremantle to Calcutta with a cargo of army stores. According to

Lloyd's War Losses, the number of people on board were forty-one crew, thirty passengers, twenty-eight military personnel and an army medical sergeant – total exactly 100. On the evening of 2 July 1944, in a favourite Indian Ocean hunting ground for Jap submarines, just south of the equator – at 03°28'S, 74°30'E – she was struck by two torpedoes on her starboard side. With fire blazing in her holds and listing badly to starboard, her captain ordered everybody into the boats, leaving on board only himself, with a US Navy gunnery officer, Lieutenant Deal, and two ratings, plus two merchant seamen, A/Bs Hess and McDougall.

After carefully checking that nobody was left aboard the freighter, these men took to No. 2 forward raft, which slowly drifted astern. But the captain saw a light on the ship and, summoning one of the motor lifeboats, which was full of men under the Chief Engineer, took command of it and headed back towards the *Jean Nicolet* to make quite sure that she was deserted. As the motor boat neared the ship's side, a submarine surfaced nearby. It was *I-8* – Captain Tatsunoke Ariizumi, the same Ariizumi who had murdered the passengers and crew of the *Tjisalak* two months before. And it had been barely a week since he and his crew had torpedoed the British ship *Nellore*, also on the Western Australia–Bay of Bengal track a few miles away to the south, and killed 79 people out of the 209 on board.

The *Jean Nicolet*'s captain cut his engine and had the boat quietly rowed back towards the raft. But it was too late. The Japanese had spotted them and the submarine came alongside the raft. The sailors slid from the raft and clung to the far side of it. They could not see exactly what happened next but there was the sound of machine-gun fire. Then the submarine reappeared and shone a searchlight on the men in the water. It came closer and threw lines to them. They climbed onto its upper casing, one by one, until only three of them were left swimming in the sea. The Japs shot at these, but did not manage to hit any of them.

McDougall followed Hess onto the fore-deck of the *I-8*. He was told to take off his life-jacket and put up his hands. One of the Japanese sailors relieved him of his watch and was about to cut off his finger with a knife so as to steal his ring, but the American managed to remove it and hand it over just in time. Then, with their hands bound, all the survivors were made to sit down cross-legged on the deck, keep their chins on their chests and ordered not to move.

218

One by one, they were taken aft. Most were never seen again, but the *Nicolet*'s carpenter risked turning his head round furtively and saw a young apprentice named King being bayoneted in the stomach and then pushed overboard. All told, fifty-seven men were dispatched in this way.

An assistant engineer named Pyle told how he, too, was robbed of his belongings and forced to sit on the fore-deck. His turn to be led aft came at about midnight. About twenty of his shipmates had already been murdered. Abaft the conning-tower, the Japs, armed with iron bars and other weapons, were enjoying some 'sport'. About a dozen of them had formed themselves into two columns and the Americans were being made to 'run the gauntlet' before being pushed into the sea. As he was pushed and kicked along the gauntlet, Pyle staggered under tremendous blows to his head. He said that one swipe in particular, to the base of his cranium, made him feel like a bouncing rubber ball. He did not realize it at the time, but his head had been split from ear to ear by a blow from either a bayonet or a sword. At last he fell into a sea of white foam. One of the naval gunners, Butler, was hit over the head with a piece of iron pipe, kicked in the stomach and cut over the eye with a sword. He managed to break free from the gauntlet and throw himself into the water. Summoning up all his will-power, he refused to lose consciousness and quietly swam into the darkness.

All the time these atrocities were taking place the *I-8* had been slowly making its way round and round the *Jean Nicolet*, firing the occasional shell at the derelict ship. Suddenly a klaxon sounded from within the submarine. Ariizumi was about to dive! Able Seaman Hess had been sitting on the fore-deck now for two hours. He had been working assiduously on his bonds with his finger-nails and had worn the rope so thin that with a mighty effort he was able to break it. And he still had a knife in his pocket that the Japs had overlooked. Quickly, with the submarine descending beneath his feet, he freed about six of his shipmates. By then *I-8*'s bows were well awash and the Americans had no alternative but to jump for it.

Taking care not to lose sight of each other, they trod water and swam about until dawn. The *Jean Nicolet* was still there, still slowly sinking and still on fire. She had been burning and sinking, hissing, rumbling and creaking, now for nearly eighteen hours. But the Japs had gone. Hess, McDougall, Pyle, Butler and twelve others swam towards their burning ship. There they found about another six of their shipmates. And they were just in time. Barely a couple of hours later, she did sink. And as she did so, amid a cloud of steam and smoke, an unlaunched raft which had become jammed miraculously floated free. The twenty-two survivors of the 100 people on board the *Jean Nicolet* scrambled onto it, blessing their luck. They clung to it for the next thirty hours, when salvation appeared in the shape of the little Isles Class trawler HMS *Hoxa*, which had been directed to the scene after their raft had been sighted by an aircraft of the Royal Canadian Air Force.

There is a degree of uncertainty about the number of survivors from the *Jean Nicolet*. Some accounts make no mention of any more men on the freighter when the Hess party returned on board, but claim instead that there were five members of the crew who had been taken below in the submarine and were eventually landed in Japan as POWs. This version must be given some credibility on the basis that the purser of the Liberty ship, one Francis O'Gara, was found alive in a Japanese camp at the end of the war. That throws doubt on the number of men in the Hess group, which was said to be sixteen, to have been rescued by *Hoxa*. To add to the confusion, the trawler was said by some to have found twenty-three men. In any event, there is still a discrepancy of one man either way, plus or minus.

Ariizumi, surely one of Nippon's most detestable submarine captains, was later given command of the revolutionary *I-400* squadron. These boats registered 3,500 tons, were 400 feet long and equipped as aircraft carriers! The intention was to use them, *inter alia*, for bacteriological warfare. The aircraft, carrying deadly cargoes of rats and fleas, bred by the million on a special 'farm' in Manchuria and infected with bubonic plague and typhus, were to bombard California and other densely populated areas on the Allied side. Thankfully, these huge boats arrived too late to become fully operational. (Although it had been an aircraft launched from a submarine which had made the war's only bombing attack on the US mainland by dropping incendiaries on forests in Oregon as early as 9 September 1942.)

In August 1945 Ariizumi was returning to Yokosuka in *I-401* under a US Navy boarding party. As she entered Tokyo Bay flying a black flag of surrender, which to Ariizumi was a sign of ultimate disgrace, he shot himself. Later, one of his crew defended his captain's murders of survivors from sunken ships on the grounds that he had received orders from naval general staff to execute them. Allied investigators were never able to trace those orders. If they ever existed in writing, they had been destroyed.

13

THE VERDICTS

The punishments handed down at Leipzig for atrocities at sea during the First World War were infuriatingly light to the point of being farcical in the view of many, on the Allied side at least. But those proceedings had taken place in a comparatively chivalrous age. The naïve trust which the Treaty of Versailles had placed in the courts of the defeated side to try, convict and sentence their own war criminals was typical of its time. And just as a family of rabbits playing in a woody glade will run for their bolt-holes in the bushes as soon as distant footsteps are heard but well before the approaching predator comes into view, so did many of those men with war crimes on their consciences vanish into well-prepared anonymity under the cover of the confusion which existed at the end of both World Wars, well before the Allies even began their investigations.

The Second World War saw escalations and magnifications of the First on many counts. Not least was in terms of the number of crimes committed on the high seas – and the degree of depravity displayed in them. It was truly as if mankind had descended into what that master of metaphor Winston Churchill described in January 1941 as "a dark and deadly valley".

With the coming of peace in Europe in May 1945, the same problems beset the victors in apprehending those of the vanquished whom they wanted to question in connection with war crimes that faced them after the Armistice in 1918. First, the task was to find them. And this time there were far more of them to find. Teams of investigators, armed with long lists of 'wanted' names, scoured Germany but had relatively little success. A Captain Gilbert Roberts, RN, arrived in Germany on 21 May 1945 with a brief to flush out former naval captains for questioning. He reported, "I found it difficult to make personal contact with many German officers who had commanded ships. Many had been killed, some were still in Norwegian waters, some were prisoners-of-war in Russian hands and others had disbanded. As all German naval communications had been disrupted many days ago and since 8 May no messages allowed between German naval personnel, B.d.U. were unable to state their whereabouts."

The difficulties facing Roberts can be borne out if we look at what seem to have been the fates of the various potential Second World War German naval criminals who have featured in this book.

Viktor Oehrn, the sinker of the *Sheaf Mead* and the *Severn Leigh*, despite having been mentioned by name at the trial of Karl Dönitz, does not appear ever to have been indicted for his own alleged war crimes. The British had captured him, then released him as part of a prisoner exchange. We can only assume that at the time his involvement with these crimes was not realized.

Hellmuth von Ruckteschell, of *Schiff 21*, was imprisoned for three years.

Heinrich 'Ajax' Bleichrodt, sinker of the evacuee ship *City of Benares*, is believed to have survived the War, but was never indicted.

Werner Hartenstein, central character of the *Laconia* Affair, was killed when U-156 was sunk off Barbados in 1943.

Heinz Eck, of the *Peleus* Affair, together with his shipmates **Hoffmann** and **Weisspfennig**, was sentenced to be shot, while **Lenz** and **Schwender** were each imprisoned for fifteen years. This was the only 'submarine' case of the Second World War to attract the death penalty.

Gerhard Matschulat, murderer of the fishermen of the *Noreen Mary*, was killed when his U-247 was sunk by the Canadian frigates *St. John* and *Swansea*.

Hans Oestermann, who sank the fishing boat *Ebb* and murdered many of her crew, was killed himself by bombing the following day.

Erich Topp, whose men killed many of the crew of the *David H. Atwater*, seems never to have paid any penalty for his crime. He was never indicted and was eventually appointed to a senior position within NATO.

Ottoheinrich Junker, who left the few survivors of the crew of the little *Tulagi* to drift for weeks in the middle of the Indian Ocean, spent three years in captivity.

On 1 May 1945 German Wireless announced important news for the German people. Three rolls of drums rumbled out from loud-speakers to millions of listeners throughout the defeated Third Reich. Then the announcer said, "It is reported from Der Führer's headquarters that our Führer, Adolf Hitler, fighting to the last breath against Bolshevism, fell for Germany this afternoon in the Reich Chancellery. Yesterday, Der Führer appointed Grand Admiral Dönitz his successor. The Grand Admiral and successor of Der Führer now speaks to the German people."

Dönitz's voice was then heard. That he was a convinced Nazi was clear from his words. He said his first task was to save Germany from destruction by the advancing Russians. That was the sole aim of the struggle, but it was being impeded by the insistence of the British and Americans in continuing the fight on the western front, and whose real purpose was to encourage the spread of Bolshevism across Europe. Thus, Germany faced no alternative but to carry on its defensive fight on both fronts. God would not forsake them, he promised.

Then came the rolling notes of *Deutschland über Alles* and other national music.

The Grossadmiral set up his Government in Flensburg-Murwik, close to the Danish border, but his 'reign' was only to last for three weeks. On 23 May 1945 he was arrested by a British SHAEF control unit. The fifty-four-year-old Dönitz entered the Nuremberg dock a year and a half later looking trim and slim, although he seemed to have aged considerably since his arrest. He spoke quietly and assuredly, but at the same time gave the impression that he was genuinely bemused and bewildered by the fact that he was on trial for anything at all. The Court heard that after taking over as Supreme Commander of the German Navy from Admiral Raeder in 1943 he had acted as Hitler's personal naval adviser. His answer to this was that it had been a strictly non-political rôle, and that his function had been purely that of a professional sailor, whose duty to the elected Government of his country was to fight the war in which it was engaged.

The stories of the *City of Benares*, *Noreen Mary* and *Sheaf Mead* were all cited as evidence against him, and mention was made of the shooting-up of a Spanish fishing vessel by Oehrn's *U-37*, although the case of the *Severn Leigh*, which was also connected with that same submarine and its commander, seems to have been ignored. But central to the Prosecution's argument was, of course, the notorious *Laconia* Order.

1. *No attempt of any kind must be made at rescuing members of ships sunk, and this includes picking up persons in the water and putting them into lifeboats, righting capsized lifeboats and handing over food and water. Rescue runs counter to the rudimentary demands of warfare for the destruction of enemy ships and crews.*
2. *Orders for bringing in captains and chief engineers still apply.*
3. *Rescue the shipwrecked only if their statements will be of importance to your boat.*
4. *Be harsh, having in mind that the enemy takes no regard of women and children in his bombing attacks on German cities.*

Did it or did it not mean that survivors from sunken ships, other than captains and chief engineers, should be fired on and if possible killed? Fleet Judge Dr Krantzbühler, the Admiral's defence counsel, argued strongly that it meant no such thing. He tried to point to his client's honourable intentions by calling witnesses who testified that it was always Dönitz's firm instruction that, above all, hospital ships must be considered to be absolutely inviolable. How could such an order square with any intention to kill helpless survivors?

Cross-examined by Colonel Phillimore for the prosecution on the thirty-fifth day of the trial, 15 January 1946, Korvettenkapitän Karl-Heinz Möhle, the former head of the Fifth *U-bootflotille* said that his reaction to the Order had been that it was not unambiguous, and that some of his commanders had asked him how the words should be interpreted. He had told them that whichever way they chose to interpret it was a matter for their own consciences. "That makes things perfectly clear." said one officer, "but it is damned hard."

Finally, it was decided that the words used in the *Laconia* Order had, in fact, carried enough weight to make the German Admiral guilty of war crimes. But their ambiguity achieved the mitigation which saved his neck. The British, American and French judges all favoured varying sentences, ranging from an outright acquittal from Judge Biddle up to twenty years from Birkett and Parker. Even the Russian Nikitchenko recommended only ten years, contrasting with the standard demand for a hanging which came from the Russians in most of the Nuremberg cases. In the end they sent Dönitz to prison for ten years, which was the lightest sentence imposed at the Trials on any of those found guilty. He accepted his sentence philosophically, but always said that he had never did quite understood how the Court had come to its conclusion. Unlike many war crimes prisoners, Dönitz was not let out early on parole. He was released from Berlin's Spandau prison on 1 October 1956, having served his full sentence. He died on Christmas Eve 1980 at the age of ninety.

By early August 1945, even before the twin traumas of Hiroshima and Nagasaki on 6 and 9 August had dealt such massive blows to Japan's national morale, none but her diehard militarists and *kamikaze* fanatics retained any will to continue with the war. Although she still possessed large numbers of troops, ships and aircraft, the Japanese homeland itself was already locked in a military and economic stranglehold imposed by the Americans and their Allies. Japanese industry, transport network and agriculture had been devastated by incessant air-raids and her stunned people were starving.

On 26 July the Potsdam Proclamation by the USA, Great Britain and China had called for the unconditional surrender of Japan, the immediate demobilization of her armed forces and the trial of all her war criminals. The Japanese Government, imbued with a wholly different religious mentality and code of honour from that of its enemies, wrestled with itself over what to do next. And so it did nothing. The lack of any response to Potsdam created in turn an enormous dilemma for the Allies. Invasion of the Japanese Islands would have resulted in the deaths of millions. Without a doubt it would have led to the bloodiest conflict the world had ever seen, with the defenders putting at least twenty million fanatical suicide troops into the field. Or should President Truman authorize the dropping of the atomic bomb and hope for an early surrender? As we know now, he opted for the latter alternative. It resulted in decades of conscience-searching on the part of the Allies, but it served its purpose.

After Nagasaki forty-five-year-old Hirohito, the God-Emperor, addressed his Cabinet and called for an end to the vacillation of the Government. Japan had no choice but to accept Potsdam, he said, if their homeland and their nation were not to be utterly destroyed. On 15 August his recorded voice spoke in an unprecedented personal broadcast to the Japanese people over the airwaves from NHK, the Japanese Broadcasting Corporation. "Should we continue to fight," he said, "the enemy's new and most cruel bomb would result in the obliteration of the Japanese nation and would also lead to the extinction of the human race." The next day the Allies accepted the Japanese surrender, but it was not until 28 August that the advance party of Americans arrived in Tokyo and another five days before the surrender document was signed aboard USS *Missouri*.

By the end of the month over 1,000 members of the armed forces, including several admirals and generals, had committed suicide. In the coming weeks many more were to follow. On 11 September the most guilty of them all, ex-War Minister and Premier Hideki Tojo, aware that he was about to be arrested as a war criminal, tried to shoot himself, but missed the vital spot. He was transfused with the blood of his enemies at a US Army field hospital and survived to stand trial, despised and ostracized by his fellow prisoners for not having committed *hara kiri*. In the end he was hung at ten and a half minutes past midnight on the night of 22–23 December 1948 and his ashes scattered to the wind.

The setting-up of the International Military Tribunal for the Far East was a tedious business. In Tokyo the former war ministry's outdated offices on Ichigaya Hill were converted into an expensively wood-panelled courtroom complex, complete with every modern appurtenance from special lighting to a glass enclosure for the translators. It was to be the workplace of platoons of lawyers, secretaries, interpreters, cameramen, reporters, typists, clerks and straight-backed, white helmeted G.I. policemen, not to mention judges, witnesses and the accused themselves, for the next two and a half years. But before any proceedings could get under way a mountainous task faced the Allies in the form of the sheer number of war crimes to be investigated. The Americans alone dealt with over 3,000 cases in Tokyo, of which ninety were eventually sentenced to death. Outside Tokyo, where the Class A major cases were heard, tribunals were set up at many other centres in the Far East – Yokohama, Manila, Hong Kong, Rabaul, Singapore, Rangoon, Djakarta, Penang and on various Pacific Islands – to deal with the long lists of lesser fry criminals. By the end of 1946 the Dutch had convicted 969 Japanese, the British 811, the Australians 644, the Chinese 504, the French 198 and the Filipinos 169, with dozens more to follow. But, just as had been the case with the Nazis, the large majority of Japanese war criminals escaped justice altogether. Lord Wright, first Chairman of the United Nations War Crimes Commission took the view that less than 10% of the world's war criminals would face trial "The majority of the Axis war criminals," he confessed, "will find safety in their numbers. It is physically impossible to punish more than a fraction. All that can be done is to make examples." In all probability, Lord Wright's 10% was at least a tenfold over-estimate.

The fortnight's period of 'grace' between the acceptance of the surrender and the arrival of the Americans in Tokyo was not spent idly at the Japanese War Ministry. For days on end giant bonfires blazed around the clock at their offices on Tokyo's Ichigaya Hill as ton after ton of paper records was consigned to the flames. At the Headquarters of the Kempei Tai (the Secret Police) and at military and naval establishments around the now shrivelled and moribund Greater East Asia Co-Prosperity Sphere, similar fires glowed in the hasty destruction of files, transcripts and books. With so much incriminating evidence destroyed, the prosecutors faced an impossible task in bringing more than a minute fraction of the guilty to justice. Even then, many Not Guilty verdicts were the result of scanty evidence. Hundreds if not thousands of persons were unidentifiable and so evaded arrest. An extract from the official list of Japanese wanted for interrogation reveals the typical difficulties facing the investigators in bringing war criminals to trial in 1945.

VERY SECRET.

No. 72   Captain – *Rakuyo Maru* – name unknown. (*Author's note*: He was dead, killed by Moxham.)

73   Commander – *Rakuyo Maru* – name unknown.

74   Paymaster – *Rakuyo Maru* – name unknown.

75   Purser – *Rakuyo Maru* – name unknown.

It appears that the only *Rakuyo Maru* suspect whose name was known was Lieutenant Yamada, who was wanted for questioning in connection with war crimes at 35 Kilo and 105 Kilo camps on the Burma-Siam railway as well as on the hell-ship.

One day during a recess in the Tokyo hearings, a young American reporter, Arnold Brackman, ventured into an air-raid tunnel at Ichigaya with a couple of friends. Ichigaya Hill was riddled with such tunnels, but this one was different. It was inside the War Ministry buildings, which had been transformed into the courthouse, and, more to the point, it appeared not to have been discovered by the occupation forces. Armed with torches, Brackman and his friends crept inside to find themselves on a wide concrete spiral stairway. It was as eerie as a tomb. They descended into the darkness. At the bottom were a pair of massive steel doors and they were open. They stepped through them into a subterranean labyrinth of corridors, offices, conference rooms and storage chambers. What they had found was the General Headquarters of the Imperial Japanese Armed Forces! The lair of Tojo himself, who now sat in the dock, literally directly above them. They wandered around in there for two hours, with the beams and shadows cast by their flashlights combining with the echoes of their footsteps and voices to create an air of spine-chilling suspense. But they did not find one desk, chair or filing cabinet. Not one piece of furniture of any description. And not one scrap of paper. The whole maze of rooms, which once must have housed dozens of people, had been stripped clean as if by a family of all-devouring vultures. And there was another huge steel door, ten feet high, with a number "3" on the front. But it was welded shut. They never did discover what lay behind it.

Of all the three 'houses' of potential war criminal prisoners, political, military and naval, it seems that the naval authorities had been the most efficient in their destruction of paperwork evidence. Coincidentally, a similar situation existed at Nuremberg. This thoroughness was, with little doubt, one major reason for the relatively small number of naval suspects indicted and tried, and on balance the comparatively light sentences passed, for war crimes at sea.

One of the few incriminating Japanese documents that was found was a directive dated 20 March 1943 and stamped *gunki* – secret. It was a single sheet numbered 24 of 70, and no other pages of the file were ever found. Nevertheless, the few words it contained spoke volumes.

"Do not stop with the sinking of enemy ships and cargoes; at the same time that you carry out the complete destruction of crews of the enemy's ships, if possible seize part of the crew and endeavour to secure information."

The tell-tale memorandum may not have disclosed the identity of its author, or even to whom it had been addressed, but it served to underline a conversation that had taken place between Hitler and the Japanese Ambassador, General Hiroshi Oshima, in Berlin on 3 January 1942. Using a map to illustrate his point, the Führer had indicated the present state of war in the Atlantic. Without victory at sea, the war could not be won and the U-boats would be the key to that victory. With America now in the war, Germany was intending to take the fight to the enemy's front doorstep. The Atlantic U-boats were being reorganized in preparation for operations off the eastern seaboard of the USA. But in the long run, said Hitler, it would be a question of simple logistics. He pointed out that America, and therefore her Allies too, had a limitless ship-building capability. No matter how many merchant ships the U-boats sank, or how quickly, there would always be more on the slips waiting to be launched. The enemy's Achilles' Heel, therefore, was not his ships' hulls, but his crew force. A ship with no crew cannot sail.

"For that reason," the Führer is quoted as saying in a document later presented as evidence against Oshima and others at the Tokyo Trials, "even merchant ships would be sunk without warning with the intention of killing as many of the crew as possible. Once it gets around that most of the crew are lost in the sinkings, the Americans would soon have difficulty in enlisting new people. The training of sea-going personnel takes a very long time. We are fighting for our existence and our attitude cannot be ruled by any humane feelings. For this reason we must give the order that, in cases where foreign seamen cannot be taken prisoner, which is not always possible on the sea, U-boats are to surface after torpedoing and shoot up the lifeboats."

Ambassador Oshima, a close friend of von Ribbentrop, was considered by many Japanese to be more Nazi than the Nazis, and had served in Germany since 1934. He agreed wholeheartedly with

Hitler's comments and said that the Japanese, too, were forced to follow the same methods. Oshima was sentenced to life imprisonment, but paroled in 1955.

The cases of War Crimes at Sea, or connected with such crimes, were a bare three among the Class A cases dealt with at Tokyo. They were:

Admiral Shigetaro Shimada – Tojo's Navy Minister. The sycophantic sixty-one-year-old Shimada was one of Tojo's toadies. Doubtless this was one good reason why, as a serving naval officer commanding the China Fleet, he was suddenly appointed Navy Minister in October 1941. Thus he was privy to the plans to invade Pearl Harbor and was responsible for authorizing the surprise attack on 7 December 1941. Units under his ultimate control massacred prisoners-of-war, transported large numbers of them aboard the hell-ships throughout the war and killed survivors from torpedoed ships. Shimada was convicted and found guilty on Count 1 – conspiring to wage a war of aggression in violation of International Law, and Counts 27, 29, 31 and 32 – waging unprovoked war against China and aggressive war against the USA, the British Commonwealth and the Netherlands. On Counts 54 and 55, which dealt with atrocities, he was found Not Guilty. We can only assume that this was because of lack of evidence. In view of the fact that he was ultimately accountable and surely must have known what was taking place, but did nothing to stop it, the Not Guilty verdicts were astonishing. How can the loss of such ships as *Kachidoki Maru* and *Rakuyo Maru* and a long list of other hell-ships have been incurred without provoking enquiry at the highest level, which was Shimada himself? And the pitifully small number of survivors to reach the Japanese homeland by sea from the *Lisbon Maru* and other prison ships to provide desperately needed labour should certainly have triggered off a barrage of searching questions. Admiral Shimada was sentenced to life imprisonment, but served only eight years. He was paroled in 1955 and died in 1976 at the age of ninety-three.

Admiral Takasumi Oka – Chief of the Bureau of Naval Affairs and from 1944 Shimada's Number Two. Fifty-six-year-old Oka was another key figure in the surprise attacks on American and Allied bases in December 1941. And, like Shimada, he had issued orders for the transportation of thousands of prisoners and slaves aboard the hell-ships. He had also administered certain prison camps on islands in the Pacific and was said to have issued orders to kill survivors of torpedoed ships. He was convicted and found guilty of the same crimes as Shimada, and also cleared of any guilt of atrocity. He was sentenced to life imprisonment, paroled in 1954 and died in 1973.

Admiral Osami Nagano – the bull-necked Nagano, at sixty-eight the oldest of the Class A naval prisoners, had been Chief of Naval Staff from 1941 and Hirohito's personal naval adviser from 1944. He had freely admitted responsibility for the sneak attacks on Pearl Harbor, Hong Kong, Kota Bharu, Manila and elsewhere, but blandly excused these actions as being questions of pure strategy. He was indicted for these attacks and for the invasion of Indo-China and the murder of prisoners-of-war. But on 5 January 1947 he cheated his accusers by dying of pneumonia and tuberculosis at the 361st US Army Field Hospital. He left a letter in which he regretted that the United States had not been informed of the attack on Pearl Harbor by 'perhaps two minutes'. In his memoirs, the youngest Class A defendant, General Kenryo Sato, claimed that Nagano's pneumonia had been brought on by inhumane treatment in Sugamo Prison. He said that there was a broken window in the Admiral's cell, which he had blocked with some newspaper, but the guards had not allowed this and had removed the paper, thus leaving the old man exposed to the bitter winter cold.

The search still continued for those named as criminals, but it was becoming increasingly fruitless. Almost two years after the end of the war in the Far East, on 23 July 1947, the Naval Liaison Officer, Tokyo signalled the Chief of Intelligence Staff, British Pacific Fleet.

Ariizumi – dead. (*Author's note*: He had committed suicide two years earlier!) Nakagawa – not yet apprehended.

On a micro-fiche in the Public Record Office at Kew a new name comes to light in connection with the hell-ships. It does not appear in any of the extensive research material that has been consulted elsewhere in the preparation of this book. It is that of one Yoshio Masuda. Apparently, he was a Lieutenant-Colonel, the commanding officer of a unit which had overall responsibility for the hell-ships.

In 1947 he was held by the Americans and due to be tried some time in 1948, such was the work-load facing the United Nations War Crimes Commission. But a memorandum from the British Staff Officer Hong Kong dated 23 October 1947 advises the Admiralty that Masuda has been passed into the custody of the British and was now scheduled for trial on 15 November 1947. But there the short account ends. The mysterious Masuda leaves our story as abruptly as he comes into it. Despite an exhaustive search through all available records in various archives, nothing appears to tell us what was done with him, or even whether the British did ever bring him to trial as planned.

Likewise, nothing appears to indicate that the criminals Yamada and Wada were ever brought to justice. One can imagine that it would not have been difficult for them, as with countless others like them, to forge completely new identities and lose themselves in the confusion of the Far East in the post-World War Two upheaval. For all we know, they might have committed suicide or they might have perished at Hiroshima or Nagasaki, or they might even have survived to this day and are reading these very words.

A widespread demand that Japan should be forced to compensate and formally apologize to the victims of the atrocities committed by its forces was an understandable development in the years following 1945, but it produced little satisfaction for any of those who had suffered, and least of all for the British. Under the 1951 San Francisco Treaty, made at the time of the Korean War, with the dangerous Cold War between communism and capitalism freezing international relationships around the globe and the USA anxious to retain its bases in Japan to peg back Russian influence, the British Far East ex-prisoners of war were awarded just £78 (about $100) each and civilian internees, which of course included merchant seamen, £48 ($60). Since 1948 the Americans had been holding $350 million in frozen Japanese assets for distribution to victims of war crimes, but only $17 million was ever paid out. The rest was returned to Japan. In effect, the Allies had waived the right to sue Japan. Article 26 of the Treaty provided that if other nationalities were awarded amounts higher than the British, then the latter would be entitled to claim an increase to parity with them. And between 1956 and 1967 many other countries' Far East POWs did obtain much more, up to fifty times more in the case of the USA. But successive British Governments have never instituted the claim which their countrymen were entitled to expect them to make. When Emperor Akihito made a highly controversial visit to Britain in 1998, the question of compensation and apology re-erupted. Lines of British ex-prisoners-of-war turned their backs in angry and disgusted silence as the royal visitor passed, and New Labour Foreign Office Minister Derek Fatchett, when challenged to resurrect the matter on behalf of the dwindling number of Far East atrocity survivors, replied that he thought it was hardly appropriate to do so over fifty years after the event. Such is the nature of politics and politicians.

As early as 1952, less than four years after the skinny five-foot four-inch body of Hideki Tojo had been cut down from the rope at Sugamo, the Japanese Government were clamouring for clemency on behalf of the war crimes prisoners held in custody. It was refused. But they tried again three years later, with the result that on 14 November 1955, just ten years and three months after the end of the war in the Far East, the *London Daily Express* reported that Great Britain had agreed to review the cases of ninety-nine Japanese currently serving war crimes sentences. Only five were refused leniency.

Such is the quality of mercy.

BIBLIOGRAPHY

Barker, Ralph, *The Children of The* Benares.

Blair, Clay, Jnr, *Silent Victory*, Lippincott, (USA), 1975.

Blair, Joan, & Clay, Jnr, *Return from the River Kwai*, Simon and Schuster, (USA) 1979.

Brackman, Arnold C., *The Other Nuremberg*, Collins, 1989.

Caidin, Martin, *The Ragged Rugged Warriors*, Severn House, 1966.

Cameron John (editor), *The* Peleus *Trial*, William Hodge, 1948.

Chapman, Paul, *Submarine* Torbay, Robert Hale, 1989.

Coutts, Ben, *Bothy to Big Ben*, Aberdeen University Press, 1988.

Coutts, Ben, *A Scotsman's War*, Mercat Press, Edinburgh, 1995.

Daws, Gavan, *Prisoners of the Japanese*, Robson Books, 1995.

Dower, John, *War Without Mercy*, Faber & Faber, 1986.

Huxley, Elspeth, *Atlantic Ordeal*, Chatto & Windus, 1941.

Lowther, W.W., *Wish You Were Here*, Walton Publications, 1989.

Kennedy, Ludovic, *On my way to the Club*, Collins, 1989.

Lyon, Hugh, *Warships*, Salamander, 1978.

Maclean, Alistair, *The Lonely Sea*, 1985.

Morison, Samuel E., *History of United States Naval Operations in World War II*, Vol VI, Oxford University Press, 1950.

O'Kane, Richard H., *Clear the Bridge!* MacDonald & James, 1978.

Peillard, Leonce, *The* Laconia *Affair*, Jonathan Cape and G.P. Putnam's, (USA) 1963.

Potter, E.B., *Nimitz*, Naval Institute Press, Annapolis, 1976.

Russell, Lord, of Liverpool, *The Scourge of the Swastika*, Cassell, 1954.

Russell, Lord of Liverpool, *The Knights of Bushido*, Cassell, 1958.

Slader, John, *The Fourth Service*, Robert Hale, 1994.

Sterling, Forest J., *Wake of the* Wahoo, Chilton Books, Philadelphia, 1960.

Tusa, Ann and John, *The Nuremberg Trial*, Macmillan, 1983.

Whipple, A.B.C., *Fighting Sail*, Time Life Books Inc, 1978.

Wynn, Kenneth, *U-boat Operations of the Second World War*, Vols I and II, Chatham Publishing, 1998.

INDEX

Grice, Cyril, 192
Grider, Third Officer George,
117, 118, 123
Grierson, Ruby, 39
Griggs, John, 116
Grimmond, Eddie, 34, 52
Grimmond, Gussie, 35, 38, 46, 53
Grimmond, Violet, 38, 53
Grouper, U.S.S., 116, 201, 202
Growler, U.S.S., 166–8, 170, 174,
175, 186
Gustard, Violet, 35, 61

Halfhide, Eric, 182, 184, 189, 237
Halse, Colonel, 111
Halsey, Admiral William, 113
Hameister, Werner, 107
Hamilton, Lieutenant G., 204,
206, 207
Hammett, Robert, 8
Harahiku Maru, 195
Harten, 89
Hartenstein, Korvettenkapitän
Werner, 1, 66, 67, 71–5, 82–5
Haupel, Roman, 69
Hauptmann, gunner's mate, 187
Hawkins, 'Freckles', 65, 68, 76,
84, 86, 87
Henderson, Billy, 87
Henderson, Edith, 35, 237
Hess, A.B., 218–20
Hessler, 75
Hetherington, Joe, 45, 49–51
Hewitt, Air Commodore, 131
Hillman, Maud, 34, 50, 54
Hirohito, 227, 232, 234
Hoffmann, Leutnant August, 104,
107, 111, 112, 223
Holmes, Captain, W.J., 166
Holmes, Terence, 52
Horton, Admiral Sir Max, 99

Howell, Lieutenant, 204
Hoxa, H.M.S., 220
Hughieson, Jack, 199, 205, 206,
208–10, 237
Huitson, George, 182
Hunt, Alf, 197, 199, 205–8, 237
Hurricane, H.M.S., 48, 50–2, 55,
60

I-37, 214
I-401, 220
I-8, 138, 218
Irvine, Ernie, 209
Irving, Joan, 44, 45, 53

Jackson, William, 148
James O. Wilder, 143
Janita, 94
Jean Nicolet, 214–20
Jolly, Mr, 13, 18
Jong, F.E., 141–5
Junker, Korvettenkapitän
Ottoheinrich, 217, 224
Junya Maru, 196

Kachidoki Maru, 162–4, 172,
174–82, 184–6, 194, 195, 231
Kamikawa Maru, 126
Katori Maru, 167
Keeley, Jack, 50
Keeter, Mechanic First Class, 118
Kefalas, Agis, 105, 106, 110
Kembu Maru, 130, 133
Kennedy, Ludovic, 100
Kennedy, Marvin, 115
Kenney, Lieutenant-General, 131,
132, 134
Kibibi Maru, 185, 186, 191, 192
Killoran, 22
Kimura, Rear-Admiral Masatomi,
130, 131, 134, 135
King John, 18, 20
King, Commander, 154

242